OUTLOOK 2000

in easy steps

Michael Price

COMPUTER STEP

In easy steps is an imprint of Computer Step
Southfield Road . Southam
Warwickshire CV33 OFB . England

Tel: 01926 817999 Fax: 01926 817005
http://www.computerstep.com

Notice of Liability

Every effort has been made to ensure that this book contains accurate and current information. However, Computer Step and the author shall not be liable for any loss or damage suffered by readers as a result of any information contained herein.

Trademarks

Microsoft® and Windows® are registered trademarks of Microsoft Corporation. All other trademarks are acknowledged as belonging to their respective companies.

Printed and bound in the United Kingdom

ISBN 1-84078-053-3

Contents

Introducing Outlook

In this chapter you will see how Outlook implements electronic mail (e-mail), personal information management (PIM) and team working processes. You will also find out what versions are available, and which one is right for your individual needs.

Covers

Chapter One

Electronic mail and PIM functions

This book discusses the need for e-mail and document management in today's information-rich environment, and shows how Outlook can be set up and used to satisfy these requirements.

Whilst using your computer, whether for hobbies, studies, or business, you will create and send or receive information of many different types, in many different forms. You may have word processing documents and reports, electronic mail schedules and timetables, tasks to perform and people to contact. With so much information available, especially where you connect to the Internet, it can be hard to remember everything that is available, and even harder to find it when you need it.

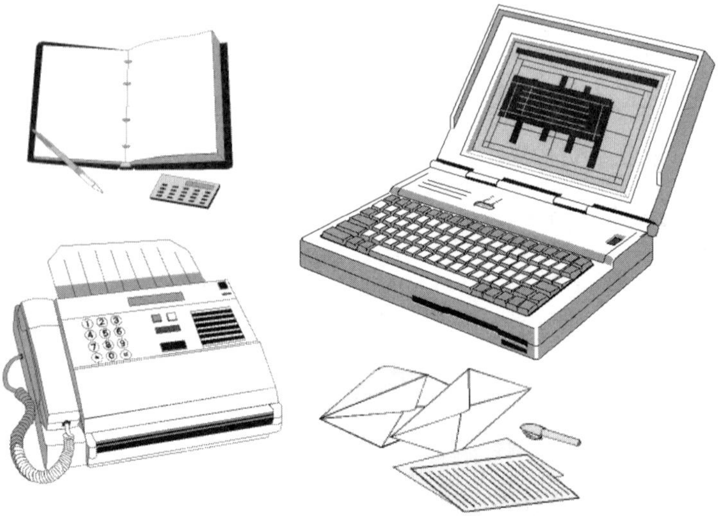

The large hard disks featured on modern PCs serve to emphasise the problem, because there is much less restriction on the size and amount of data that you can afford to keep. The range and variety of computer applications allow you to manipulate and process this information, creating even more information to manage.

If you are working with others in a formal or informal team, then you may find that you are spending most of your time searching for information that they require and preparing it in a form suitable for transferring. You may have to look in many locations to collect the information that you need.

Where Outlook fits in

Both Outlook 2000 (from Office 2000) and Outlook Express 5 (from Internet Explorer 5) are discussed throughout this book.

The data you need can be spread out in many different places and different forms. Details of meetings may be written on your calendar or in your planning diary. Reports and letters may be stored on the hard disk in your PC. You may have additional information, comments, suggestions and corrections in the form of e-mail messages from others, plus a record of the e-mails that you have sent.

You may already have separate applications that help you with some of these tasks: an e-mail system to handle electronic messages, an Internet newsreader, a PC based fax system, or an electronic personal information manager such as Schedule+. These systems will each have their address book to keep details of the senders and the recipients, hence often carrying duplicated information.

You won't have to lose your existing e-mail message files or your current address book details. Outlook will migrate them for you.

Outlook is a desktop information management program that is designed as one product, to help you co-ordinate and manage all the different categories of data that you deal with. It uses a standard interface, and enables you to control and schedule your tasks, data, e-mail and contacts. It can even keep track of the documents you create. It provides support for Internet news, and it works with your office applications and your Internet browser.

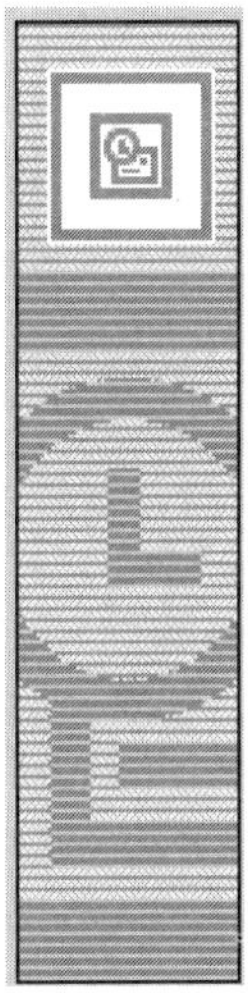

With Outlook you can manage personal or business information, on your own stand-alone system, or as part of a group connected by a network or linked through the Internet.

In Outlook, information is organised in folders, and its activities are divided into sets of functions related to these folders. So, for example, the Inbox folder displays your messages and allows you to forward them or to send replies.

The following sections look at the individual parts of Outlook, so that you can see how they all interrelate and fit together.

The parts of Outlook

Outlook offers you many components and functions, and presents them in a variety of different views. This startup screen has been selected to show you as many of the parts of Outlook at one time as possible.

The default startup view shows the Inbox viewer, or you can select the Outlook Today overview (see page 11).

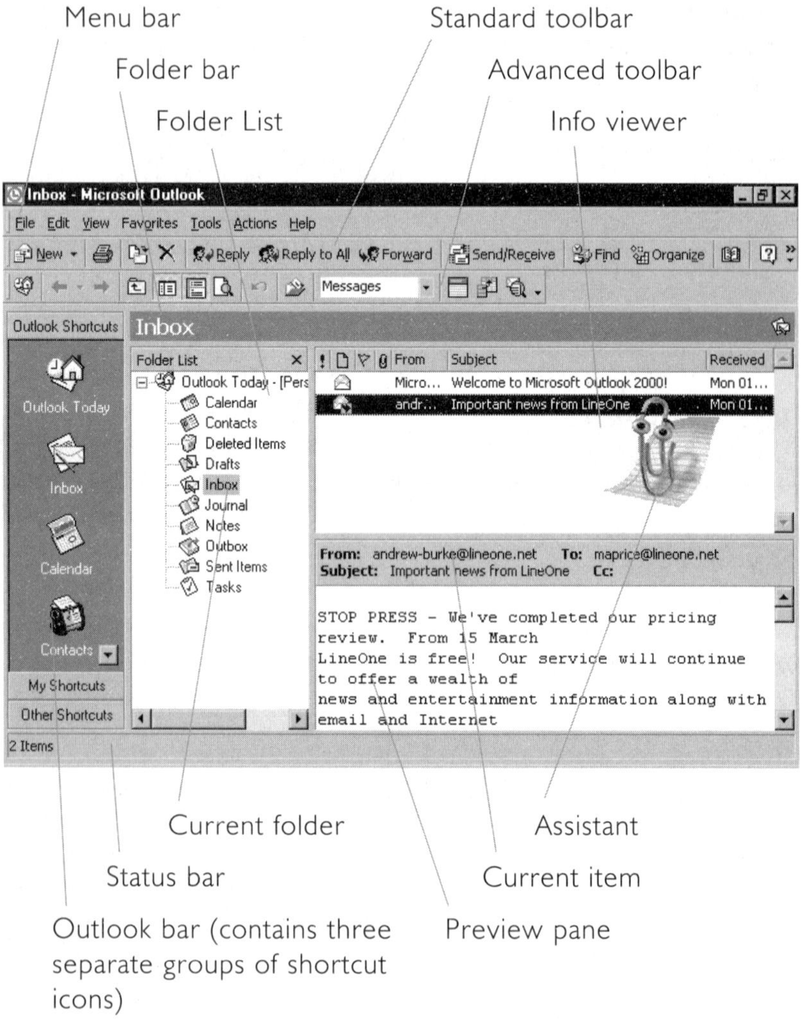

Outlook functions can be reached from the shortcuts on the Outlook bar or from the Folder List.

The exact look and content of the screens that you see will differ, depending on the version of Outlook installed and on how much you customise the display to suit the tasks you want to perform.

Outlook Today

The default start up with the Inbox is ideal if you want to go straight to work on your e-mail. If you use the full functions of Outlook however, you may prefer the alternative startup display. This is Outlook Today, which gives you quick access to the main functions.

The information window gives a high level view of the day's activities, highlighting the events and tasks that you will be facing. There are extracts from your calendar and your task list, plus a summary of your mail. You can change the amount and the type of information presented, for example to show the week ahead.

You can change Outlook startup in other ways also. See Chapter Three for examples.

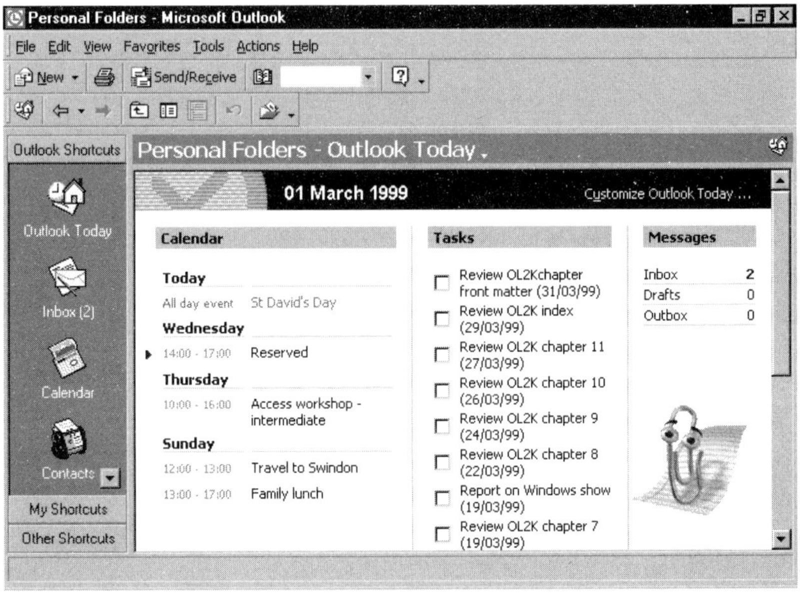

Other parts of Outlook are also available, including the Menu bar, the Standard toolbar and the Outlook bar. The remaining parts are hidden to reduce the level of screen clutter, but you can choose to display any that you wish.

Outlook Express also offers a Shortcuts bar, as an easy to use alternative to the Folder List.

Outlook Express has a similar high level display window, which gives you quick access to its mail, news and address book functions, but it does not include the other Outlook scheduling and information management facilities.

Outlook folders

You can add your own folder entries, to organise your mail.

Outlook stores your mail messages, sent and received, the details of your schedule and other information in a series of folders. These are known as your personal folders. The folder list is normally hidden, but you can request it to be displayed so that you can see the structure:

1. Click View on the Menu bar.
2. Select Folder List from the menu displayed.

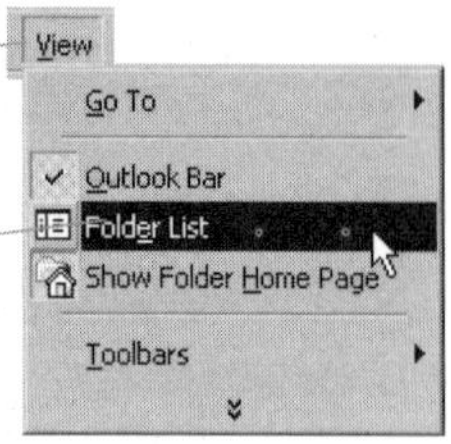

You can switch to any part of Outlook by double-clicking the folder name.

You can use the Outlook folders to switch between the various functions as an alternative to the Outlook bar. However, if you'd rather use the shortcuts, hide the Folder List:

3. Select View and Folder List again, or click the Close icon, and the action will be reversed.

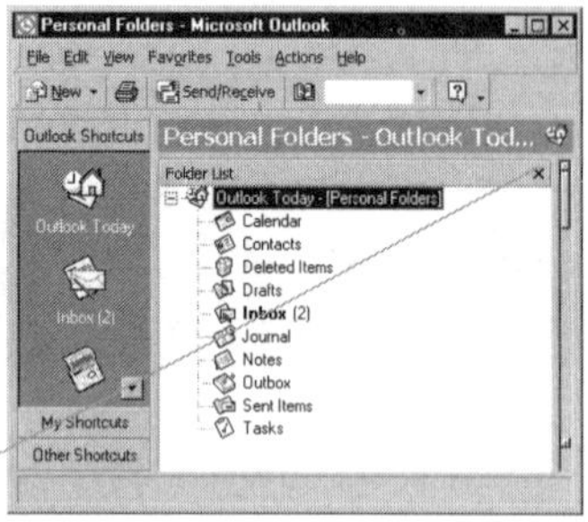

Chapter Six has more details of these Outlook files, and how to manage them.

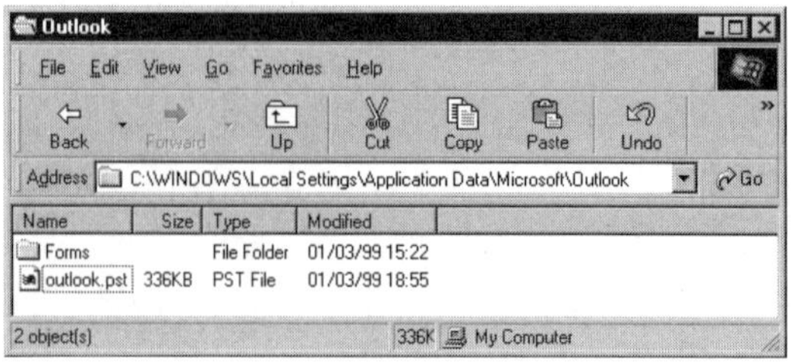

Outlook does not use the normal Windows file system to create Outlook folders, but uses a special file that holds all the contents of all the folders. This file is stored in the Outlook application data folder on your hard disk. Other special Outlook files contain the settings and configuration data required to control the way that Outlook works for you. (Chapter Six has more details of these Outlook files, and how to manage them.)

Menu and toolbars

Toolbars change as you switch functions, to include related tools and features.

Menus and toolbars in Outlook 2000 are automatically personalised – ie, as you use Outlook, individual features are dynamically promoted/demoted in the relevant menus/toolbars.

At first the menus will be abbreviated. To expand them manually, click on the chevrons at the foot of the menu:

(The lesser used features display in a paler grey.)

Toolbars display on a single row if possible, and overlap if there isn't enough room on screen. To display the lesser used buttons on a separate fly-out, click:

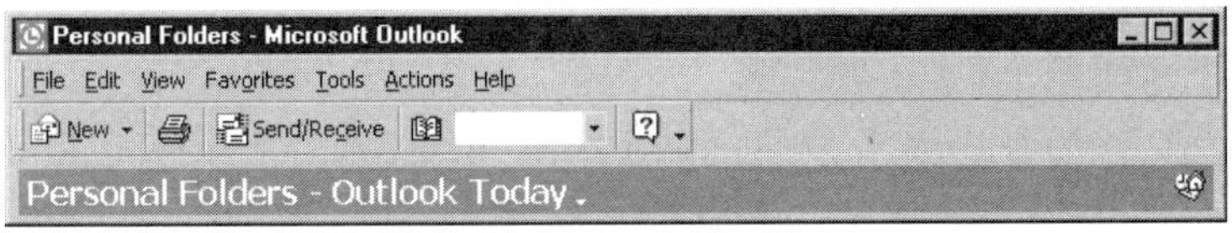

Across the top of the Outlook window you'll find the Menu bar with items such as File, Edit, and View, which display lists of commands and submenus. Below the Menu bar is the Standard toolbar, with buttons to give you quick access to the most used commands.

The actual contents of these bars are not fixed. For example when you change to the Inbox, you'll find that the toolbar is tailored to suit that specific part of Outlook.

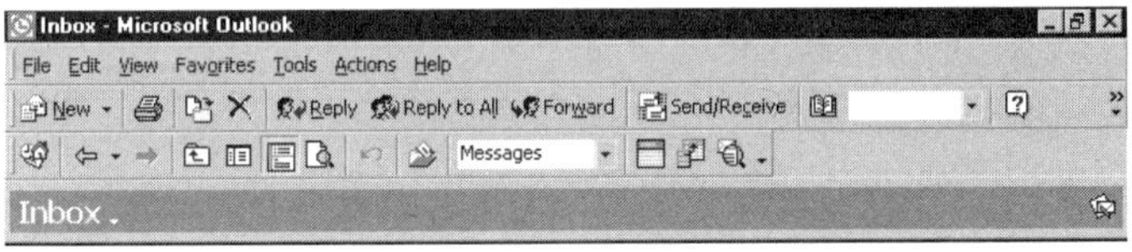

Display the Advanced toolbar to get quick access buttons for additional options. Follow these steps to display/hide an additional toolbar:

1. Select View from the Menu bar.

2. Click on the Toolbars option.

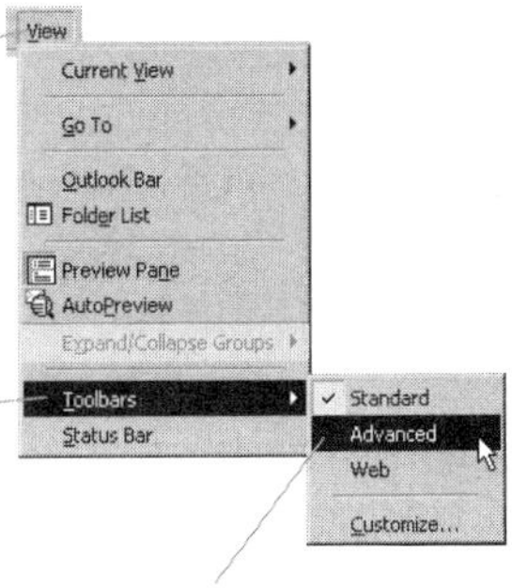

3. Click the name of an un-ticked toolbar to display it. (To remove a toolbar from display, click on a ticked toolbar.)

Inbox and e-mail

The Inbox is the folder where Outlook stores all your incoming messages. It is often chosen as the initial startup screen for Outlook, because it is a natural starting point to the day's work. It lets you receive new messages, review your existing messages, and take the necessary actions. The Inbox accepts various message types including e-mail, faxes, meeting requests and task assignments. It will also hold subfolders to group together the items that belong to a particular project or area of interest.

The Inbox preview pane lets you scroll through the selected message. Double-click the title to see the whole text.

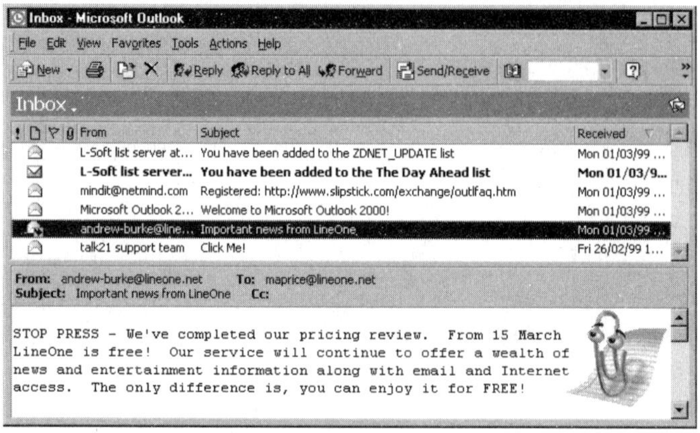

From the Inbox folder you can carry out any e-mail related task. The toolbar shows the main activities but there is a complete list in the Actions menu.

1. Select Actions from the Menu bar. Choose a task to perform.

2. Create new messages or faxes, search for specific messages, flag items for follow-up, forward messages to others, or issue replies to your messages.

All these e-mail actions and more are described in Chapters Four and Five.

Calendar and Taskpad

The Outlook Calendar will be one of the more used Outlook screens since it shows your schedule – a day, a week or a month at a time. It also reminds you of forthcoming events such as holidays and courses.

There are separate View options for the Calendar and the Taskpad, so you can adjust them to show the details you need.

1 Date navigator.

2 Diary/planner area.

3 Taskpad area.

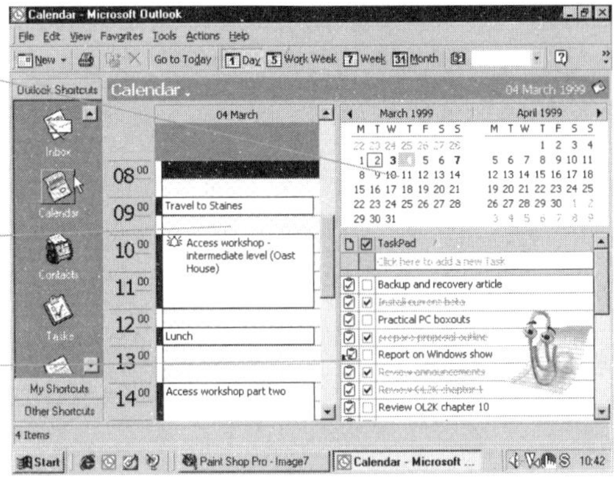

The Calendar will also display your task list for a selected period, giving you a summary of the jobs that you must carry out, or that you have assigned to another to perform, and showing you the latest status.

Use the Calendar to enter the details of your one-time or recurring meetings and appointments, and to set aside time for activities. If you are working with a team on a network, the Calendar can schedule meetings using the 'busy time' information for groups of people.

Dates and times can be entered in words: eg, "next Tuesday" or "noon". Outlook translates to the exact values.

4 Subject and location of appointment or meeting.

5 Start time and end time, and reminder for advance warning.

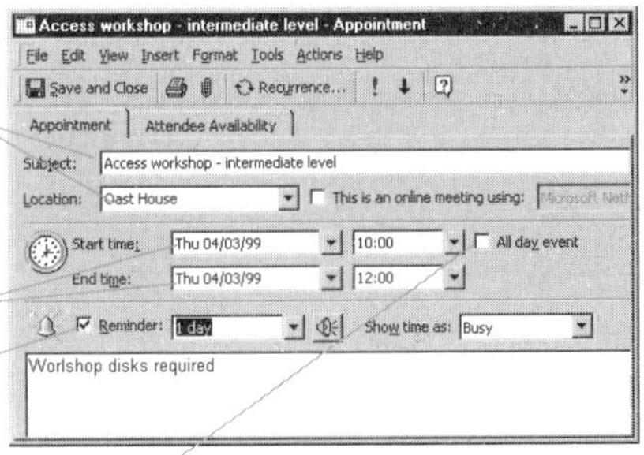

6 Type of meeting (all day, on-line, recurring, etc.).

Tasks list

For activities that are more complex than meetings or appointments, you may prefer the Tasks application in Outlook, to keep track of your business or personal projects. The task list can be a simple to-do list, or you can specify start and end dates and other details. The list shows the tasks by status:

When you mark a task as complete, it stays on the list but the description gets struck through, so you know it's done.

1. Completed task.
2. Overdue task.
3. Assigned task.
4. Scheduled task (not yet due).

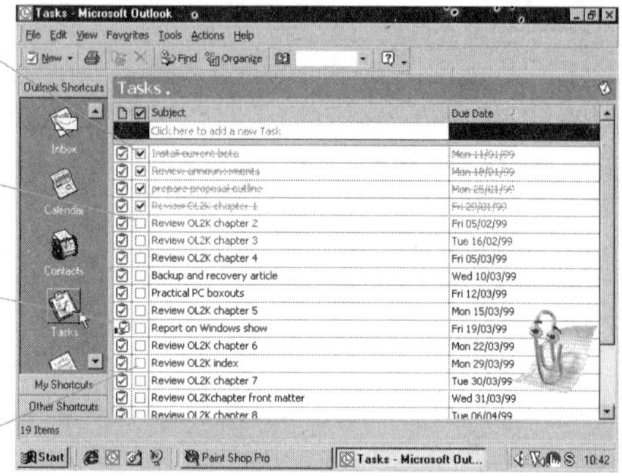

You will be warned when a task becomes due. You can dismiss the reminder and carry out the work, or you can postpone the reminder, for a few hours or days, and be reminded again.

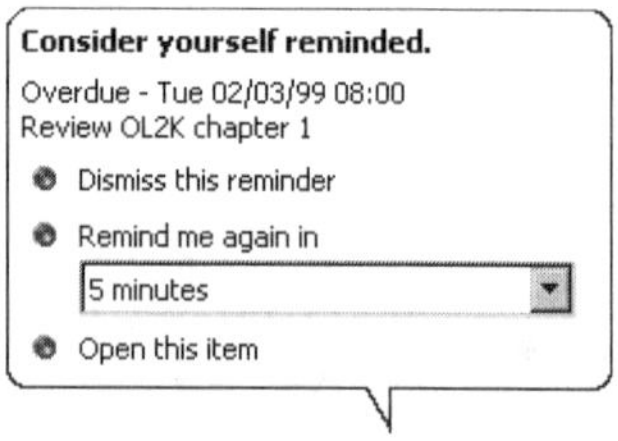

With the Task list, you'll never forget another anniversary, but you'll have to enter the dates first!

The task list is an ideal place to keep billing information when you have to account for your time, or to keep track of your business mileage and other expenses.

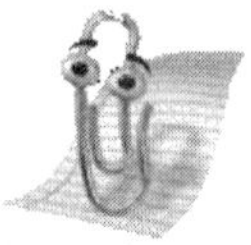

When you assign tasks to others, you can keep records of their progress in your own task list, through e-mailed updates and completion reports and updates. Status reports can also be sent out to anyone interested in the progress of the project.

Contacts manager

You can use Contacts for addressing in all your Windows applications.

Contacts holds phone numbers, fax numbers, mailing addresses, e-mail addresses, web pages and any other communication details you may want. It takes existing details from your current name and address lists, so you won't have to retype information. You can show the contents in many different styles to suit the needs of the moment, and use the details for other Outlook functions.

1 Name and address.

2 Phone numbers or fax numbers.

3 E-mail id's.

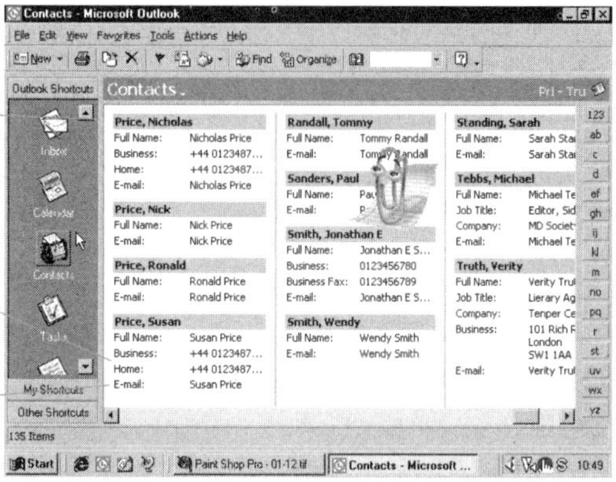

Contact details from e-mail and electronic business cards can be added without retyping.

When you make a new contact, you can add the details to the list. The Contacts function will minimise the amount of typing that you have to carry out.

4 Press the New Contacts button on the toolbar.

5 Type the full name, address, phone and fax numbers, and any other contact details that you may have.

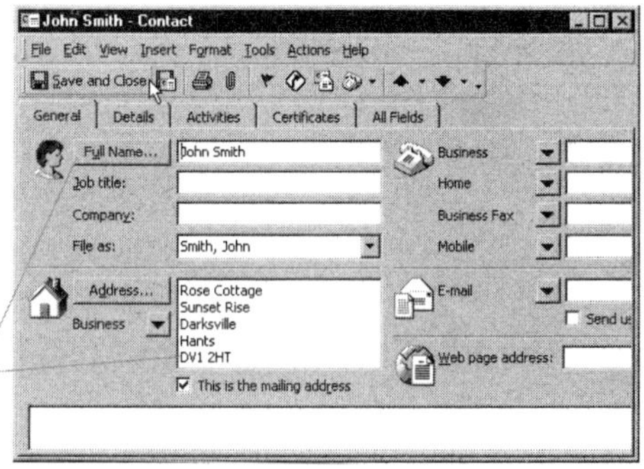

Just type names and addresses as they come. Outlook will ask if things are not clear.

6 Outlook separates out address lines and post codes, and rationalises telephone numbers.

Journal records

Journal will only record items for contacts located in the main Contacts folder.

Large numbers of tasks (or several concurrent projects) can be hard to organise, so you can set up the Journal to automatically keep track of chosen activities. The Journal will log all Outlook communications of the types you select, for the contacts you specify. It will also optionally log all activities on documents or spreadsheets.

The Journal does not log the contents of the items, but records their names and the times at which they were created or transmitted.

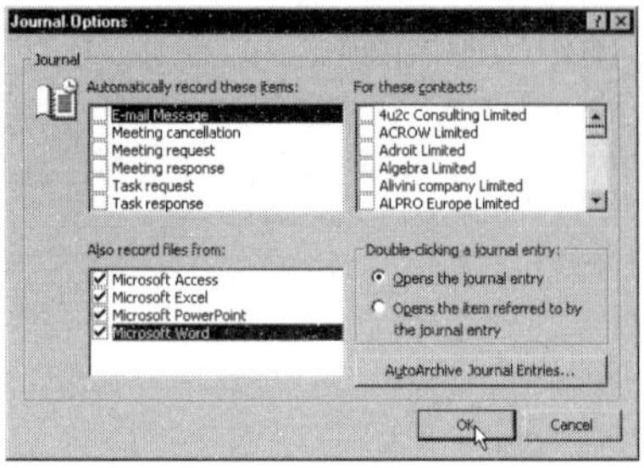

Outlook records activities for the Office 97 and Office 2000 versions of applications only.

The log will start off small but can grow very quickly, especially if you log your documents. You can limit the number of items displayed by restricting the time period, or by selecting particular contacts. You can also assign categories or project names to particular messages and use these to limit the view.

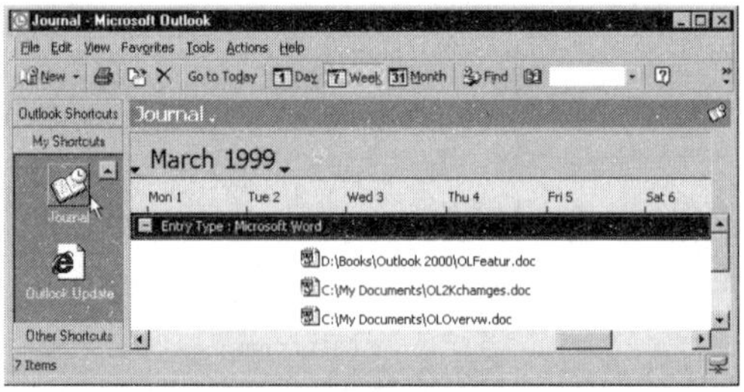

The Notes function is another way to keep track of tasks, especially ad hoc and unstructured activities. See Chapter Ten for more details.

Add records manually for existing documents or to keep track of items that are not scheduled for automatic recording. Use the Journal to keep track of any activity, not just Outlook or Office activities. For example, make a record when you receive an important letter, or take an important phone call, and use the details to help you create task reports or generate progress reports.

For less complex situations, the Activities tab in the Contacts manager may provide all the information you need, as Outlook reminds you when you open the Journal for the first time.

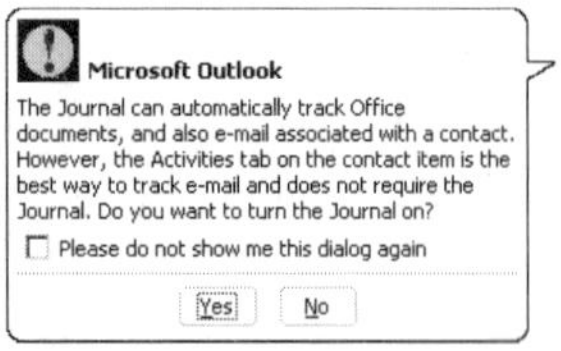

Beyond Outlook

Check also Outlook Add-ins which give extra functions. See Chapter Eleven.

There are some functions not included in Outlook itself, that you will find very useful in dealing with your mail and your schedule. Outlook provides the means for you to start up these external functions, using the Go To menu list:

1. Click Go on the Menu bar, and select Go To.

2. Expand the list if necessary and select the function you want.

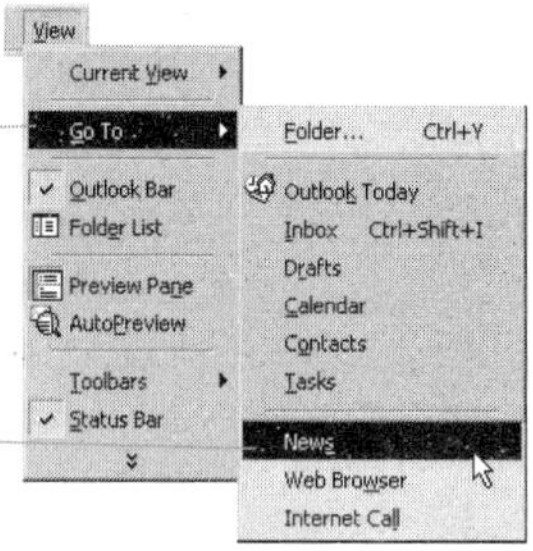

You will find out more about newsgroups in Chapter Seven.

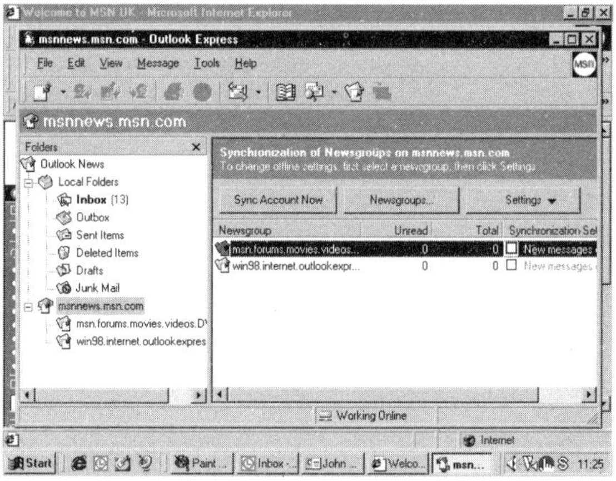

News starts your Newsreader where you can read messages and add your comments in various news groups. Outlook uses your existing newsreader, or sets up the Outlook newsreader, which is a news-only version of Outlook Express.

See chapter eight for details of Net Meeting.

Web Browser starts Internet Explorer 5, or your alternative web browser, and dials up your ISP if you are not already connected.

Internet Call allows you to initiate or participate in a meeting over the Internet, using Net Meeting with IE4 or an equivalent product for your web browser.

Which version of Outlook?

The full Outlook is not always the best choice. It depends on what functions you actually need.

If e-mail is the most crucial application for you, and you do not feel the need for scheduling or team work tools, then you could use Outlook Express, which concentrates on the e-mail and Internet newsgroup functions. The e-mail folders, and address book entries that they control, can be easily migrated to the full Outlook application, if you decide to upgrade at a future date.

If you are connected to a network and work with a group, you will have network server software such as Exchange Server. Outlook 2000 works with this software, allowing you to view the calendars and the time allocations for the group. You will also be able to delegate access to your personal folder, so that a co-worker can monitor your messages while you are busy or away.

You should select Outlook Express if you:

1. Prefer a simple, easy to use system.

2. Require only Internet e-mail and newsgroups.

3. Use Microsoft Office 98 for the Mac (includes Outlook Express).

This will give you a full e-mail service, but without the PIM functions.

You will be able to update to the full version of Outlook at any time in the future, if your requirements change. You will be able to retain all the messages and folders that you created in Outlook Express, and to migrate all the contact details and Internet links.

You should select Outlook 2000 if you:

Most examples assume you have Internet e-mail. Networks have many possible options, so if in doubt check with your Network administrator.

1. Need advanced e-mail and work group features.

2. Require personal or group scheduling and task management.

3. Use Microsoft Office 2000 or Microsoft Exchange Server.

Check your system against the installation described in Chapter Two, and see if there are any additional components you may need.

When you have selected the version of Outlook, there may be further choices to make, depending on the type of network or Internet connection that you are planning to use, and the way in which you need to communicate with other people, fellow workers, clients or associates. Outlook checks your existing system and makes these choices for you, if possible, or presents you with options and explanations to help you make the choice.

When you install your version of Outlook as described in Chapter Two, it detects the settings needed and selects the specific components required. If you find that Outlook has already been installed on your machine, use this chapter to help decide whether you have all the components you need. It describes the steps to follow if you find you need changes, showing you how to add or remove components, and it describes how to manage Outlook's startup.

The subsequent chapters take each function in turn to examine in more detail, working through examples and illustrating the options available. Most of the chapters apply to all versions of Outlook, and all types of e-mail service. Chapters Eight to Ten however deal with the PIM functions that are exclusive to the full version of Outlook. Chapter Eleven looks at examples of add-on functions and utilities for Outlook, from Microsoft and from others.

Updating your software

Outlook will detect existing e-mail and treat it as valid data, even if it was just a trial.

The first releases of Windows and Microsoft Office included e-mail clients and scheduling software as separate products. If you have Windows 98 or Internet Explorer 4 installed on your PC, you will have Outlook Express 4 with improved e-mail features. This product is also included as the e-mail client in the software supplied by some Internet service providers, for example MSN.

Recognising the need for greater integration, Microsoft developed the Outlook product to provide similar e-mail functions to Outlook Express, with the addition of scheduling and information management.

Outlook 97 was included as an integral part of Microsoft Office 97 and of Microsoft Exchange Server. Outlook 98 was later released as an upgrade, available initially as a separate product, for free download from the Internet. There were also CD versions supplied on the cover discs of various PC magazines. The free offer was later replaced by another free offer, this time limited to registered users of Office 97, Outlook 97, and Exchange Server.

See in Chapter Two how to access the Microsoft web site to download Outlook or its add-on components.

Internet Explorer 5 includes Outlook Express 5. Outlook 2000 is integrated with Microsoft Office 2000 and may be available as a separate product or included in future releases of Microsoft Exchange Server.

Even if you are not using Office 2000, it may be worth checking at the Microsoft Office Update web site, to see what offers Microsoft may make from time to time for this latest version of Outlook.

Installing Outlook

In this chapter you will see how to set up Internet mail, why and how to install Outlook, how to replace any existing e-mail or personal information management (PIM) applications, and how to add or remove components.

Covers

Chapter Two

Prerequisites to Outlook

You should apply the latest service releases to your operating system before you install Outlook 2000.

You need to consider the applications and software that are already installed on your PC, to ensure that they will work effectively with Outlook. There are four main areas:

1. Microsoft Windows operating system
   The examples in this book assume you have Windows 98 installed on your PC, but the recommendations apply to PCs with Windows 95 and IE5.
   There may be differences in details such as installation procedures and software tools for PCs with Windows NT workstation or Windows 2000 Professional.

2. Office applications
   Your word processing, spreadsheet and other applications will exchange information with Outlook. It is best if these applications are designed to work with Outlook, like the applications in Office 2000.

Even if your applications don't directly support Outlook, you may be able to import and export data.

3. Internet software
   You will need Internet Explorer 5 or another Internet browser, plus any software provided by your chosen ISP.

4. E-mail software
   You need the appropriate version of Outlook. This may be included with the Office or Internet software, or you may obtain a separate stand-alone version.

Make a list of the applications and software on your PC and keep this available for reference, in case any problems arise when you start using Outlook. Technical support staff will need to know what is installed to identify the cause of any error.

To run this software you must have the appropriate hardware components on your PC. You'll need the following items or their functional equivalent:

1. PC with Intel 486/66 processor
   This is the minimum, but a Pentium processor is recommended for Internet access and networking.

2. 8Mb memory (Windows 95/98) or 16Mb memory (Windows NT 4.0 or Windows 2000)
   Again, these are minimums, and at least double, perhaps four times would be much better.

3. 65Mb disk storage
   This does not include the storage needed for mail and for Internet pages. Allow about 15% of the hard disk.

4. Data or data/fax modem 28.8 kbps
   With e-mail and Fax, 14.4kbps is fast enough, but Internet activity needs more speed, 33.3kbps or 56kbps.

Choosing your ISP

If you are starting out with a new PC, you will find the software for Windows and your applications pre-installed, but you will need to set up your access to the Internet and establish your e-mail account.

You can use any ISP that you wish, but Microsoft makes it easier to get started with some of the more popular options.

If you are planning to use one of the major Internet service providers, Windows 98 includes the procedures necessary to establish an account or to provide the details of your existing account. To view the list of services supported:

1. Press Start, Programs, Online services.

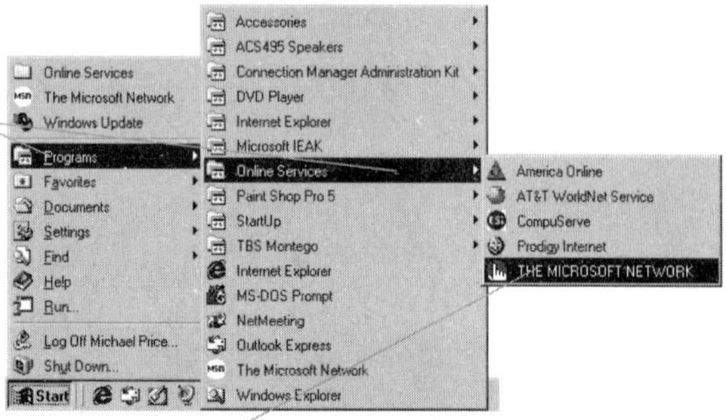

2. Choose the service you want to try: AOL; AT&T; CompuServe; Prodigy; or MSN.

If you already have an account with one of these, make sure that your account name and password are ready to hand. If you are planning to use one of the free trial offers that give you a month's free usage, the package will provide the information needed.

Note that you are not restricted to the above services, but you will require a setup procedure from the ISP concerned if you want to connect to a different service. You may also need special software. Check with the help line for the service to confirm the process.

If you will be connecting to the Internet through a local area network, you'll need information from your network administrator, such as the name of the proxy server and the port number.

Your administrator may also provide special settings to configure your browser for corporate networks.

Setting up your Internet service

Check that the ISP has a local phone number for your area, a lo-call number charged at local call rates, or best of all a free (0800) number.

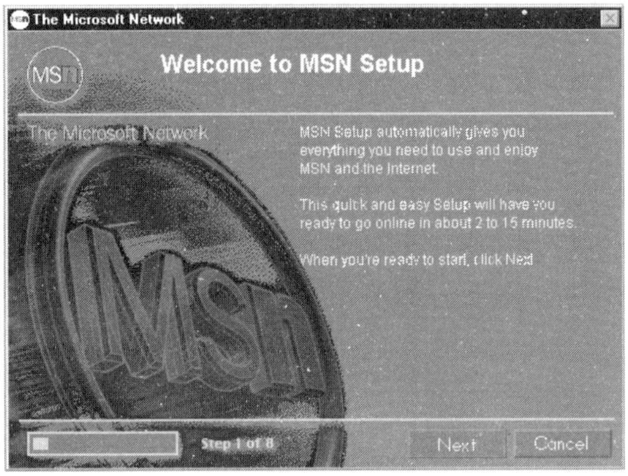

Select the service you are using, and you will be taken through the process for defining your account. For example, if you choose MSN (the Microsoft Network), you are taken step by step through the procedure:

1. Specify your country and location information.
2. Review the ISP agreement, since you'll be agreeing to its terms when you press Accept.
3. Insert the Windows CDROM for the required files to be copied onto your hard drive.
4. Enter the user id and password information for your existing account, or the details for a trial offer or new account.

You may be asked for a credit card number, so be sure to cancel the trial if you change your mind.

Restart the PC and the appropriate icons will be added to the desktop. Connect to the ISP for the first time, to finalise details such as the telephone number to dial for future connections and to establish your account, and if appropriate set up your web space.

Making the Internet connection

There are entries in the Dialup Networking folder for all the services defined on your PC.

Start the browser by selecting the icon on the desktop or the Quick Launch toolbar on the taskbar. You may also find entries added by your ISP, such as the MSN icon on the desktop and the MSN quick start icon on the system tray. Starting the browser initiates the sign-on process.

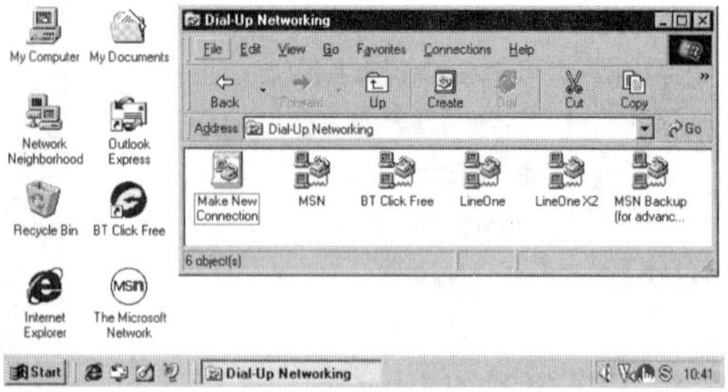

Press Cancel if you want to work off-line (eg, to view web pages that you have previously downloaded).

1. Enter your user id and password, and press Connect.
2. Dialling begins, and the modem connects to the ISP security server.
3. The server checks your id and password. When this is completed, it passes control to the browser and you see your start up Internet page.

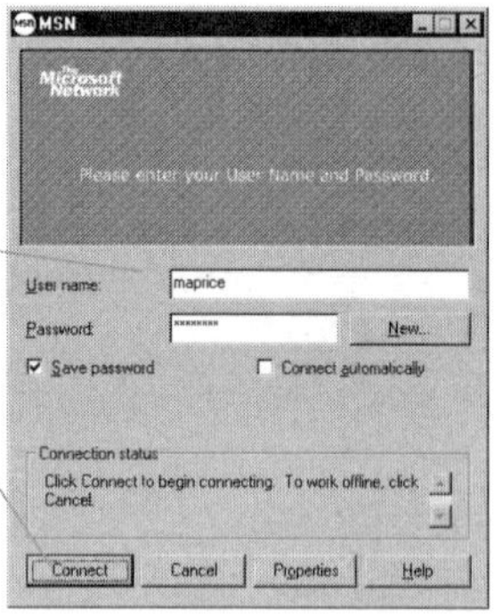

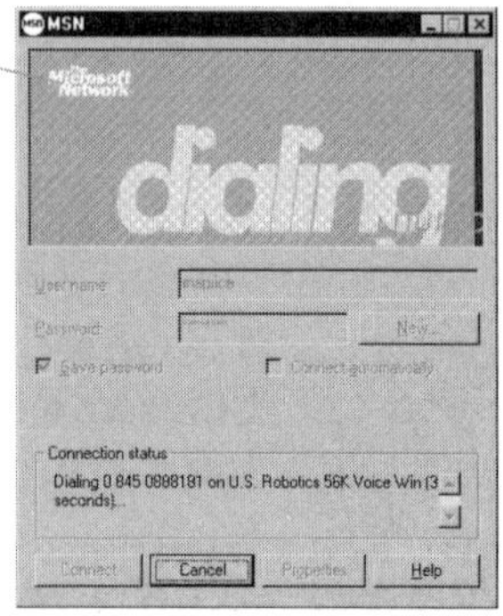

If you are part of a local area network, you may not have to dial up to use the Internet.

The browser will always switch to the same page on the Internet, giving you the latest version. The default page is likely to be related to your ISP, but you can select any Internet page as your start up or Home page, in your own web space or at another web site.

...cont'd

You'll see a page like this if you choose MSN home page for the UK as your starting point.

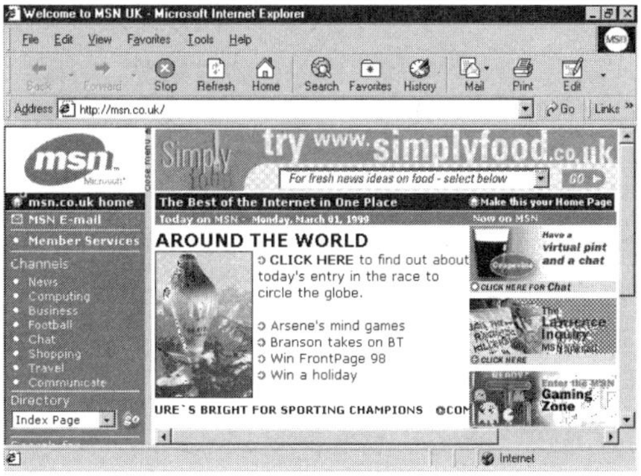

You don't have to belong to a site to display its pages, except for those pages restricted to members only.

Choose the areas or topics that interest you, to get a quick news update every time you connect to the Internet.

To select a new home page, you must change the Internet options. Follow these steps:

1. Select Tools from the Menu bar.

2. Select the Internet Options entry.

Press Use Current, and the web page you currently have open becomes your new home page.

3. Type in the URL web page address, for example: http://www.msn.co.uk/

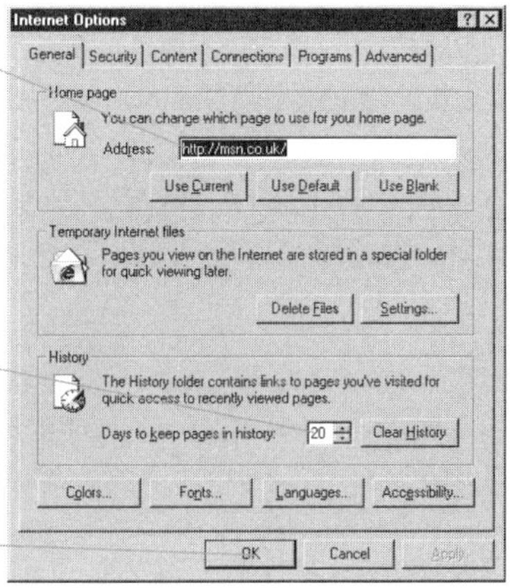

4. You can tell the browser how long to retain links to the pages you visit.

Press Blank to start the browser without fetching any page from the Internet.

5. Press OK to save settings.

Internet mail

You can also use the News function to read and take part in newsgroup discussions. See Chapter Seven.

With your browser open, you can switch to the e-mail service to read or send messages.

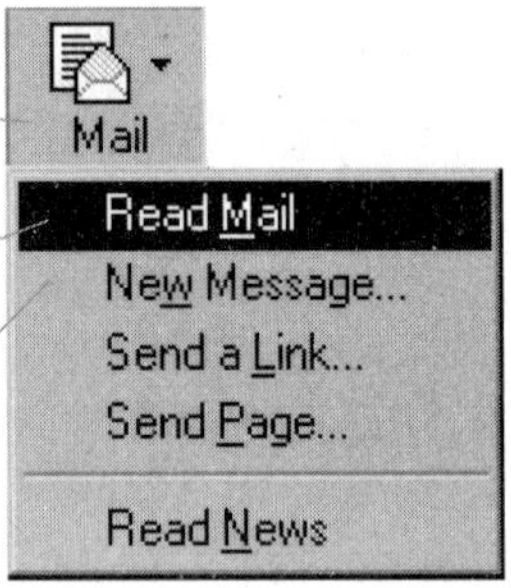

1 Select Mail from the Menu bar.

2 Select Read Mail to review the messages in your Inbox.

3 Choose New Message to create and send an e-mail message.

This will start the e-mail client software defined for your Internet service. For MSN and IE5 this will be Outlook Express. The layout of the screen depends on the way your system has been set up, but a typical setting will show the Folder List, your contacts, the Inbox and a preview showing the contents of the message currently selected.

You do not have to sign on to the Internet to view the contents of your Inbox, or to compose messages and replies. You must be connected to receive new mail or to send the messages after you have composed them.

Outlook Express

Outlook Express can be run separately: it does not require you to start your Internet browser software.

You can run Outlook Express from the Start menu, or from the icon on the desktop, or from the entry on the Quick Launch toolbar.

Outlook Express by default starts up in the high level, summary view with links to all the parts. It does not dial up to the Internet or mail server immediately, but you can set it to check periodically for messages, and it will request to dial up at those times.

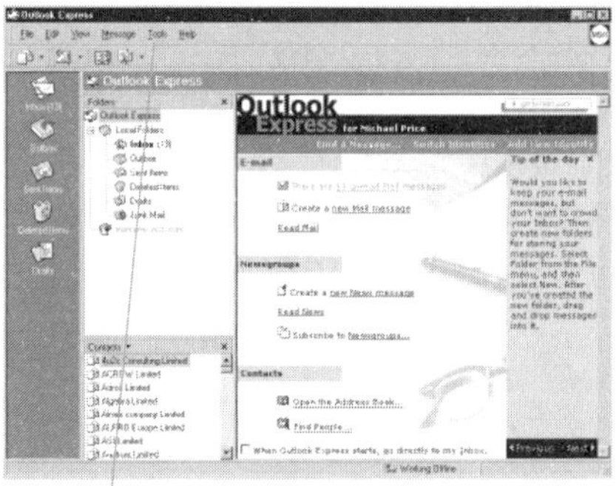

To change the startup actions and control the dial up connection to the mail server:

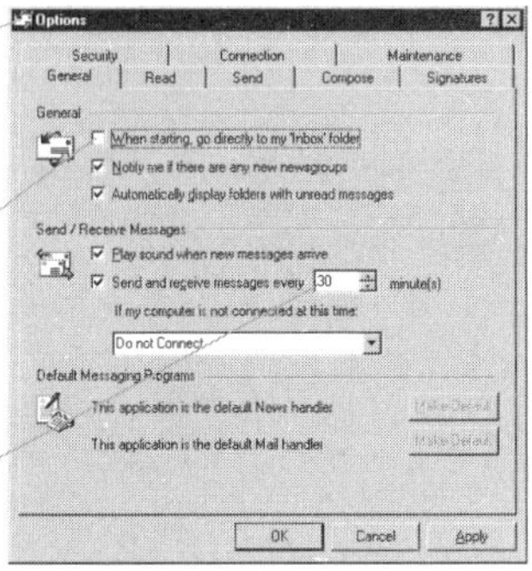

1 Select Tools from the Menu bar, and select the Options entry.

If you clear the delay period box, you will have to press Send and Receive when you want to check for mail at the server.

2 Check the box to start up in the Inbox folder rather than the Outlook Express window. Set the delay period between checks for mail.

3 You can display the Outlook bar with its shortcut icons, as an alternative to the folder list for navigating through Outlook Express.

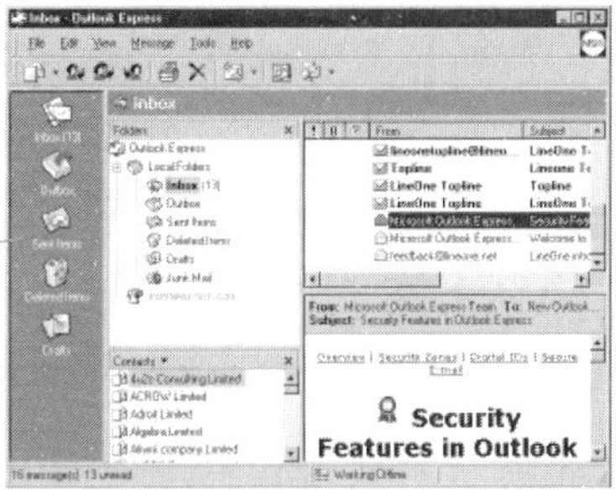

Changing identity

You can create different Identities in Outlook Express. If you and another member of your family share the same PC, each of you can view your own mail and your own contacts by creating an identity for yourself.

To add a new identity:

Hot tip: Your contacts and mail are not entirely private, but this method does avoid information being intermingled.

1. Select File from the menu bar, then Identities and then click Add New Identity.

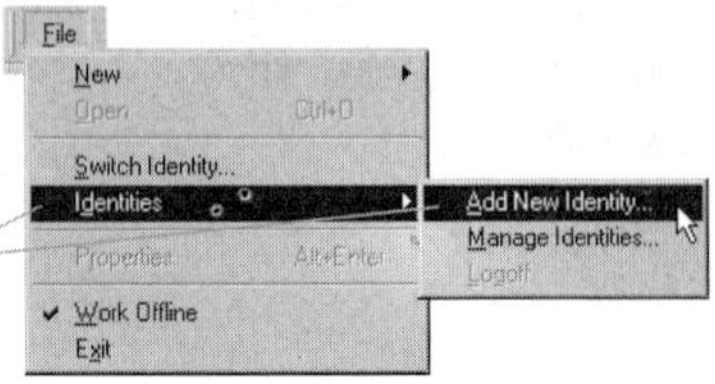

2. Enter the name for the new user. The connection wizard will ask for e-mail account details.

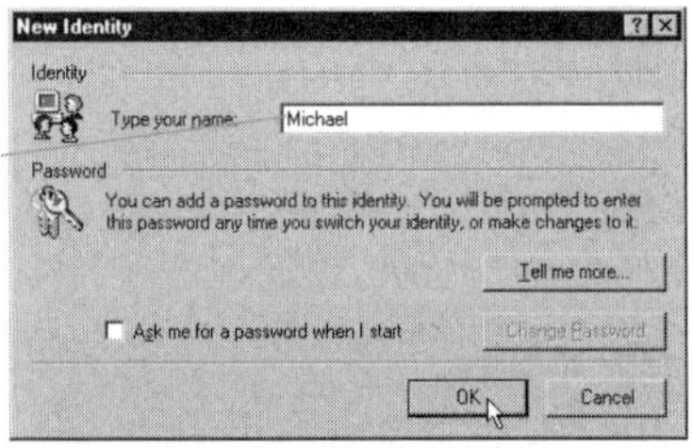

As well as a private address book, there is a Shared folder that can be used as a group address book, or as an area for exchanging contact information.

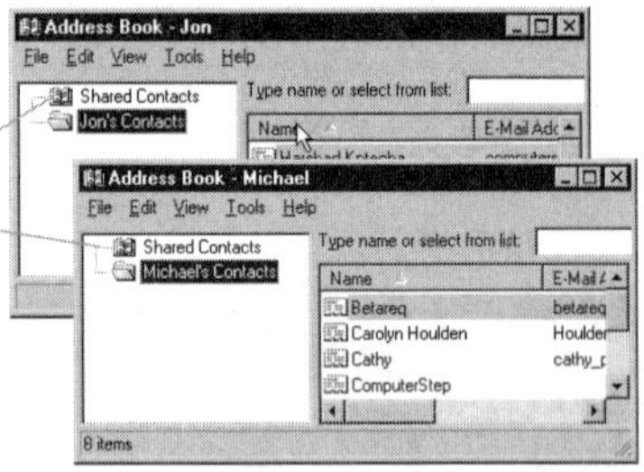

You can switch between identities without having to restart Outlook Express:

Hot tip: Only the default contact and mail details are migrated to Outlook 2000 when you upgrade.

3. Select File from the menu bar, then click Switch Identity.

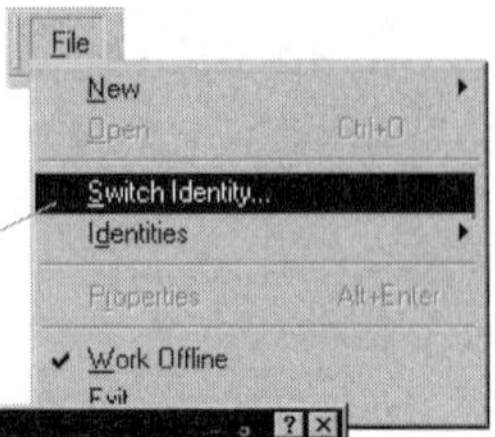

4. Choose another identity, or select the main default identity.

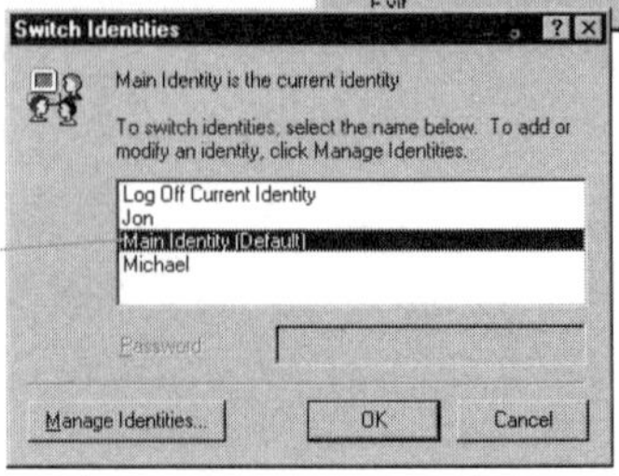

Upgrading to the full Outlook

See Chapter One for advice on which version of Outlook to choose.

If you decide that you need additional management and scheduling functions, you can replace Outlook Express (or any other e-mail client installed on your PC) with the full version of Outlook.

If you have already used your existing e-mail client, you will not lose any of the message logs, and you will not have to re-enter any names and e-mail addresses that you may have accumulated, since the installation procedure takes care of transferring these to your new system.

Setup will determine all of the components you need, and set up Outlook for No E-mail, for Internet Mail Only or for Corporate and Workgroup, based on your PC configuration.

Outlook is provided as a part of Microsoft Office 2000, so you may already have the full version. However, the version of Outlook included in Office 97 and known as Outlook 97 had several shortcomings, so you should upgrade that version to Outlook 2000.

There are several ways to install a copy of Outlook 2000:

1. Run Setup from the Office 2000 CDROM and install Office, including Outlook as a component.
2. Install Outlook as a separate product from the Office CDROM or the Outlook CDROM.
3. Install Outlook as an included component of the Microsoft Exchange mail.
4. Connect to the Internet and run the active setup to install or update Outlook 2000.

The following section describes the installation of Outlook as part of Office 2000. The installation processes are similar for the other methods, once you have selected the product and started the setup itself.

Installing Office and Outlook

Ensure that the latest version of IE5 is installed with your Office 2000 installation.

This is the most usual method of installing Outlook, since you will have all the components of Office, at the same level of upgrade.

To carry out the installation, insert the Office CDROM and Setup will automatically run.

1. Enter your personal details and the CD key for the product.

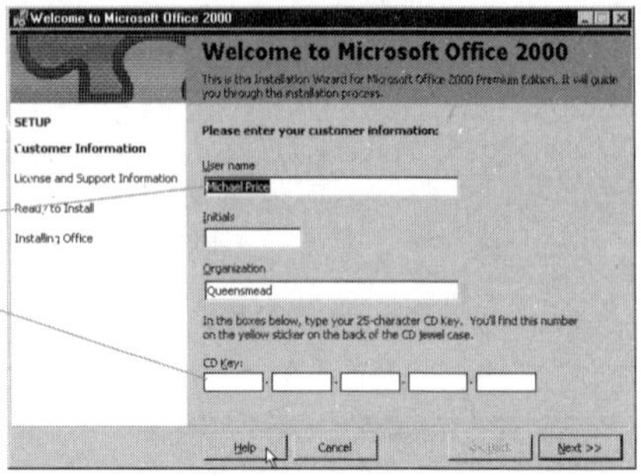

2. As always, you must accept the terms and conditions.

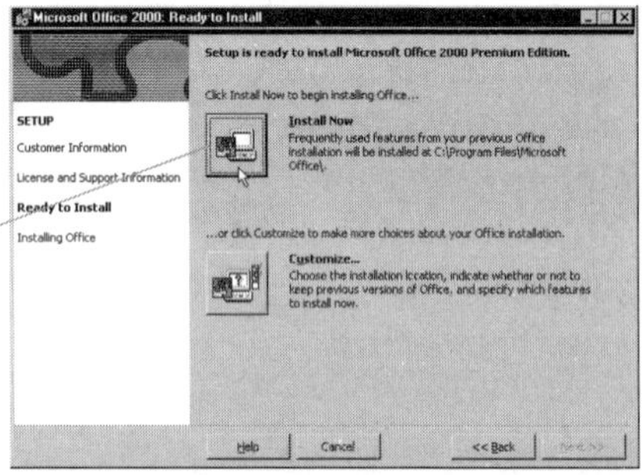

To be sure it will be installed at this time, click the Customise option, and explicitly select Outlook 2000.

3. Select the default installation and the applications used in your prior version will be replaced by Office 2000 versions.

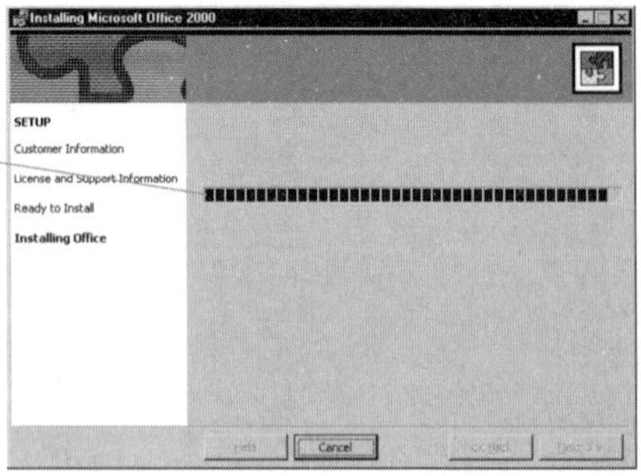

4. The required files are copied without further intervention. You must allow the system to restart upon completion of the file copying.

The Office 2000 Setup program uses a different approach from previous versions. All applications are enabled for selection, but those not previously active are not immediately copied to the hard disk. If you decide to use them in the future, they will be copied on first use.

Running Outlook for the first time

Outlook recognises it is being started for the first time and looks for any existing e-mail applications and folders that may need converting.

When you have installed Outlook, you can start it using the Start menu entry, or from the new icon on the desktop.

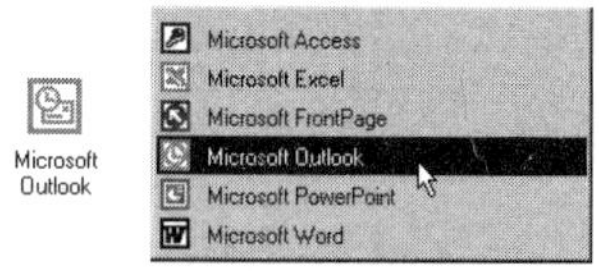

The startup wizard guides you through the steps in configuring Outlook 2000. It lists the e-mail packages found on your PC. If one of these was your active e-mail system, choose it so that it will be converted to Outlook.

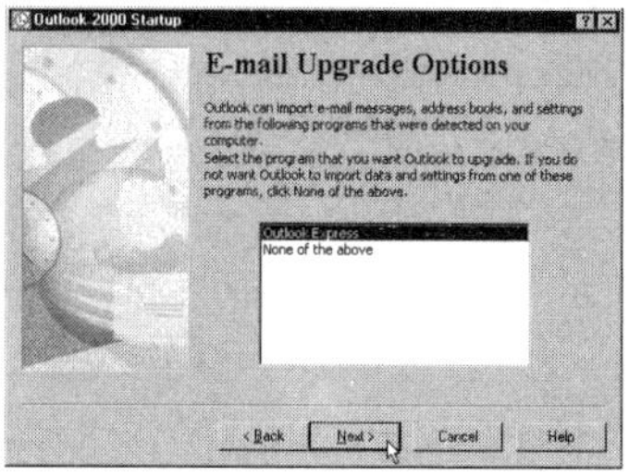

The e-mail account and server details that are extracted from the previous files are displayed. This allows you to check the values and click the Change Settings box to make any adjustments needed.

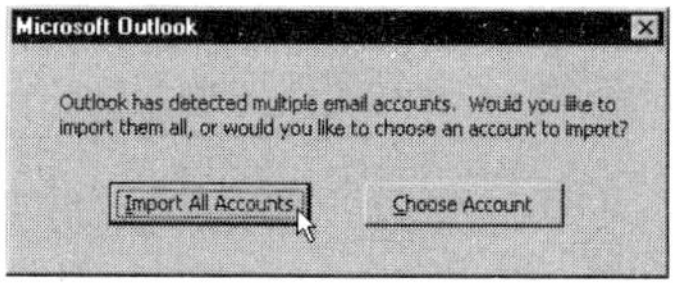

Optionally, the e-mail messages and the name and address list from the previous system are copied to your new Outlook folders.

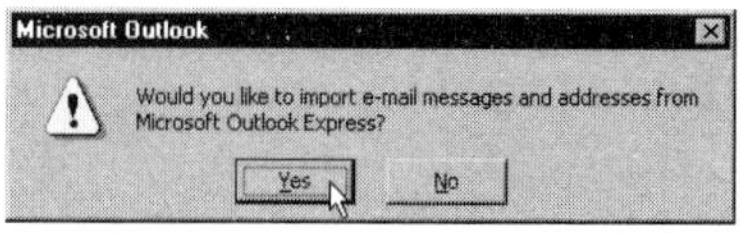

You should register your new version of Outlook as the default for mail, news and contact information.

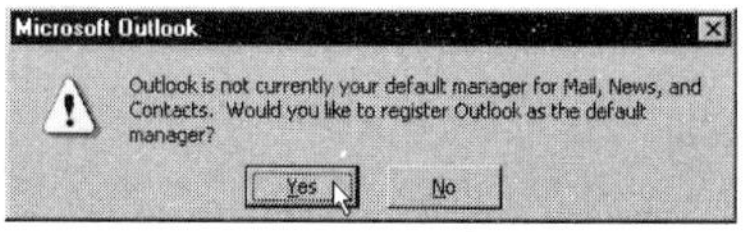

To start using Outlook to send and receive messages, see Chapter Three.

Outlook Express remains on your hard disk because it will be used by Outlook for accessing newsgroups, but it should no longer be used for e-mail. Check that the default e-mail system in the settings for your Internet browser reflects this change.

The old entries for Outlook Express are removed from the desktop and from the quick launch toolbar, and Outlook is ready for use, on its own or from the Internet browser.

Changing Setup

Chapter Eleven lists all the add-ins available from Microsoft, plus add-ins from other sources.

When you re-insert the Office CDROM in the future, or run Add/Remove and select Office 2000, the Setup program detects that Office is already installed and starts in maintenance mode.

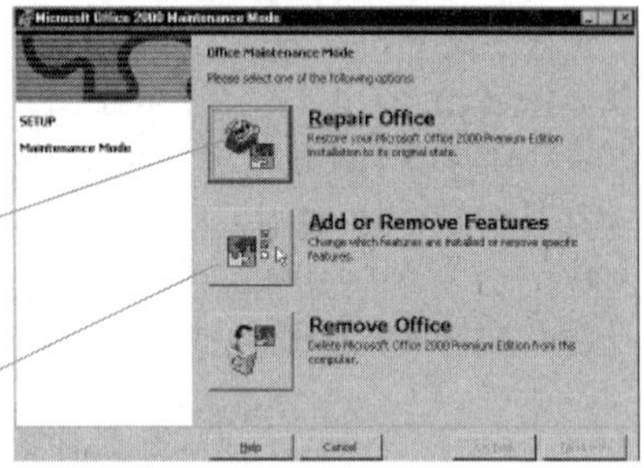

1 Select Repair Office to return your installation to its original settings.

2 Select Add or Remove features to change the installation.

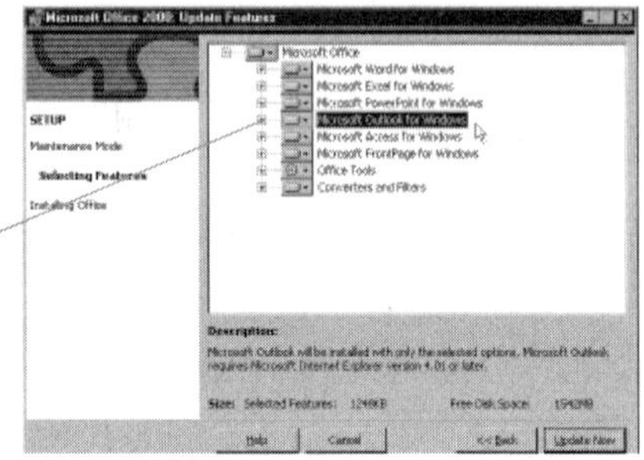

3 Select the Outlook entry and click the [+] to list the features.

This displays all the components of Outlook, and shows you how they are installed. To view or change the installation options for an item:

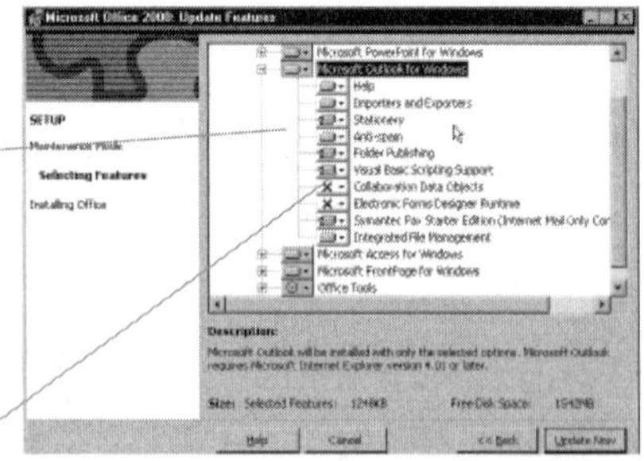

4 Right-click a feature to display the options.

Features may be installed to run from disk, run from CD, or to be copied on first use. The latter option means that the Office CD should always be near to hand, in case it is needed.

Controlling Outlook startup

The Outlook help file lists command line switches which allow you to start Outlook in a specific mode or with a specific form or folder. To find the help details, search for the words "Control start up", using the Office Assistant.

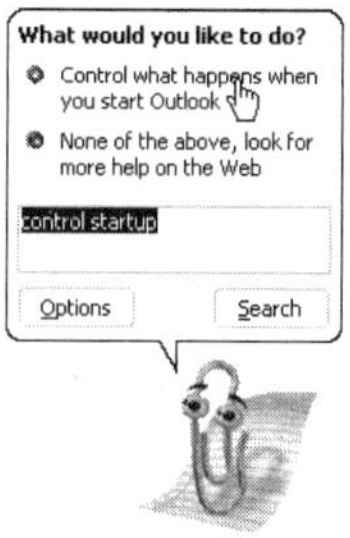

The switches include:

/folder	Hides the Outlook Bar
/select path/folder	Display the named folder
/c ipm.note	Create an e-mail message
/c ipm.post	Create a post
/c ipm.appointment	Create an appointment
/c ipm.task	Create a task
/c ipm.contact	Create a contact
/c ipm.activity	Create a journal entry
/c ipm.stickynote	Create a note

Paths that include spaces, such as C:\Program Files**, must be enclosed in quotation marks.**

To specify a folder in Outlook, precede the path with "Outlook:\\"**.**

There are some additional switches (not discussed in the help topic) which clear and regenerate certain types of item in Outlook. These could be very useful for resolving problems with the particular types of item, but they will delete information from the folders, so make sure to backup Outlook before trying these switches.

/CleanFreeBusy	Clear free/busy information
/CleanReminders	Clear reminders
/CleanViews	Restore default views
/ResetFolders	Restore missing folders
/ResetOutlookBar	Rebuild the Outlook Bar

See Chapter Six for information on Outlook backup and folder archive.

Using switches

Create a shortcut on the Desktop, to start Outlook with the switches.

Command line switches are used when Outlook starts up. The easiest way to add switches is to create a shortcut to the Outlook program:

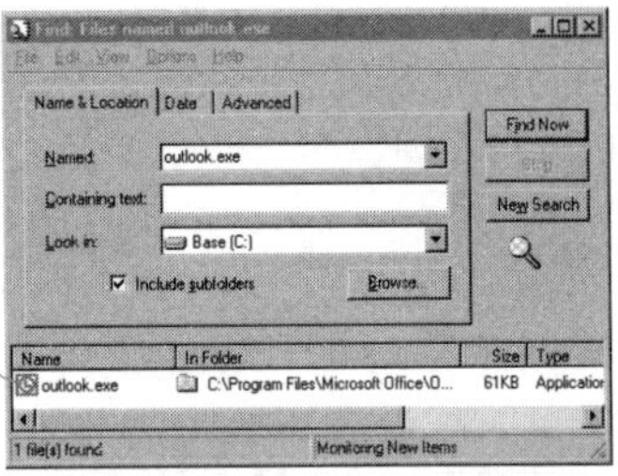

1. Use Windows Find to locate the Outlook.exe file.
2. Right-click and drag the file to the desktop to create a shortcut.

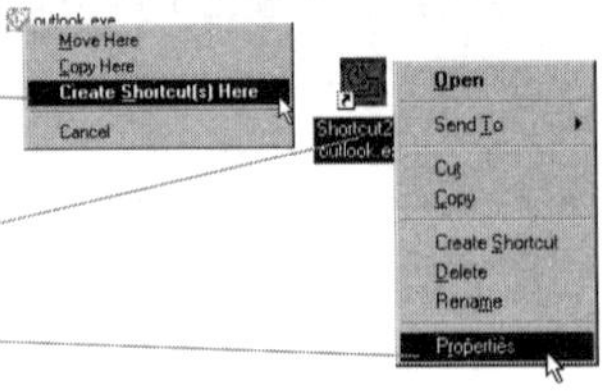

If you have installed Windows 98 and are currently using Web style (rather than Classic style), single-click (rather than double-click) on the Outlook shortcut in step 5.

3. Right-click the shortcut and select Properties.
4. Enter the command line switch after the file name in the Target box and press OK.
5. Double-click the shortcut to start up Outlook with the specified switches.

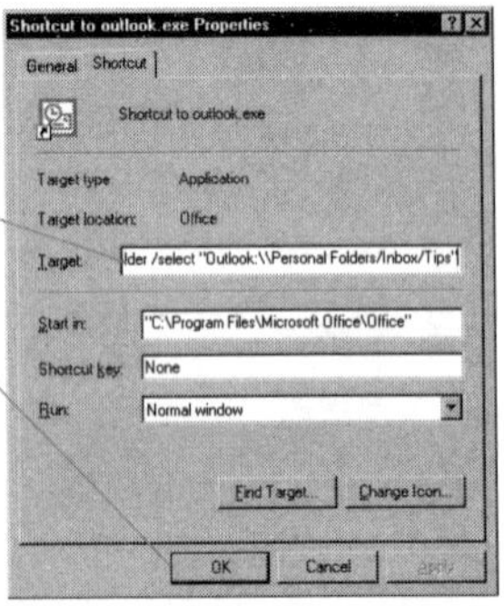

Chapter Ten shows how to start up Outlook to create a Note.

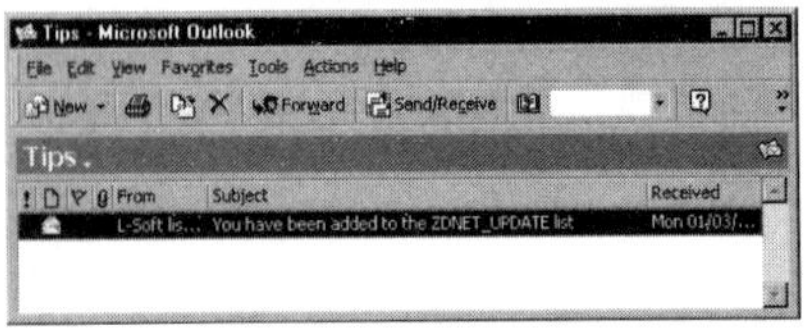

For example, if you have added a new folder to your Inbox, called tips, and you want Outlook to start up with the Tips folder (and without the shortcut bar), enter these command line switches:

/folder /select "Outlook:\\personal folders/inbox/tips"

To start in Outlook with the My Documents folder open:

/folder /select "C:/My Documents"

Using Outlook

In this chapter, you'll see the different ways of starting Outlook – on its own or from the Internet browser. You will also see how to set up the Outlook environment, and how to switch between Outlook and other Windows applications.

Covers

Chapter Three

Starting Outlook Today

When you start Outlook, it will begin at the e-mail Inbox folder by default. This is ideal for e-mail and Internet mail, but for other activities you may prefer to start with Outlook Today, which provides a general interface to the mail, calendar, tasks and contacts functions.

When you start Outlook, you do not need to be actively connected to the Internet.

1. Select Outlook Today from the Outlook bar and click the Customize Outlook Today button.

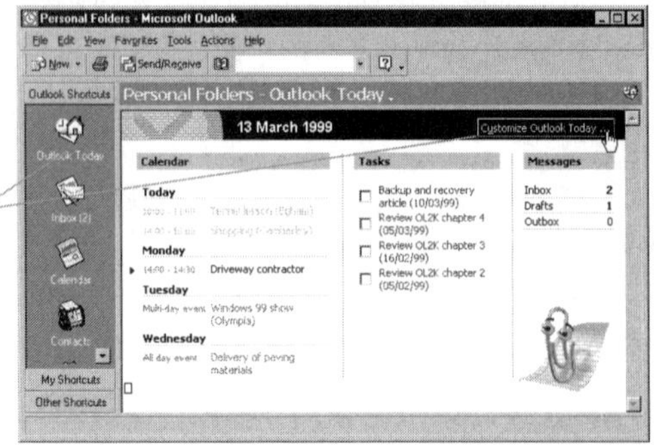

2. Click in the Startup box to go directly to Outlook Today.
3. Set the number of days (1–7) in the calendar display.
4. Choose a full task list or today's tasks only.

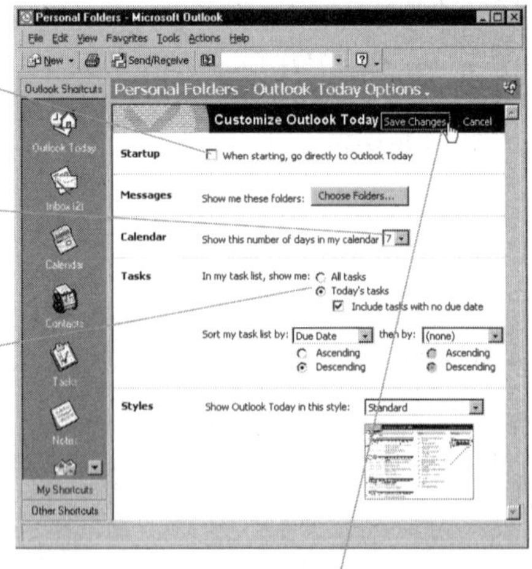

You can change the style of Outlook Today's window.

5. Press the Save Changes button to go back to the Outlook Today window.

The next time that you start Outlook, the Today window, with your selected settings for calendar and task lists, will be displayed first.

Outlook Express also offers you the choice between Inbox and a high level function window, as the initial startup display screen.

Starting Outlook automatically

If you set Outlook to start up at power on, avoid connecting automatically to the Internet.

Outlook will quickly become an essential part of your system, and you may decide that you want it to start automatically every time you start the system. You can achieve this by adding Outlook to the Startup folder.

1. Right-click the Start button, and click the Open entry.

If you are currently using the Web style view (rather than the Classic style view), single-click (rather than double-click) on the icons in step 2.

2. Double-click the Programs icon and then double-click the Startup icon to open the folder.

3. Right-click the Outlook icon, drag it from the desktop and Drop it in the Startup folder.

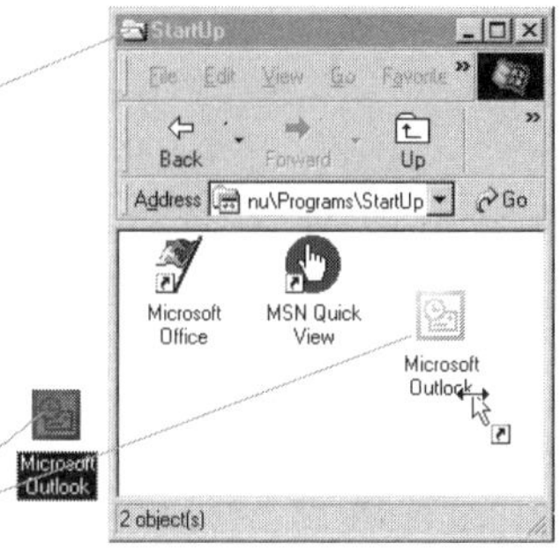

4. Select the entry to create a shortcut, and Outlook will be added to the startup list.

Close the folders when you have made your update to the Startup folder.

Whenever you restart the PC, the programs in the Startup folder are executed, and so Outlook will automatically start up and display the Today windows or the Inbox, depending on the options you chose.

'Close all items' is a quick way to tidy up, when you have been busy opening and actioning your e-mail and other Outlook items.

Though there are many different ways to start Outlook, closing is much simpler. You just click the Close button on the top right, or select File, Exit.

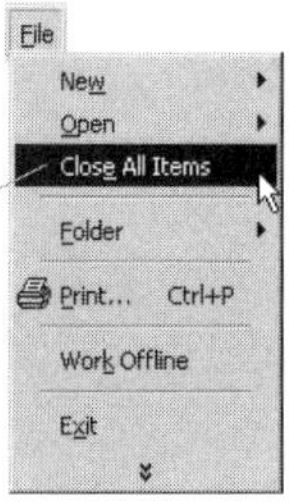

If you're not quite ready to Exit, you might try the File, Close All Items option. This, as its name implies, will close all the open Outlook items (messages, task, appointments etc) but leave the Outlook program active.

Getting help

Outlook 2000 uses the Assistant as the interface to the help system.

The easiest way to get help is with the Office Assistant. Familiar to users of Office 97 and Office 2000, it provides in-context help and guidance, and useful tips. It is often as handy as the humble paperclip it emulates, but it does sometimes get in the way. To work with the assistant:

1. Press Help on the toolbar if the Assistant is hidden.

2. Click on the Assistant to reveal its message box.
3. Enter a question and press Search.
4. Click the Assistant again to remove the message

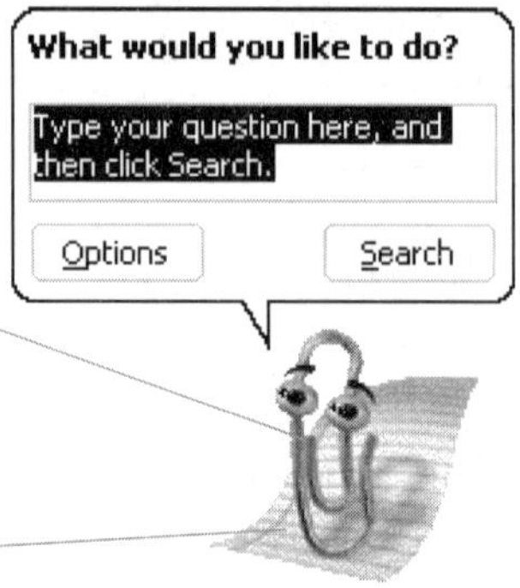

To choose a different Assistant, with its own style and animations:

You can change the shape and the style of the Assistant, but the help offered stays much the same.

5. Click the Assistant, select Options and click the Gallery tab.
6. Press Next or Back to find the Assistant you prefer, and then press OK.

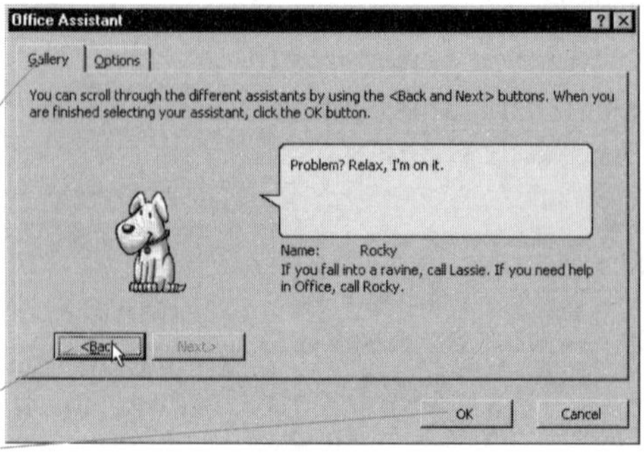

You may need the Office CD, if that Assistant is not installed.

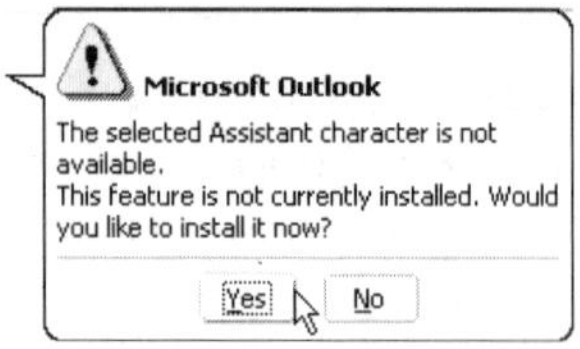

If the animated assistant gets in the way, you can switch it off.

You can temporarily hide or show the Office Assistant while you're working in Microsoft Outlook. You can also turn off the Office Assistant and use only the Help window.

To turn the Assistant on or off on a temporary basis:

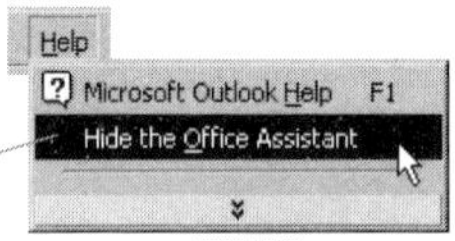

1 Select Help from the menu bar and click Hide the Office Assistant.

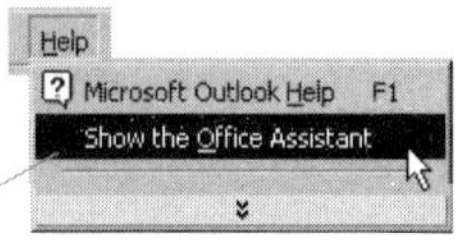

2 Click Help, Show the Office Assistant to reverse the action.

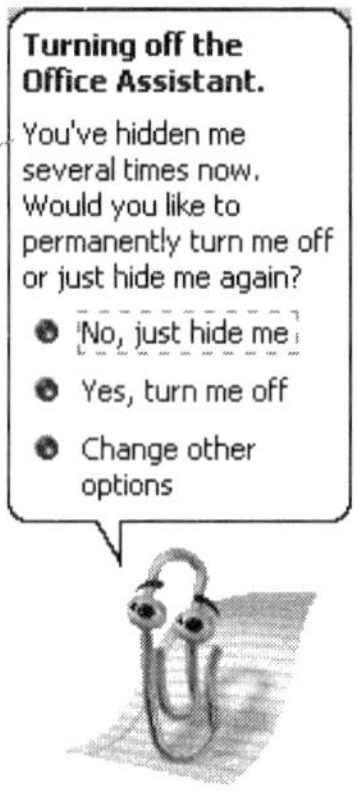

3 If you hide the Assistant several times, it may offer to retire!

4 Otherwise, to switch the Assistant off permanently, open the Options panel, click the Options tab, and clear the 'Use the Office Assistant' box.

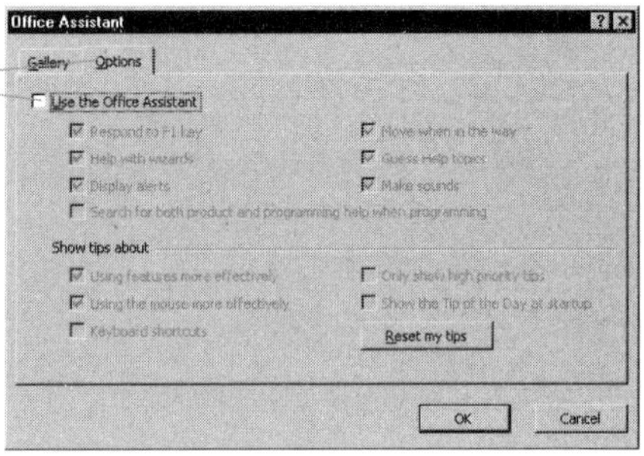

Now you can use the normal Help features such as Contents, Answer wizard and Index to locate the information you want.

You can reinstate the Assistant at any time, by selecting Show the Assistant from the Help menu, as described above.

Help on the Web

Outlook and Office 2000 use Web pages on the Internet as an extension of the Help system.

If you don't find the information you need in the Help files, you can switch to the Internet to continue your search.

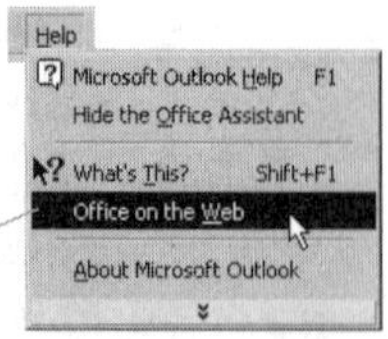

1. Click Help and choose Office on the Web.

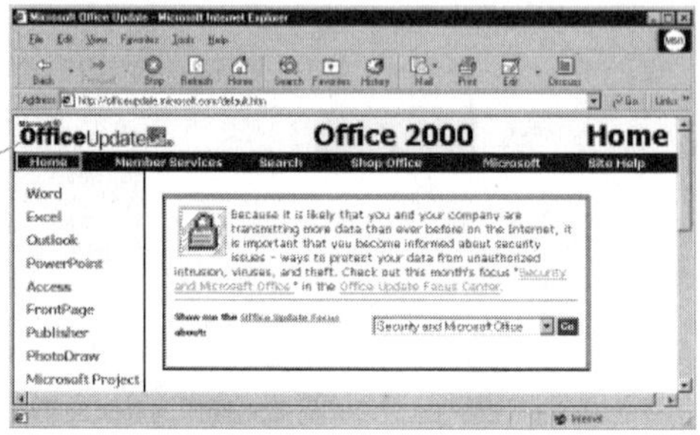

2. Your browser will display the Office Update page.

The actual contents will vary, but will highlight particular Office features, and you can issue searches for answers to your questions.

You don't have to go that far to get help. Brief but helpful descriptions, known as screen tips, are shown as the cursor pauses over an icon. If these tips do not appear on your system:

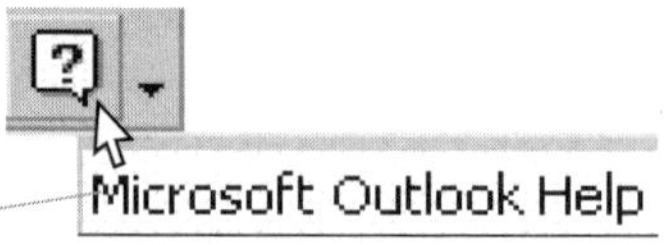

Changes you make here may apply to all the toolbars in Windows, not just Outlook.

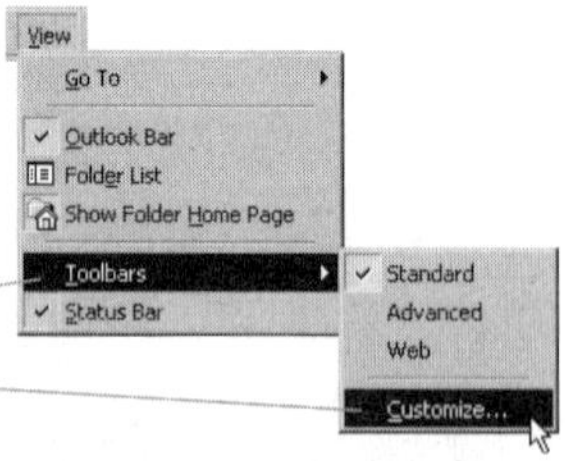

3. Select View, Toolbars and then Customize.

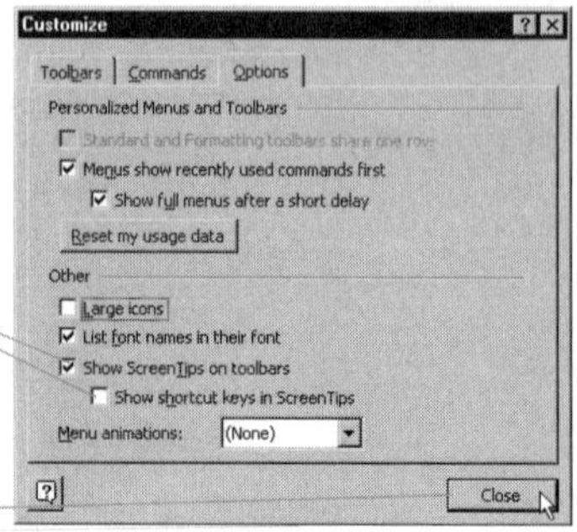

4. Select the Options tab, and click Show Screen Tips. You can also choose to Show shortcut keys.

5. Press the Close button to save the changes.

Outlook bar

The sidebar concept originated with Outlook but has now been adopted for the other Office 2000 applications.

Use small icons to get more shortcuts visible at a time. **See page 50.**

Shortcuts on the Outlook Bar can be links to ordinary file system folders, as well as Outlook folders.

Down the left hand side of the display is the Outlook Bar. This may hold two or three groups of shortcut icons.

The Outlook Shortcuts group allows you to select Outlook Today or one of the five main Outlook functions (Inbox, Calendar, Contacts, Tasks and Notes). You can also select the Deleted items folder to see items flagged for disposal.

To see all the shortcuts in the groups:

1. Press the up and down arrows to scroll the entries on the bar.
2. Click on the group name to display another shortcut bar.
3. Click on a shortcut in the group to activate it and display the folder contents.

The My Shortcuts group (called Mail in some versions of Outlook) accesses your work areas for outgoing mail messages, Draft form, already Sent, or ready to go from the Outbox. It also accesses the Journal function, and provides a link to the Outlook Update web site.

The third group, usually called Other Shortcuts, links you to the PC file system, and other components, through My Computer, My Documents and the Favourites folder.

If the File System is missing, you must add Integrated File Management. See page 174 to add components.

You can add a new group to the outlook bar, for example to access project folders, and you can insert additional shortcuts into any group:

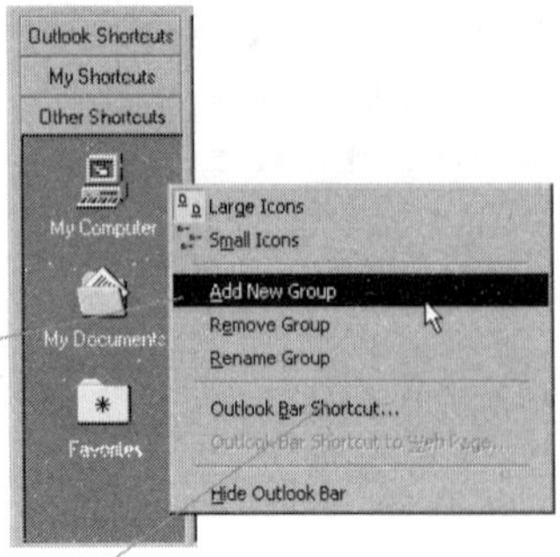

4 Right-click the Outlook bar and click Add New Group to make space for more shortcuts.

5 Right-click the Outlook bar and select Outlook Bar Shortcut, to add new Outlook or file system folders.

If you are on a network, you should add the network drives and public folders that you have access to.

If you are using Outlook Express, you will find just one shortcut group that combines the Outlook and Mail shortcuts. This Outlook bar can be used in place of the folder list that is normally used in Outlook Express to navigate through the functions.

Outlook Express does not support shortcuts to the file system folders or to network drives.

You cannot add new groups to Outlook Express, or have shortcuts to file system folders, but you can add new shortcuts to Outlook folders to the Outlook bar:

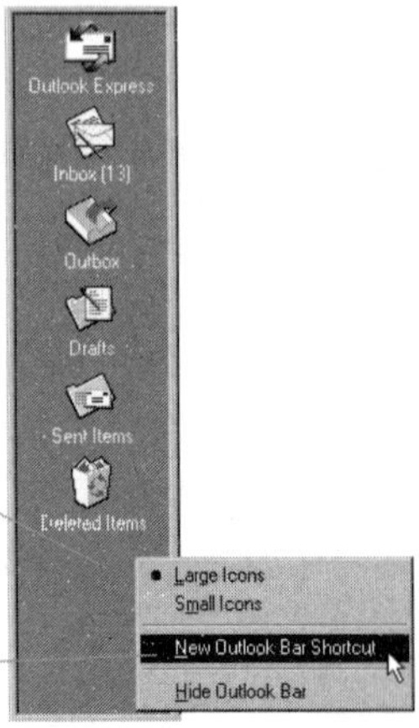

6 Right-click the Outlook bar to display the menu.

7 Select New Outlook Bar Shortcut to add a shortcut to an Outlook folder.

Outlook navigation

Try out the ways of moving around in Outlook, so you can quickly go wherever you want.

With so many different functions, and so many ways to switch between them, you could easily lose your place. One way to keep track, especially if you are used to the Internet way of working, is with the Advanced toolbar.

If this is not currently displayed:

1. Select View from the menu bar, click Toolbars, and select the Advanced toolbar.

The Advanced toolbar has several buttons that help you move around from item to item.

With the buttons on the Advanced toolbar, you can:

- Go back to the previous item in the list of visited folders

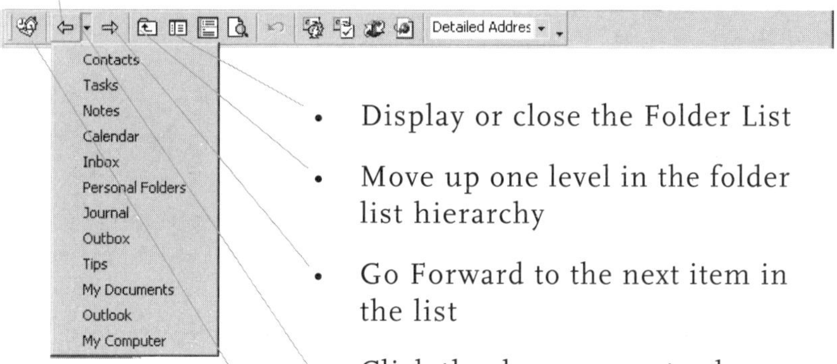

- Display or close the Folder List
- Move up one level in the folder list hierarchy
- Go Forward to the next item in the list
- Click the down-arrow to show a list of folders and other components
- Go straight to the Outlook Today window

If you need a larger info window, you can hide the Outlook bar and use this toolbar list instead.

Notice that toolbars in Outlook are floating, so you can drag them to any position on the display window. They can be made vertical as shown here, but the icons and the text on the buttons are designed for horizontal use, so this is not normally the most useful position.

Adjusting the toolbars

You don't need the Advanced toolbar if all you want are forward and back buttons. Add them to the Standard toolbar.

You can use the fly-out as an alternative way to add buttons to toolbars. Click:

on the toolbar. Place the mouse pointer over Add or Remove Buttons. In the menu that appears, select/ deselect buttons.

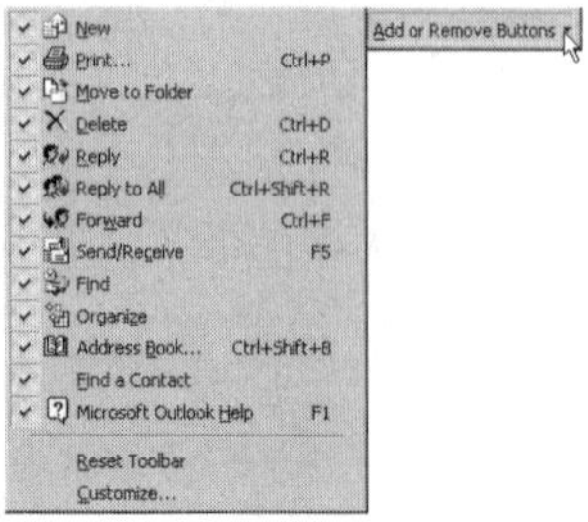

You can change the text or images on buttons. **See page 49 for details.**

1. Select View from the Menu bar, then Toolbars, then Customize. (Customize can also be found at the bottom of the Add or Remove Buttons flyout. See the margin for this.)

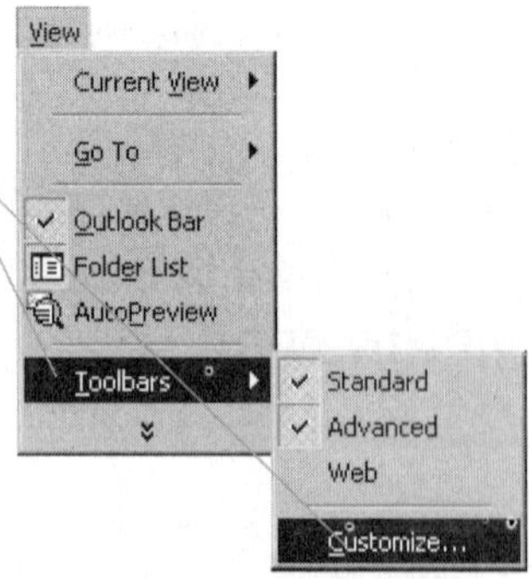

2. Select the Commands tab, the Web category, and the Back command.

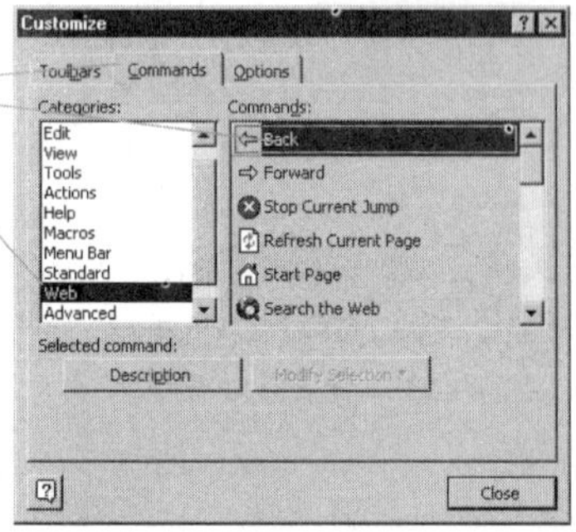

3. Click the Back command and drag it towards the toolbar.

4. Drop the Back command onto the Standard toolbar.

5. Click and drag the Forward command.

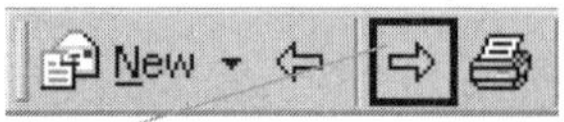

6. Drop the Forward command onto the Standard toolbar.

The Back and forward buttons will appear on the Standard toolbar for all Outlook functions.

You can add other buttons in a similar way. However, the toolbar can get long, and it may overflow to a second line for some of the Outlook functions. When you switch to the Inbox for example, there are additional buttons, some with long descriptive text. The toolbar does overflow on PCs with standard resolution displays.

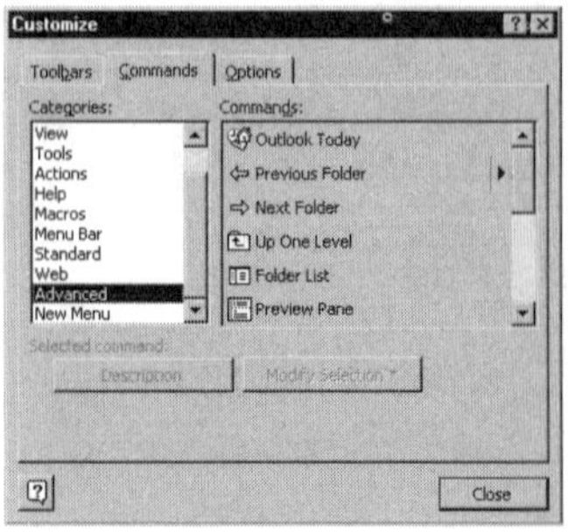

Some change options are unavailable for buttons that display a list or a menu, and so appear greyed out.

To change the image and the text for the tool bar buttons:

1 Switch to the function that uses the toolbar buttons you want to change, and right-click the toolbar.

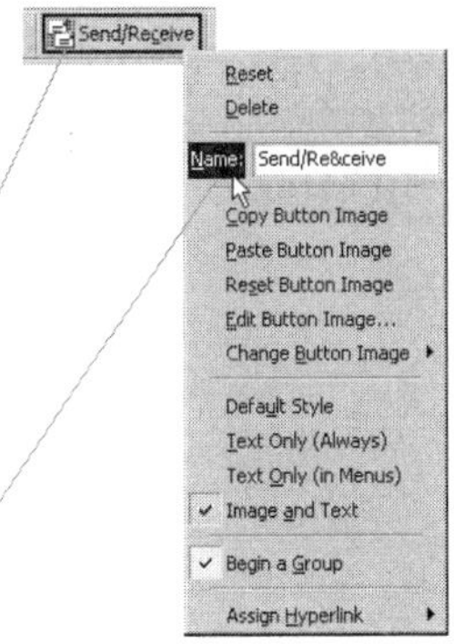

2 Select Customise, and drag the panel out of the way, so that the toolbar is clear.

3 Right-click the button to display the Change menu.

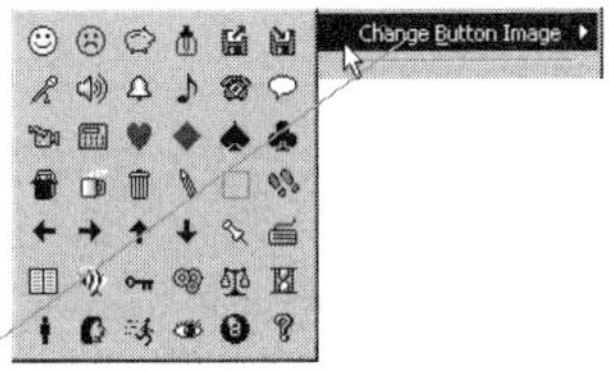

4 Modify the descriptive text name for the button, if required.

5 Change the button image. Change to one of the selection of images that Outlook offers, use Copy/Paste from a bitmap image, or Edit the image directly.

6 The name text can be shown alone, or with the image. The Default setting puts the image alone on the button.

To cancel changes and return to the original settings, right-click the button and select Reset.

Select the Default for all the buttons on the toolbar if you want to avoid them overflowing onto a second line, and use the Screen Tips (see page 44) to remind you of their names and purpose.

Starting functions

The Today window offers the main functions, but the Outlook bar has the full list.

Since there could be many entries on the Outlook bar, you may want small icons to make them all visible at once:

1. Right-click one of the Outlook shortcuts bars.

2. Select the icon size. The change applies to the selected bar only.

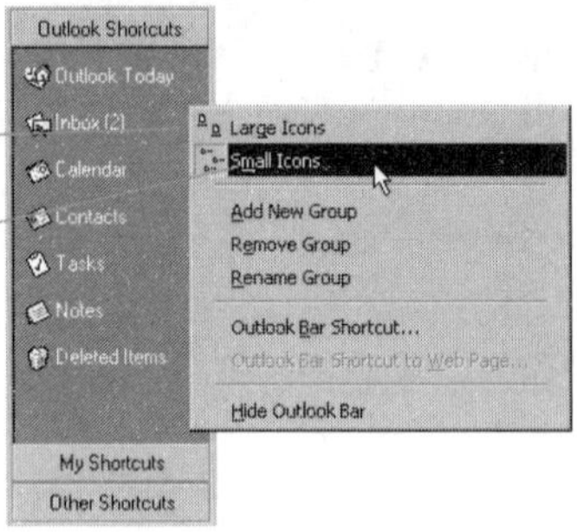

You can also switch Outlook functions using the Go To command:

3. Select View, Go To from the Menu bar and select the function.

4. Shortcut keyboard combinations are offered for some functions (eg, Inbox is Ctrl+Shift+I).

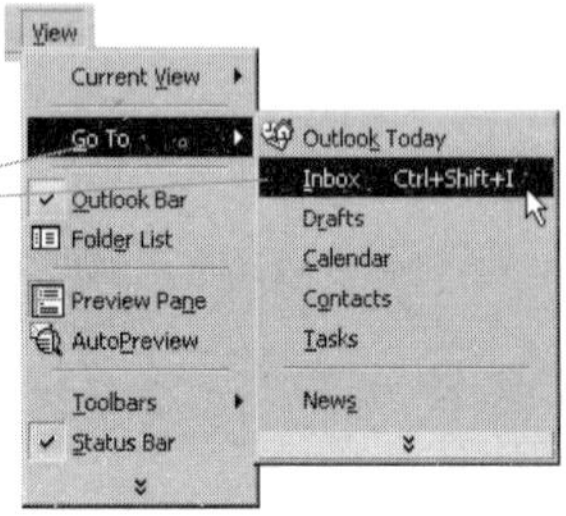

Create new items from any part of Outlook, as the need arises.

When you need to start a function to create a new Outlook item such as a message or a contact entry, use the New Item button as a shortcut:

5. Click the down-arrow next to the New Item button, and select the type of item (ie, Contact, Task, Note, etc).

6. Note the series of shortcut keys (eg, Ctrl+Shift+N for a Note).

Working with Office

Outlook allows you to deal with your other documents, using applications such as Word or Excel, without having to switch back to the Windows desktop.

Access documents in My Documents or any file system folder on the Outlook bar.

1. Select the Other Shortcuts bar and click My Documents to display your work in progress.

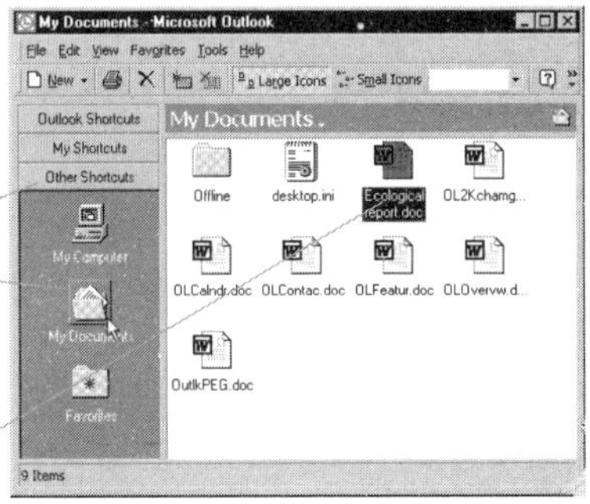

2. Double-click the icon for the document you want to open.

You can also access Outlook functions from within Office 2000 (see page 186).

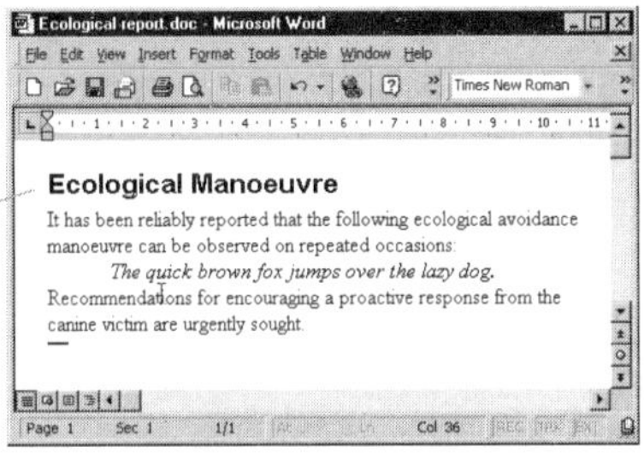

3. The related application starts up and loads the document, ready to edit.

If you have problems locating a particular document in your file folders, change the Current View and select the Document Timeline, to view by the date it was last modified.

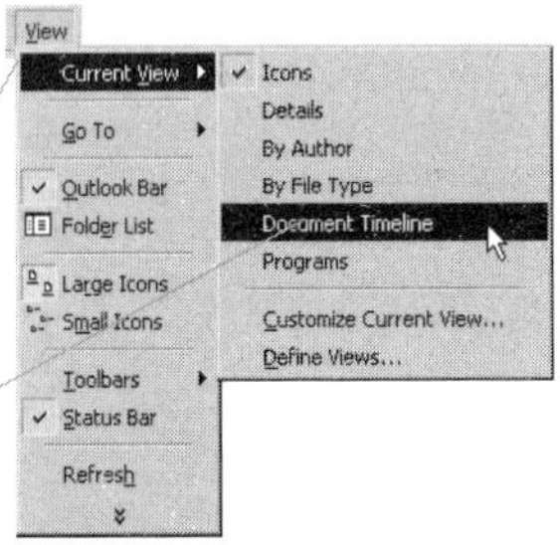

4. Select View from the Menu bar, Current View, Document Timeline.

Customise the current view to list by the date created, if that will help you find the document.

5. Select day, week or month and scroll to the period when you changed the document.

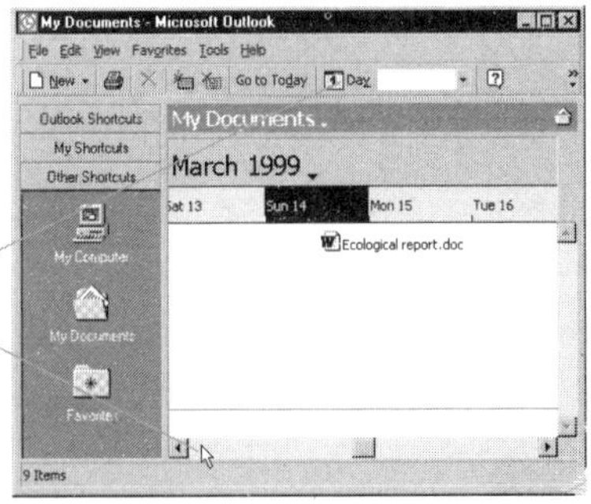

Other applications

Treat the Other Shortcuts bar like a small version of the Windows desktop.

The My Computer button on the Other Shortcuts bar allows you to work with all the applications and facilities on your system, just like the equivalent icon on the Windows desktop.

1. Open the Other Shortcuts bar. Select My Computer to display the disk drives.

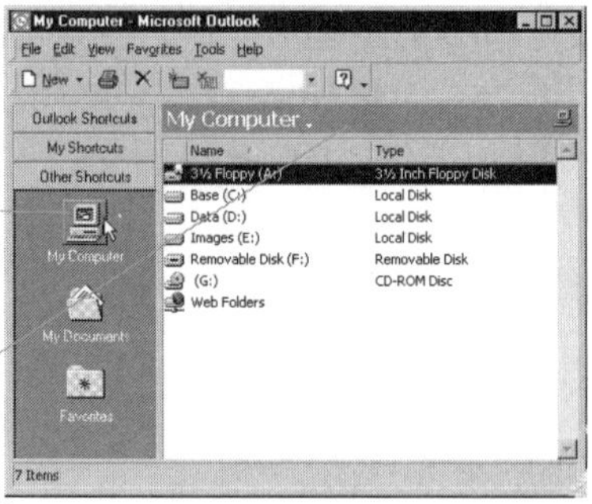

2. Click the folder bar to display the tree structure. Click the pin to retain the tree view.

3. Explore your drives to locate documents, copy and print files or run applications, just as in Windows Explorer.

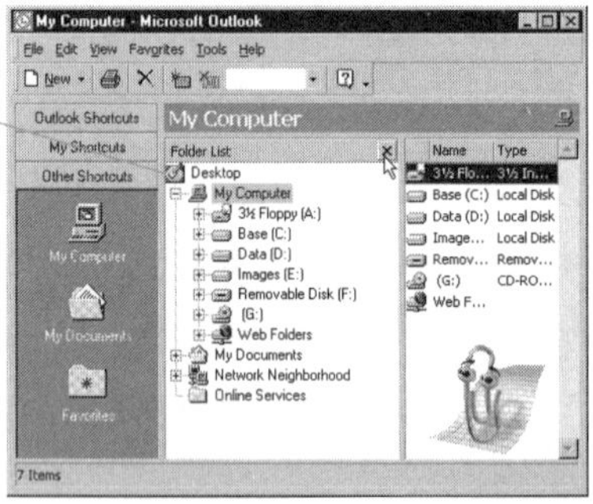

If you have started an application, return to Outlook by selecting an item from the Taskbar. If you have several Outlook items active, select the right one using the task list:

The active item and the function name are shown, to help you choose between repeated icons.

4. Press and hold the Alt key, press the Tab key until an Outlook item is selected.

5. Release the Alt key to switch to the selected item.

Using Electronic Mail

This chapter works through the basics of e-mail: sending a message, making copies, receiving messages, saving and printing messages, seeing how your messages make their way through the Internet, and replying to messages.

Covers

Chapter Four

Creating your message

There's a variety of address formats, and some are case sensitive, so type the e-mail address exactly as given.

Electronic mail (e-mail) is the computer equivalent of exchanging memos and notes. You can communicate with anyone who has access to the Internet, either directly through an ISP or through an office or college network. All you need is the e-mail address, in the form of:

userid@network

name/number (eg, johns; jsmith; 76543.123)

address of network (eg, msn.com; aol.com; london.uk.co)

required separator (say it as AT)

You can send and receive e-mail from any part of Outlook, but the normal starting point is the Inbox, which stores received messages. Start Outlook, and follow these steps to create a new message:

Chapter Three shows you how to start Outlook in the Today window or the Inbox folder.

1 Select Mail from Outlook Today, or click Inbox on the Outlook bar to show the message list.

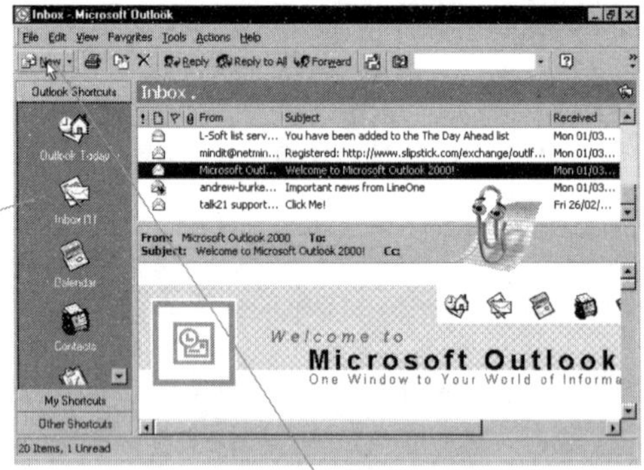

2 Click on the New Message button on the toolbar to start creating a message.

The Inbox will contain a list of messages right from the start. They are mainly those transferred from your previous e-mail system during Outlook setup, but there will be some messages, even if this is the first time that you have run an e-mail system on your machine. These are informational and marketing notes, sent to you as part of the IE4 and Outlook setup, or added by your Internet service provider or by other software vendors.

Contacts keeps track of e-mail addresses and adds the details for you. See Chapter Five.

3 Enter the e-mail address for the recipient, using the standard userid@network format, and add addresses for people getting Cc or Bcc copies (see page 57).

4 Enter the Subject, which becomes the message title.

- Recipient
- Copies
- Blind copies
- Subject
- Salutation
- Message text
- Sign off
- Signature text

Netiquette conventions for e-mail and news group messages differ between groups. If in doubt, be informal but polite.

5 Issue a suitable greeting to the recipient, and introduce yourself if sending to someone new. This is considered good netiquette.

6 Type the text of your message as the addressee should see it. The example uses the default plain text, with a simple, mono-spaced font. This is the best format to use if you do not know the types of e-mail system used by the recipients.

Keep to plain text message formats unless you know that your recipients can handle the more fancy options.

7 End with your name and personal details, such as title or telephone number. You needn't put your e-mail address, since Outlook attaches this to the message when it is sent.

Checking spelling

While you are creating or changing your message, you can check the spelling. Unlike some e-mail clients, you will find a proper UK dictionary among the languages offered.

1 Select Tools from the Menu bar, and pick Spelling, or press the shortcut function key F7.

Each spelling (or typing) error in the message is detected in turn, and you may be offered one or more possible words, though sometimes no suggestion can be made.

2 Locate the correct spelling (or retype the word) and Change the text. Change All for a repeated error.

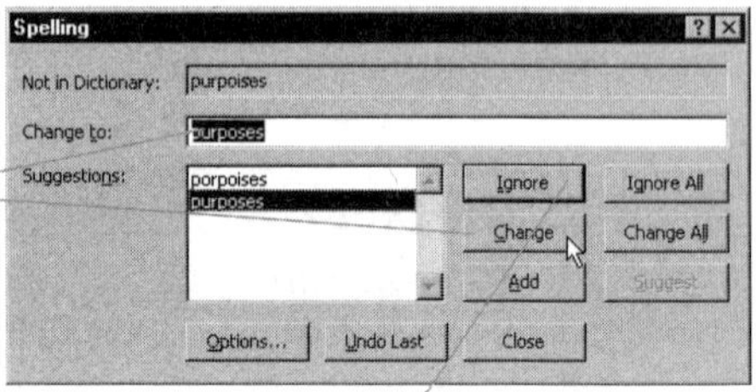

3 If the word detected is just a code or other value, press Ignore, or Ignore All if there may be more occurrences.

4 For proper names and for words not found, press Add to include them in the supplementary dictionary.

There can be several different language dictionaries in Outlook: see 'Office 2000 in easy steps' for more on this.

5 Press Options to change the settings, edit the supplement or to choose a different language.

6 Spell check terminates when all the errors have been detected and processed (or when you press Cancel).

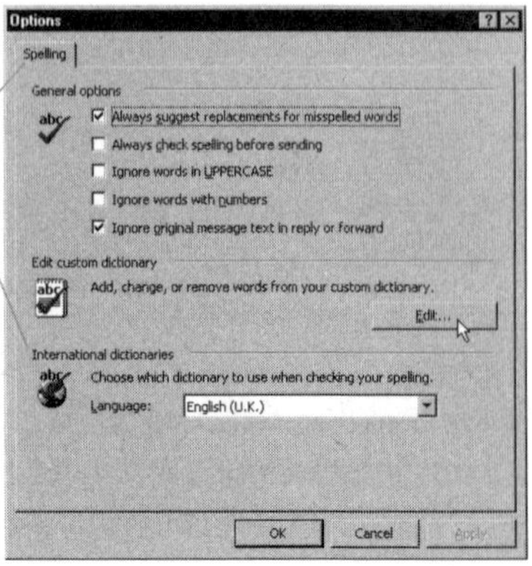

Message headers

When you create a new message, you may notice that some of the boxes are not displayed on your screen. To redisplay them:

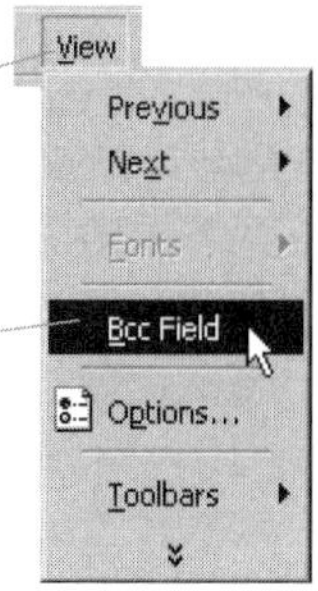

1 Select View from the Menu bar.

2 Click the Bcc field for blind copies.

The Cc box specifies carbon copy (or courtesy copy) recipients, who will receive a copy of the message. Their names and e-mail addresses will be listed with the message.

Copy your own Id on messages where you need a particular record kept.

The Bcc box specifies blind carbon copies. A copy of the message is sent, but these recipients are not listed. This may sound strange, but it is a useful technique when you want to send copies of messages to a log kept for record keeping or personal use.

Click the priority buttons on the toolbar, to draw attention to their relative importance. Just press to select, and press again to deselect. The two buttons give three combinations, which represent High, Normal and Low priorities.

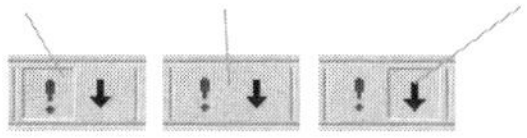

The high and low indicators appear on the message lists for the recipients, and the priority field can be used to sort the messages. Priority indicators can be a good method for highlighting tasks, but only work effectively when used selectively and on agreed criteria.

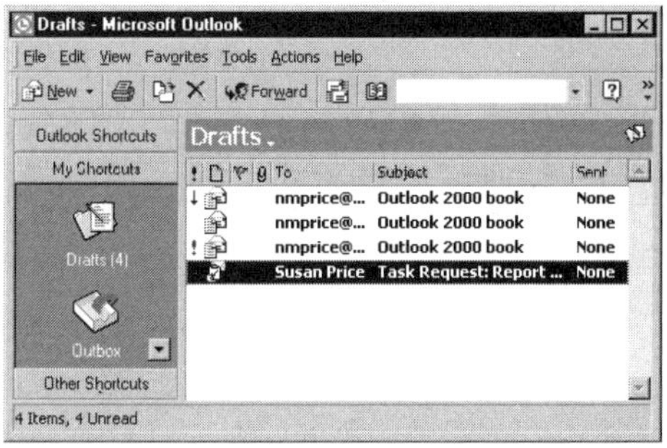

Saving messages

Outlook saves your messages periodically, while you are creating them.

Outlook automatically saves open messages every three minutes, storing them in the Drafts folder. They are removed when the message is sent, or when you Close and discard.

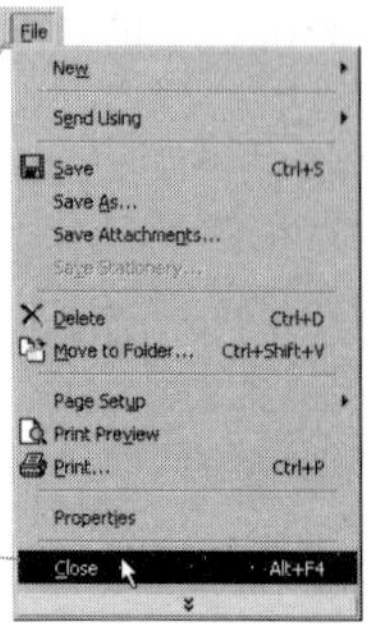

1 Select File from the Menu bar, and Close to stop editing the message.

2 Outlook displays a warning message, asking if you want to retain a Draft copy.

3 Select Yes to save and end, No to discard and end, or Cancel to Close.

Turn automatic saving off or on, and change the time, or the target folder.

4 Select Tools from the Menu bar, then Options, and choose the Preferences tab.

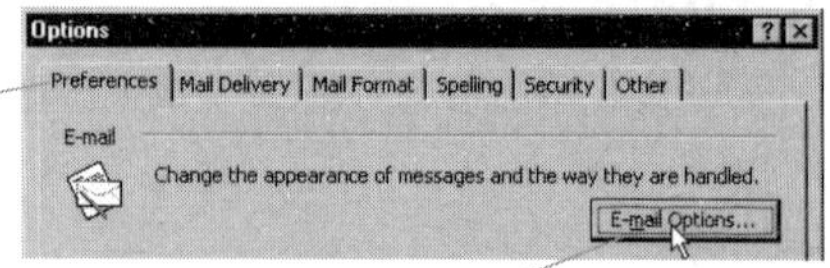

5 Press E-mail Options, and then select or clear the 'Automatically save unsent messages' box.

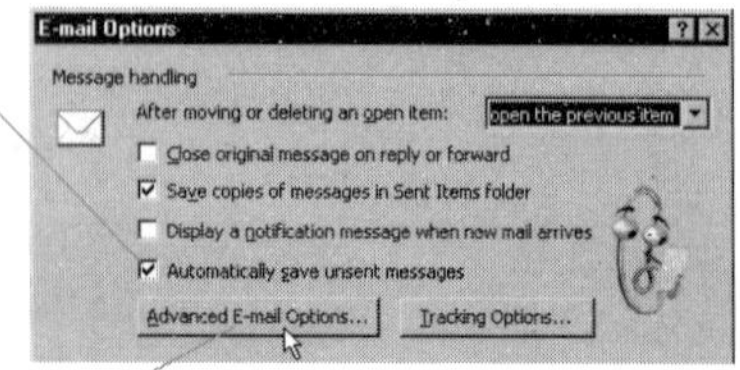

6 Press Advanced E-mail Options.

7 Change the folder where messages are stored or change how often the message is saved.

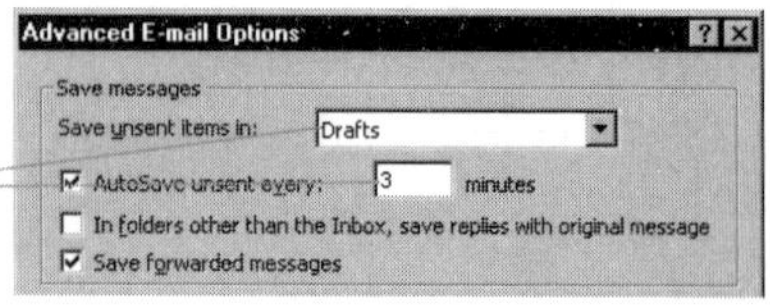

Sending messages

You can see from the count when a message has been added to your draft folder, without having to open the folder.

If the button you want doesn't appear on the toolbar, click:

The rest of the buttons display in a separate flyout. The ones you often use get added to the toolbar (for more on this, see page 13).

When you are ready to continue creating your message, the Draft folder allows you to pick up from where you left off:

1. Select My Shortcuts, Drafts and double-click the message to reopen it.

2. Outlook reminds you that this message has not yet been sent.

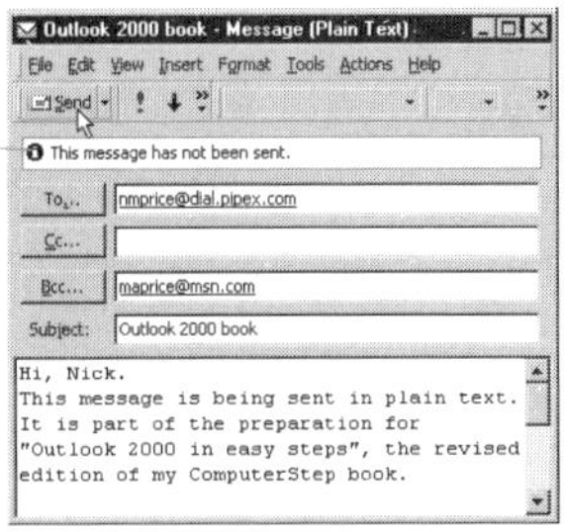

3. Enter the rest of the contents of your message. If Automatic save has been switched off, press the Diskette button to make a manual copy in the Draft folder (see the HOT TIP).

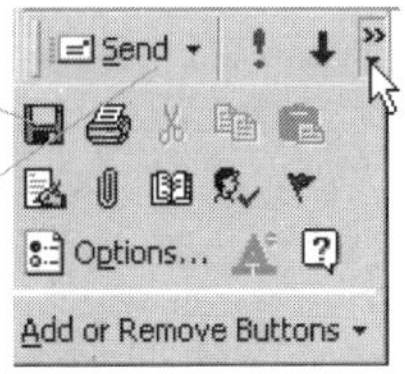

4. Complete your message and when it is ready, press the Send button.

5. Select My Shortcuts and check the Outbox count. Open Outbox to see the message titles.

If your PC is connected to a local area network with a mail server, messages will be immediately transferred to the server. For Internet Mail Only users, Send really means "make ready to send", and the message waits as a pending item in the Outbox.

You can Recall messages that have been sent to the mail server, as long as the recipient has not yet read them. You cannot recall messages over the Internet.

Transmitting your message

Sending Internet mail is a two stage process. Select Send, and then connect and select Send and Receive to complete the job.

With Internet mail, the message in the Outbox will not be sent until you have connected to the Internet and explicitly or implicitly asked to transfer mail. If you end Outlook without doing so, Outlook reminds you that there is mail waiting to go.

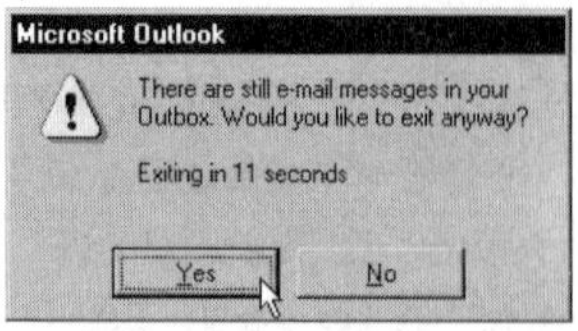

When you restart, you will see from the Outlook Today window and from the My Shortcuts bar that there is unsent mail. You can rectify this from any part of Outlook. To send the mail over the Internet (and receive any mail waiting there for you):

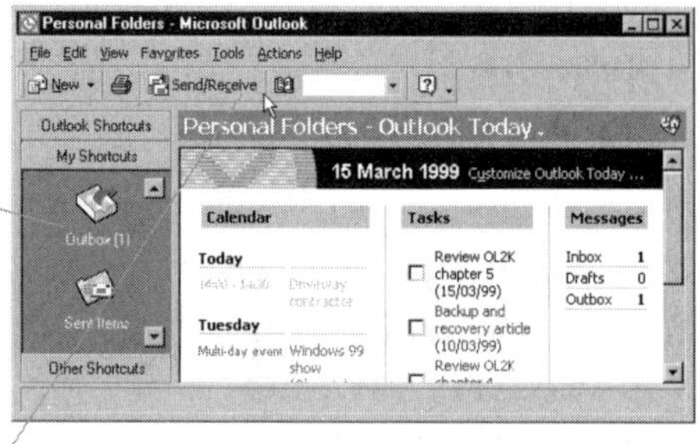

1. Outlook Today shows the count of unsent mail.

2. Press Send and Receive to start the Sign-in program for your ISP.

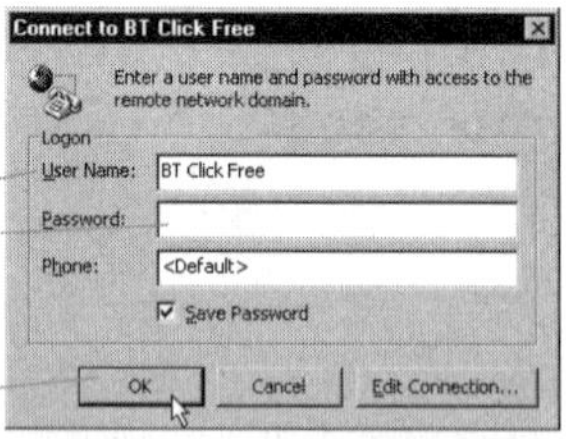

3. Enter your user id and password if necessary, and press OK to connect.

The Sign-in program dials the phone number for your ISP, verifies your user id and password and connects to the mail server.

The Outbox messages are copied over the modem to the mail server, on their way to the recipients.

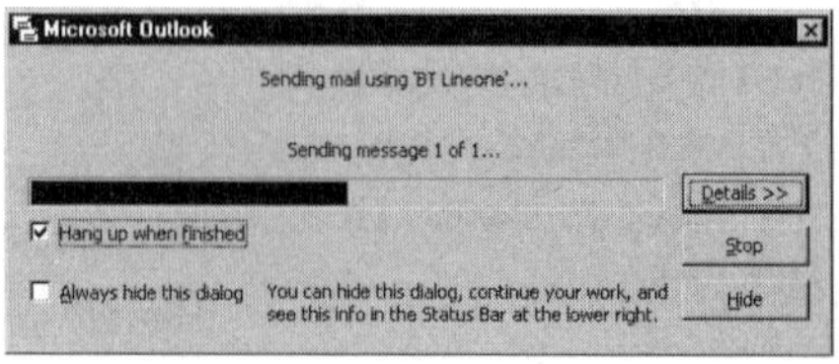

The first time you connect, click the box for Windows to remember your id and password.

If you don't want to keep copies, the E-mail Options (see page 58) can turn this off.

The messages are removed from the Outbox to show that they have now been sent. Copies may be saved in the Sent folder in My Shortcuts.

When the messages have been transferred to the mail server, and any waiting mail has been downloaded, Outlook will normally disconnect from the Internet, and the mail server handles the rest of the transfer.

4 Select the My Shortcuts bar to check that the message has been moved from the Outbox.

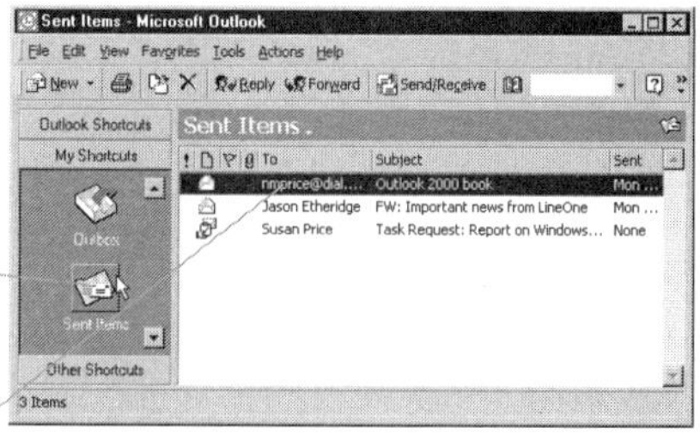

5 Open the Sent folder to see the message titles.

The preview pane shows the contents of the selected message, without opening it.

You may sometimes want to send mail without collecting any waiting messages, for example when you are using a different PC than usual, or when you are in a particular hurry and don't want to risk a large download. Outlook offers this option, though it isn't on a toolbar button.

6 Select Tools from the Menu bar and then choose Send.

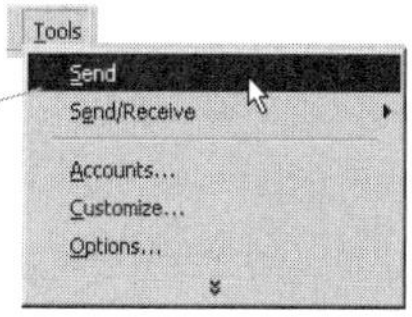

7 Connect to the ISP mail server using the Sign-in program, as described previously.

Outlook empties the Outbox folder, transfers messages to the Sent folder and the mail server, and then disconnects from the Internet without waiting for incoming mail. You will download this mail as usual the next time you press Send and Receive and connect to the mail server.

Receiving messages

If you select Send and Receive when there are no messages in the Outbox, the Sign-in program starts up to connect you to the server, this time to query for any incoming mail awaiting download. To obtain your mail:

1. Press the Send and Receive button on the toolbar.

2. Connect to the Internet and allow Outlook to download any messages that may be waiting.

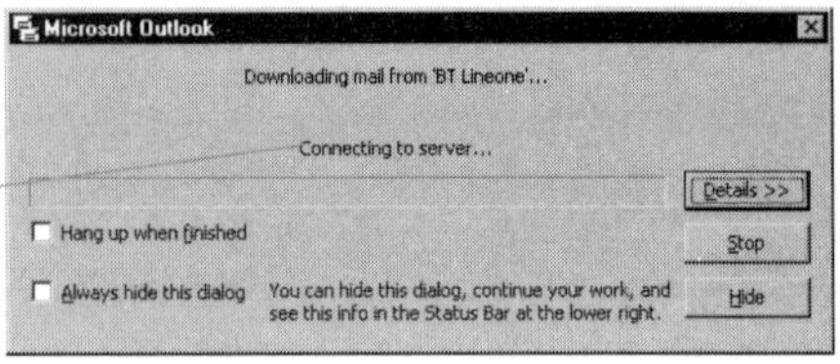

3. Select Inbox from the Outlook Shortcuts bar, and note that new messages are shown in bold font.

4. The Cc to sender that was included with the first message is sent back by the mail server, as if it were an ordinary incoming message.

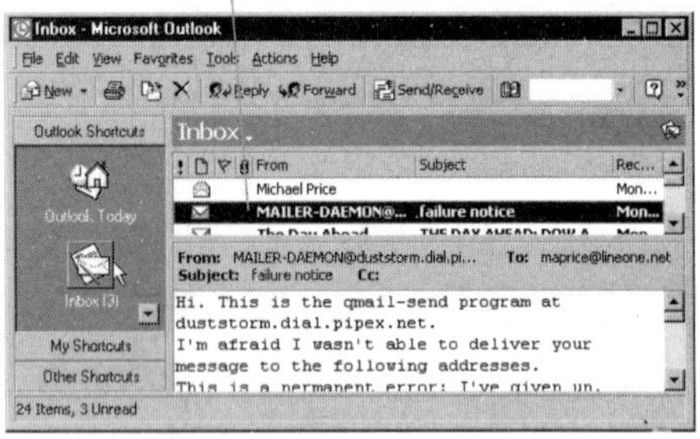

5. The second message in the example is a failure notice, indicating a problem with the message previously sent.

Only one message is sent to the server, which generates the Cc and Bcc copies needed, to minimise the communications time.

Outlook will do the checks and selects for you, using the rules wizard to filter your mail (see Chapter Six).

You can deal with many e-mail messages straight from the list. The subject titles will help you pick out what's important, and with the preview pane set up, there's often no need to open a message to get the main points. You can then pick out the messages that are important and open these to take the appropriate actions.

Reading the message

When you identify a message that needs action, open it to see the full contents on a larger window and get toolbar buttons that offer the likely actions that might be called for. To open the message:

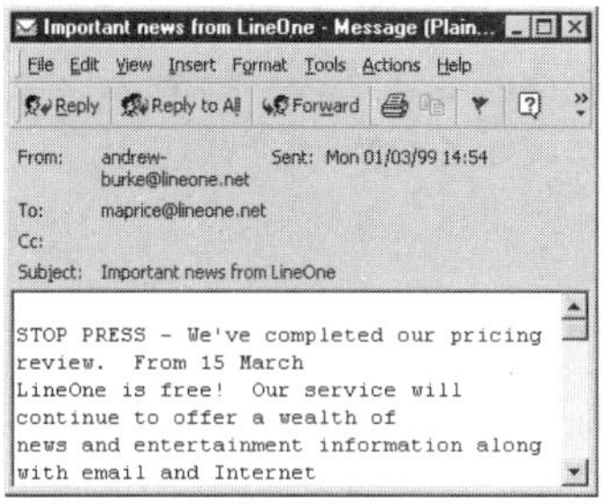

1 Open the folder with the message, and double-click the message title.

2 Read the message and decide on your action.

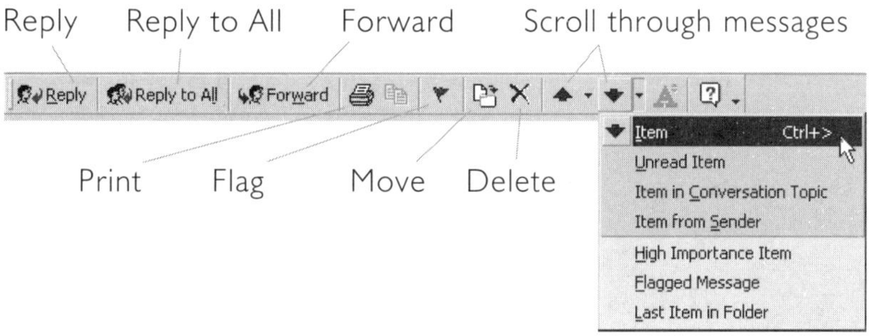

The toolbar shows the main actions at your disposal. For example, you could mark a message for follow-up when the appropriate time arrives. To apply a flag to this effect:

There are Other flags to use: Review, FYI, Read, Forward, etc.

3 Press the flag button, and set the flag, for example to Follow up.

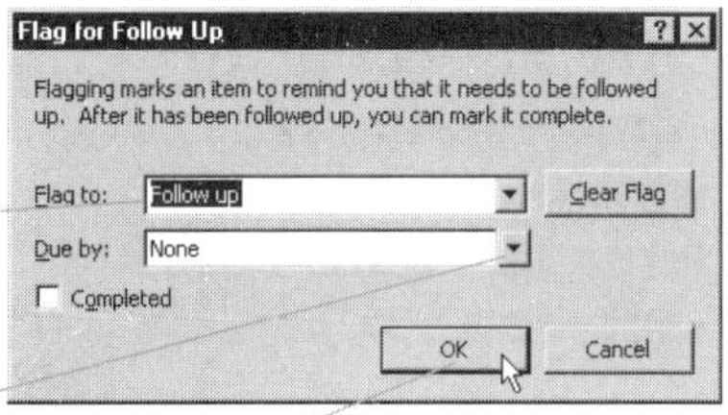

4 Set the Due date and time for a reminder.

5 Select OK, then File, Close to end the message review.

Routing messages over the Internet

Examine the route messages take over the Internet, to see where delays and errors could arise.

Sender

1 Create the message, in the Draft folder.

2 Sender presses Send to transfer the message to Outbox folder.

3 Press the Send and Receive button.

4 Encode message and the attached items for transmission.

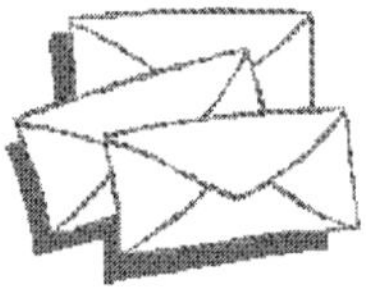

5 Dial the Sender's ISP mail server.

6 Transmit the message to the Mail Server.

7 Transfer the message to the Sent Items folder.

Delays can occur at various points in the flow: waiting to connect (step 3), over the Internet (step 9), waiting to connect (step 11), waiting to read (step 16), waiting to reply (step 18).

8 Disconnect Sender and Mail Server. Transfer the message to the Sent Items folder.

9 Forward the message to the network address (or issue Failure Notice if invalid address).

Problems may arise during encode and decode on systems with different capabilities.

Messages may be forwarded by many Internet servers before they reach their final destination.

Recipient

10 Store message at the ISP in Recipient's mail box (or issue Failure Notice if invalid id).

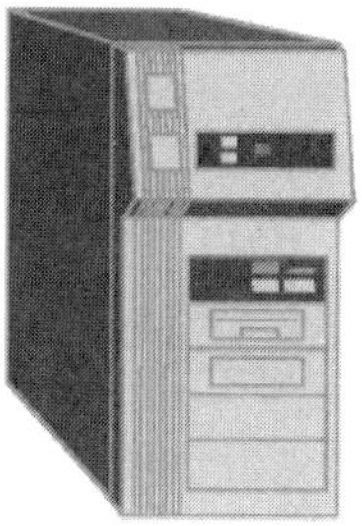

11 Recipient presses the Send and Receive button.

12 Recipient dials the ISP mail server to collect mail.

13 Transmit the message from the ISP mail server.

14 Decode message to standard text and attachments.

15 Filter and store message in Inbox or in another folder selected by rules wizard.

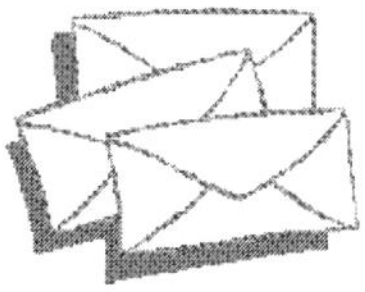

16 Open and read the message and view attachments.

17 Create a reply to the message, in the Draft folder.

18 Repeat the whole process to send the reply.

Replying to one and all

You can reply to sender, even if you were just copied on the original message.

When you receive a message, the header contains the e-mail addresses for the sender and the recipient, and for any Ccs. This makes it easy to respond:

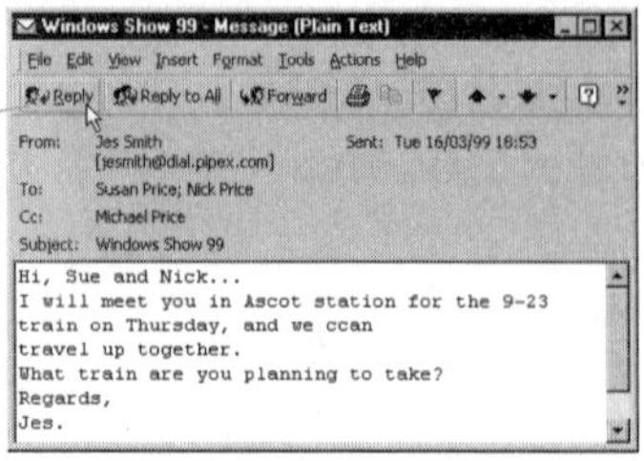

1 Click the Reply button to start a new message.

2 The sender's address is added and the title has RE: prefixed to it.

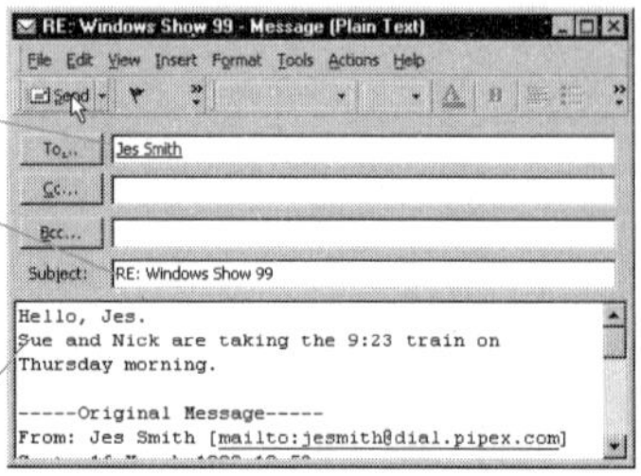

3 Insert new text, or comment on the text of the original message, then press Send to store the reply in the Outbox.

Your reply automatically picks up the information from the original message, including the full text, indented to distinguish it from new text. You can delete sections of the old text, and insert lines with your comments at relevant points, to make your response more direct.

Another level of > sign gets added on each exchange, eg:

- response to reply
- >reply
- >>original text

As alternative ways to distinguish the reply, Outlook applies prefixes to the original text, or sends it as an attachment. To change the settings for replies:

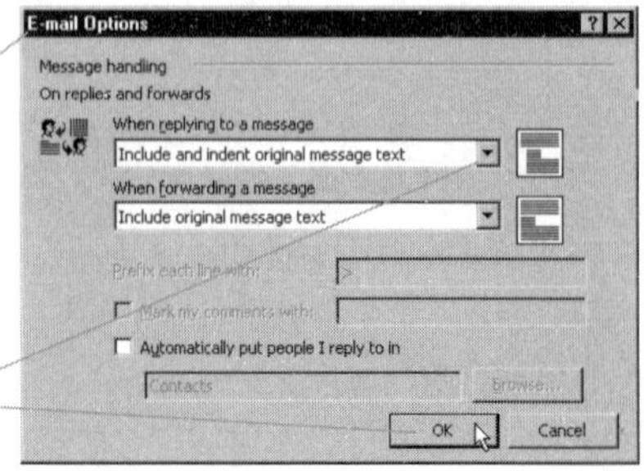

4 Select Tools>Options> Preferences>E-mail Options for message handling.

5 Click the down-arrow to pick an action, then press OK.

Replies to all are sent to every address in the To box and the Cc box, so check in case there are unexpected addressees.

Replies can be sent to all the addressees shown on the original message:

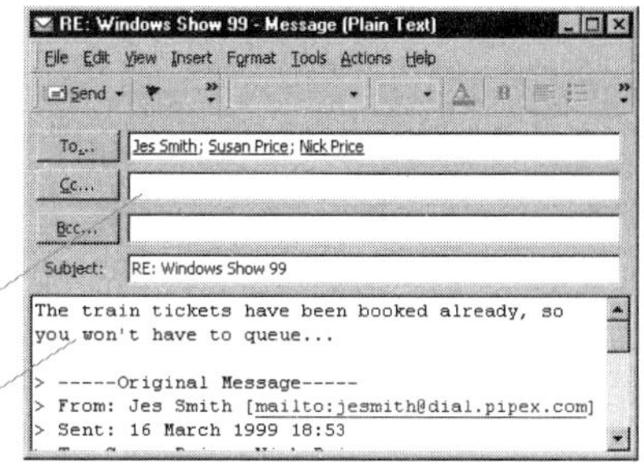

1. Click Reply to All to respond to the message.
2. Review the To and Cc box entries.
3. Enter your text and comments and press Send to save the message in Outbox.
4. The message symbol on the Inbox list changes to show you have replied.

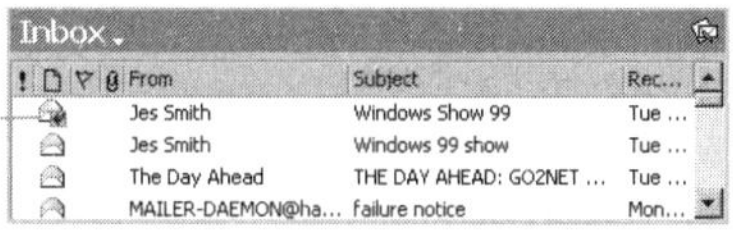

To inform others of the e-mail conversations taking place, select Forward and enter the e-mail addresses in the To or Cc boxes. The letters FW: are used as the title prefix.

If there are a number of messages to forward:

The reply will remain in the Outbox until you Send and Receive.

5. Select messages from the Inbox folder, using the Ctrl key or Shift key.

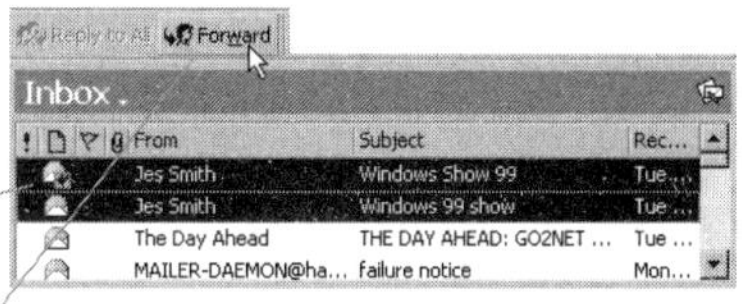

6. Press Forward, and enter the e-mail addresses and any descriptive text. The selected messages are sent as attachments.

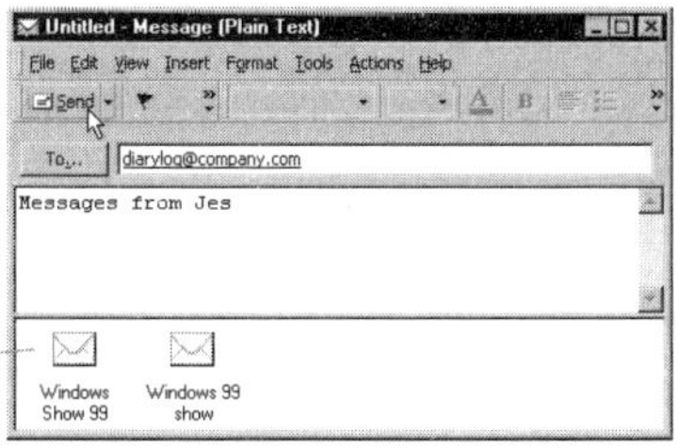

Adding your signature

Outlook allows you to specify a block of text to attach as a signature for the messages you send. To define the text for your signature:

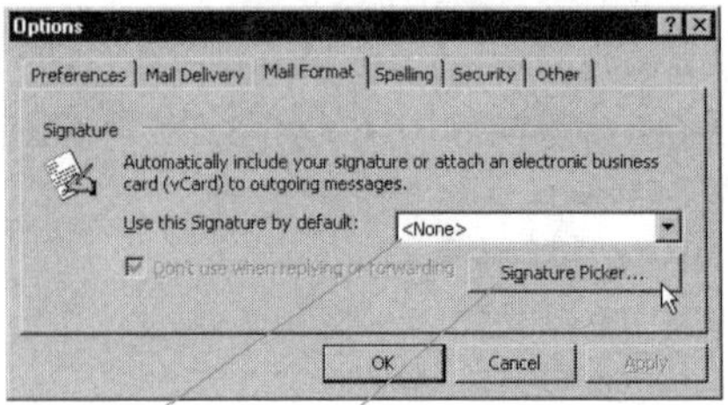

1 Select Tools from the Menu bar and choose Options.

2 Choose the Mail Format tab and choose a signature file from the list.

Have a number of different signature files to provide details for various purposes and situations, and insert the one that is appropriate to a given message.

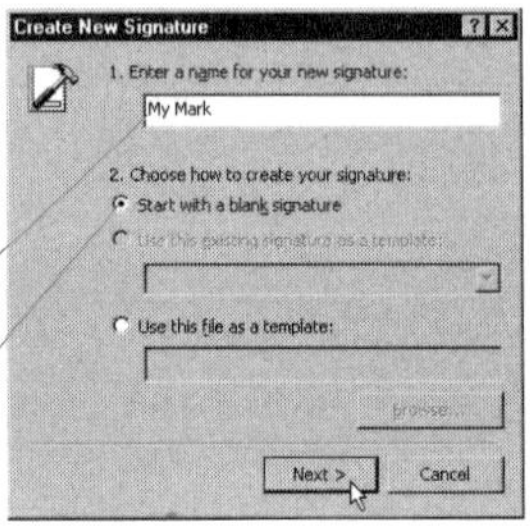

3 If there are no files shown, press Signature Picker, and select New.

4 Enter a name for the text file that you will be creating.

5 Choose to start with a blank signature.

You might like to add a comment or thought for the day, as part of the signature.

6 Type the text that will form your e-mail signature.

7 Press Finish, OK, to save the text block.

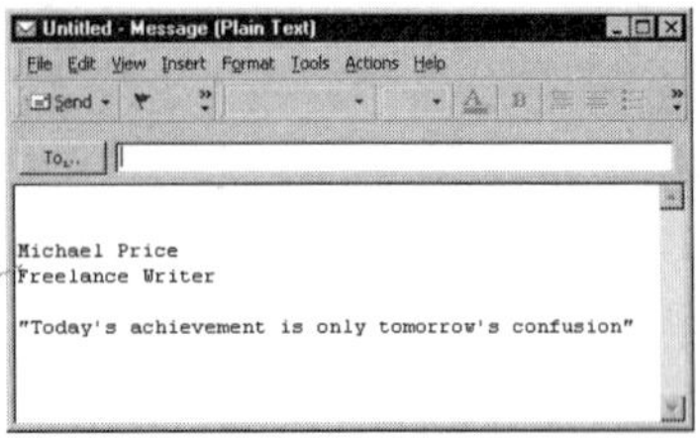

The next time that you create a message, it will have your signature text attached.

Attaching files

When you send an e-mail message you can attach files of any type, including documents, spreadsheets, images and even presentations. The file names appear as icons at the end of the message. When the message reaches its destination, the recipient can save the files to disk, or open them directly from the message. This assumes that the software needed to process the file type is installed. For example, to open a Word file requires a copy of Word or one of the Word viewers. To attach files to an e-mail:

Use the file types and the search features to help locate the files to insert.

1. With the message open, and the cursor positioned in the text, choose Insert from the Menu bar and then select File.

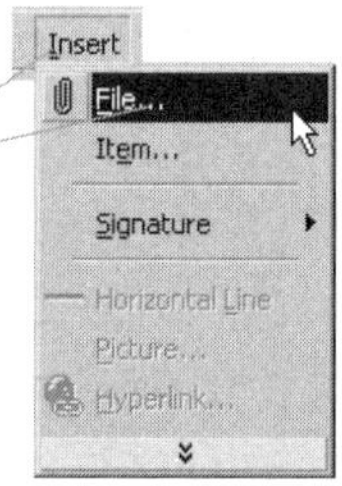

2. Locate the file folders. Select the file names, and press Insert.

3. Text only files are inserted into the body of the message, at the cursor location, and form part of the message.

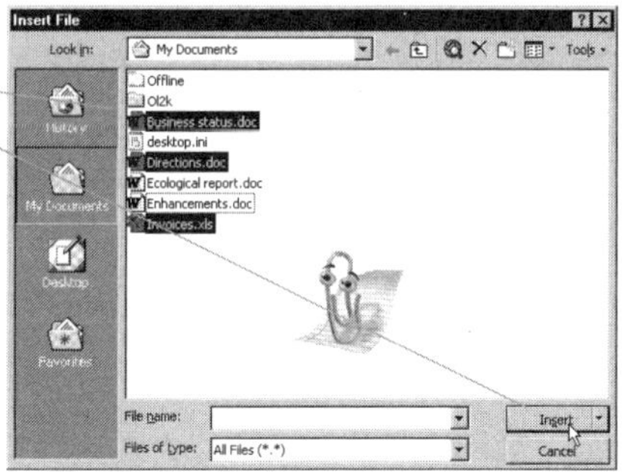

Add items from any Outlook folder. Use Insert, Item and choose messages or other items from Outlook folders. Attached items may not be viewable if the recipient does not use Outlook for e-mail.

4. Attachment files are sent along with the message, with icons as place markers.

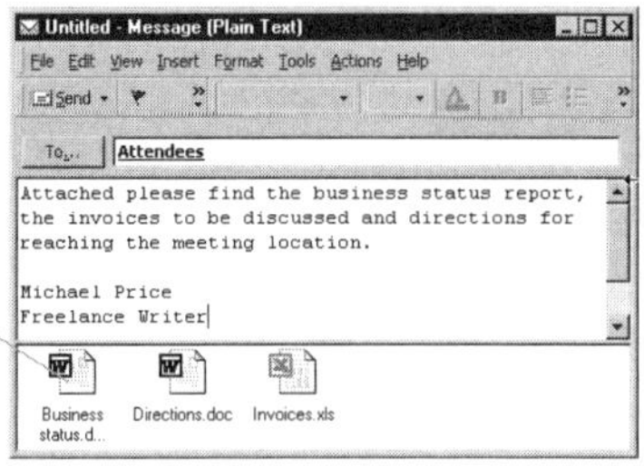

5. Press Send to transfer the message and the selected files to the Outbox.

Inserting pictures

HTML and Pictures are very effective, but rely on the recipient having Outlook or a similar e-mail system to handle formatted messages. They also make the messages larger and hence slower.

Messages that use the rich text HTML format can have pictures, lines and hypertext links inserted directly into the body of the message, in the appropriate position and viewable immediately. To attach a picture:

1 Open the message, select Format from the Menu bar and change to HTML.

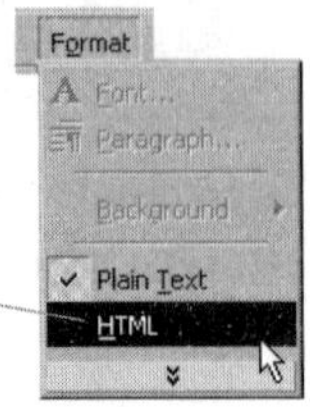

2 Position the cursor in the text, select Insert from the Menu bar and then click Picture.

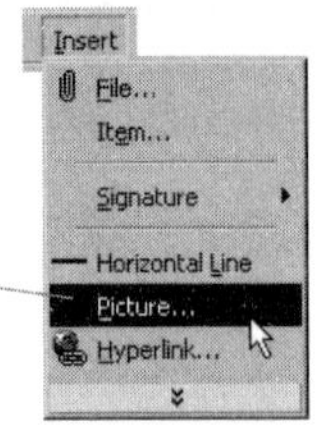

3 Enter the file path and name in the picture properties, using Browse to locate it, add a title, and press OK.

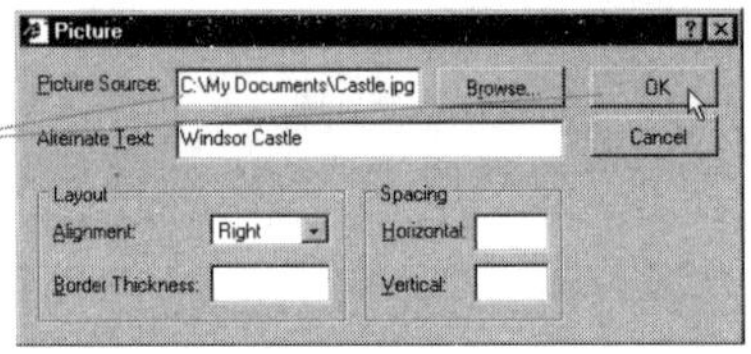

4 Click on the picture and drag the picture handles to resize it as required.

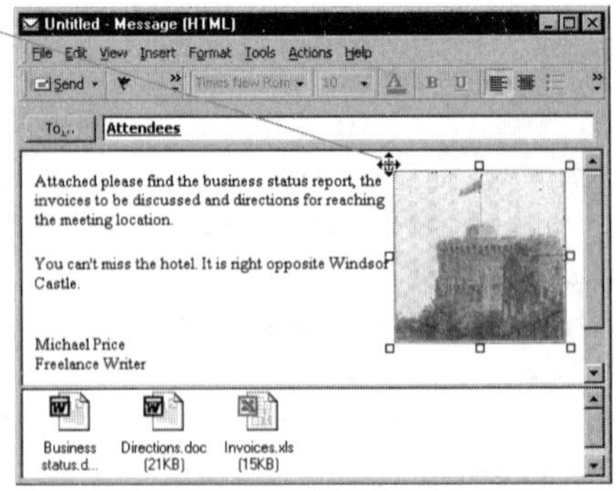

5 Right-click the picture to redisplay the properties panel and adjust the alignment, borders and spacing.

Files are encoded in transfer over the Internet, and decoded on receipt.

6 Press Send to transmit the message and the files together.

Fancy stationery

HTML format predefines images and text to create stationery, templates or backgrounds for messages.

The list contains types of stationery that you have used previously.

Enhance your messages using e-mail stationery. To view and select the stationery you want:

1 Select Actions from the Menu bar and New Mail Message.

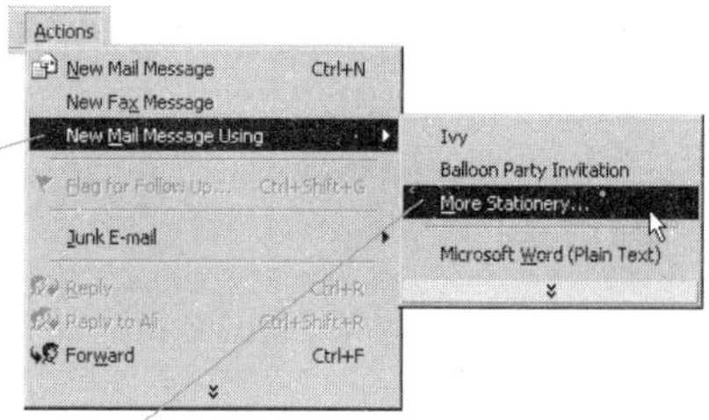

2 Choose a stationery type from the list, or request more stationery choices.

3 Review the types in the preview panel, select one and click OK.

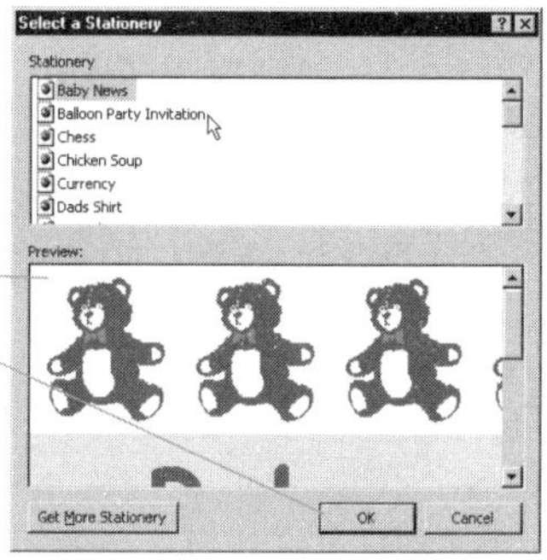

4 The stationery forms the background, and may add text and fonts to help set out the message content.

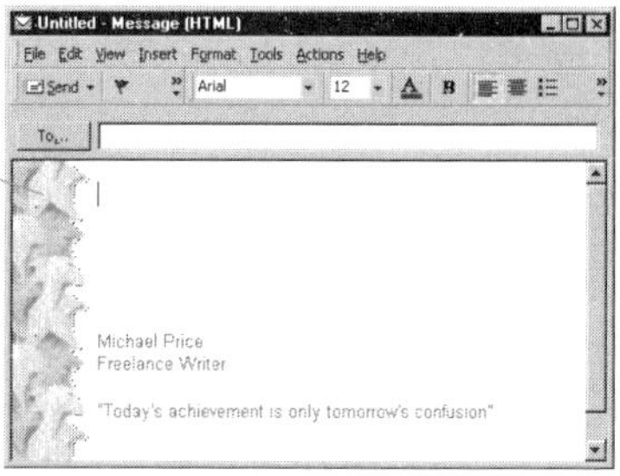

You can select a stationery type to become the default for your messages.

5 Select Tools and Options, and the Mail Format tab.

6 Choose the type in the Stationery and Fonts area.

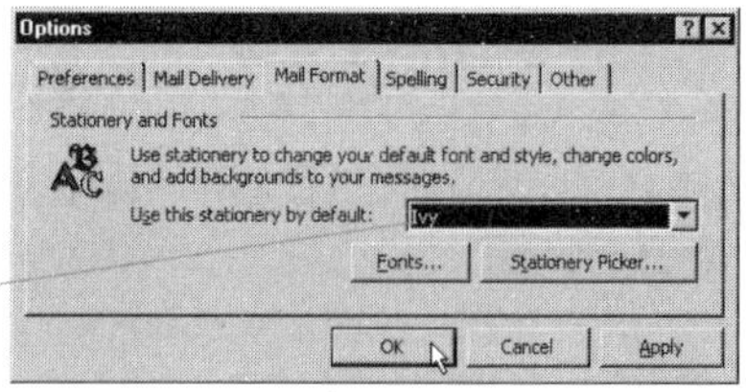

Receiving attachments

The Inbox list shows there are attachments with a paperclip symbol beside the message title.

When you receive an e-mail with attachments, you can save the attachments without opening the message.

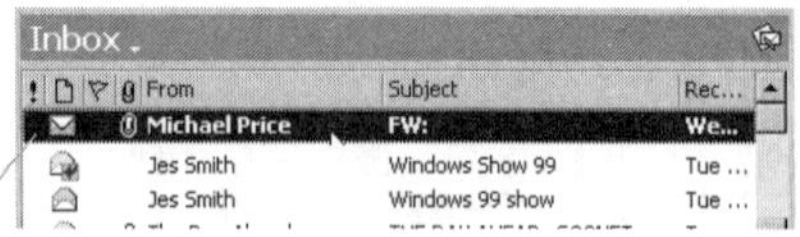

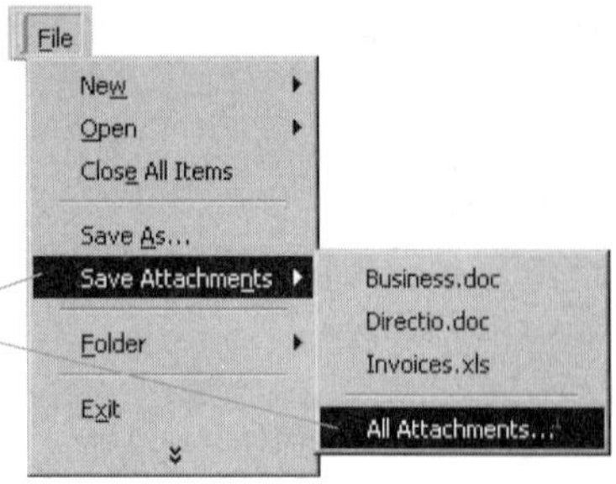

1 Select the Inbox entry, click File, Save Attachments and choose the file you want to save.

Inserted pictures will be displayed, if you have the required viewer. Otherwise, you will see the descriptive text instead.

2 Double-click the Inbox entry to open the message.

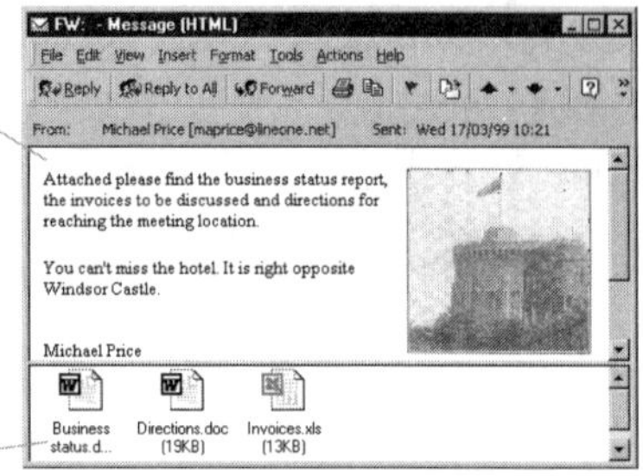

3 For registered file types, double-click an attachment icon to run the associated program to process the contents.

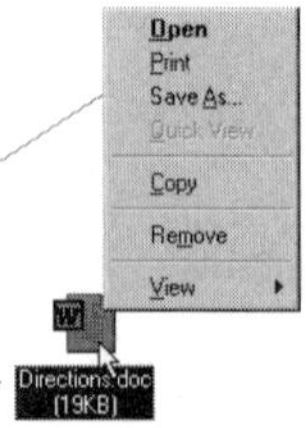

4 Right-click the file icon to open, print, copy, save or view the attachment in the message.

The Sent folder on the sender system will also contain extra copies of the files attached to the message.

Attachments can take up more disk space than you might imagine, because there are several copies. While the message remains in the Outlook folder, you will retain copies of the files, even if they have been saved to a file folder on your hard disk.

However, you can select Remove from the quick menu shown above, to eliminate the attachment icon and the file contents from the message and the Outlook folder.

Managing contacts

This chapter looks at keeping track of contact details, starting with e-mail addresses for messages, and adding-in all the other details about the people you meet and deal with.

Covers

Chapter Five

Name and Address Books

Lists of names and addresses are requirements for many applications. They are used in word processing to produce address labels or with mail merge and form letters. Fax software needs names and fax numbers, telephony software needs names and voice phone numbers. Diary and personal planner systems also need name and address lists.

With Internet Mail Only, and no network, you will not have a post office address list.

Some applications have their own dedicated address books, but there are several types of more general purpose address books that may be used as a common resource by many applications.

Post Office Address List

If you are part of a local area network, you may have access to a Post Office Address List. The Post Office is on the network server and contains the mailboxes for the network users. The Address List associated with this contains names, job titles, e-mail addresses and other details about the network users.

Personal Address Book

In addition to the group address book, you may find a personal address book. This is intended for names and e-mail addresses of the people you need to contact more frequently. This could include some of the people in the main company list, as well as people from outside your organisation that you contact via Internet mail.

Windows Address Book

If you use Outlook Express, the personal address list function is provided by the Windows Address Book. This can be used in Outlook Express and from Windows and other applications.

See pages 75–83 for details of Windows Address Book and pages 84–92 for details of Contacts Manager.

Contacts Manager

The full version of Outlook includes its own address book, the Contacts Manager. This replaces the Windows address book, supporting the same functions. In addition to names and e-mail addresses it contains much more information about the person (eg, multiple business / personal addresses, telephone and fax numbers, comments and descriptions).

Windows Address Book

The Windows Address Book stores information about people and organisations that you deal with. The data recorded can include e-mail addresses, mailing addresses, phone and fax numbers. It also provides Internet directory services, which allow you to search for the address details of people and businesses on the Internet.

Windows Address Book can also be opened from the Inbox, from your web browser, and from the Windows Start menu.

Windows programs (including Outlook Express) use the address book to save you having to enter contact details, letting you pick up the information needed by reference to a name or by clicking in a table. There are several ways to open the Address Book in Outlook – for example:

1. Press the Address Book button on the toolbar.

2. Select Tools from the Menu bar and then Address Book.

3. If the Outlook Express window is displayed, Click the Address Book link to open it.

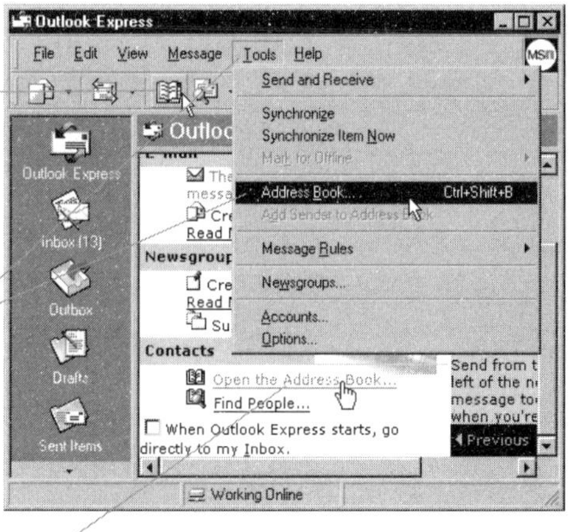

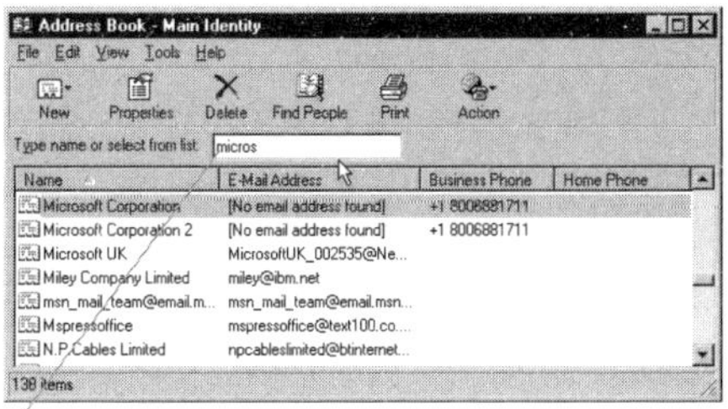

4. The Address book starts up, showing the list of entries, with the toolbar giving the functions needed to search for specific entries, add new entries or change the details recorded for the contact.

Adding names

You can add the details for a new contact as a new entry directly into the Address Book:

Press tab to go from box to box. Leave the box blank if you don't have (or don't need) that item of data.

1 Press the New button, and New Contact.

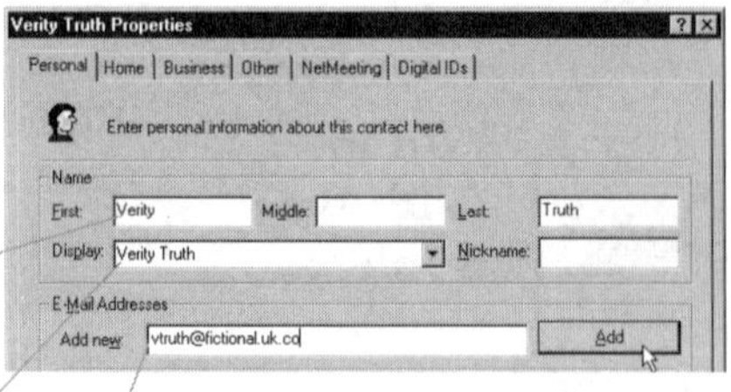

2 You enter the first, middle and last name.

3 Your messages will show the generated display name in the To or Cc box.

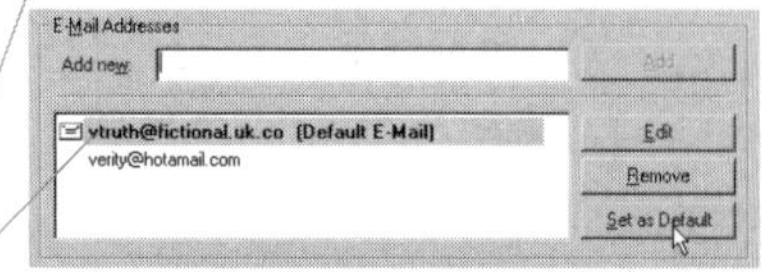

4 Enter the e-mail address and press Add. You can put more than one e-mail address per contact.

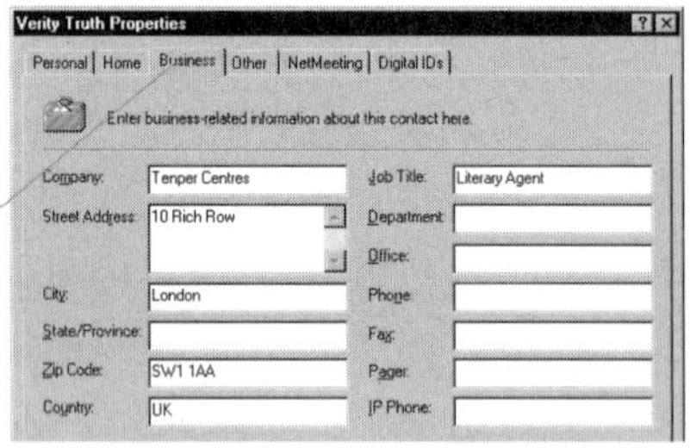

5 Select Home or Business tabs to add mailing addresses and phone numbers.

Select the entries and press the Delete button, to remove unwanted items.

When you press OK, you will see the new contact added to the address book.

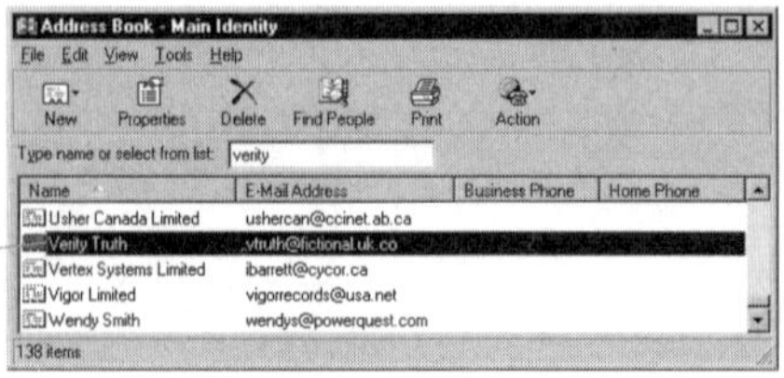

To modify the details for a contact, select the entry and press Properties to redisplay the entry forms.

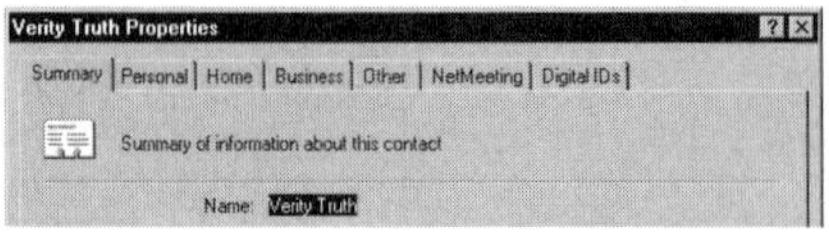

Addressing e-mail

The address book makes it much easier and more accurate to send e-mail. Just pick entries off the list. When you start creating a new message:

If you have a lot of entries in the book, type the first few letters of the name, and Outlook will reposition the list.

1 Press a Select button (To, Cc or Bcc).

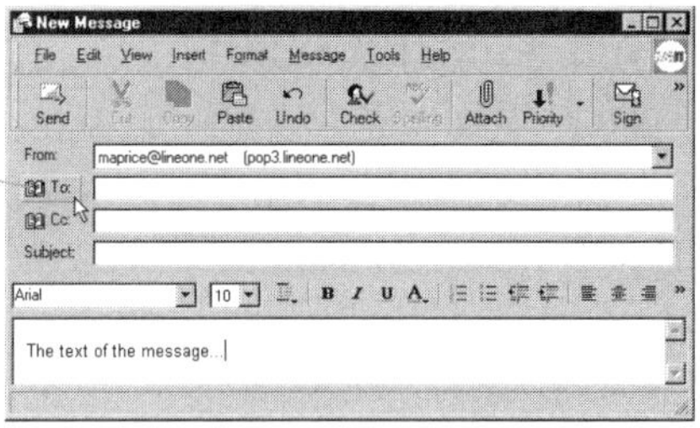

2 Choose a name from the list and click the To, Cc or Bcc button to add the name to that respective box.

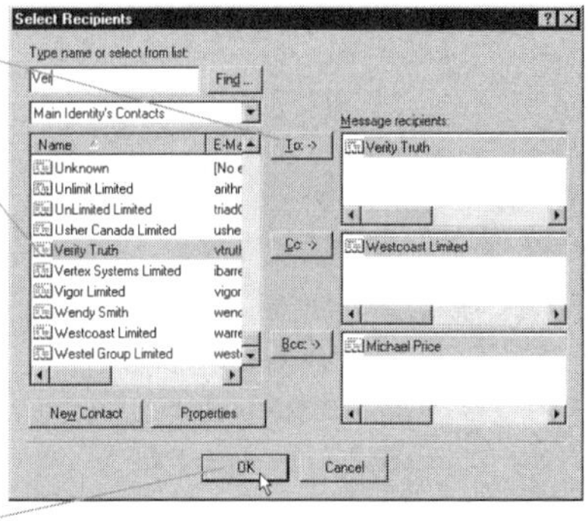

3 To change your mind about an entry, just click the name and press Delete.

Add new contacts or modify existing details. Changes are immediate.

When you press OK, you will see the display names added to your message. The e-mail addresses themselves are hidden from view.

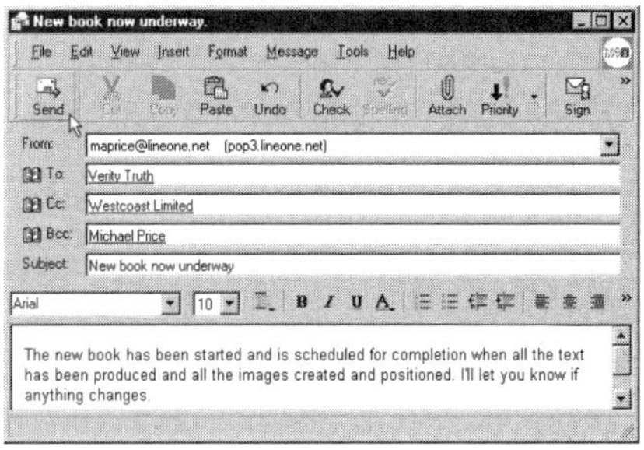

You can locate the details without opening the address book. Type in part of the name, and press the Check Names button. Outlook will look up the name in the book, and enter the matching entry. If there are several possibilities, you can select the correct one from the list of candidates that will be provided.

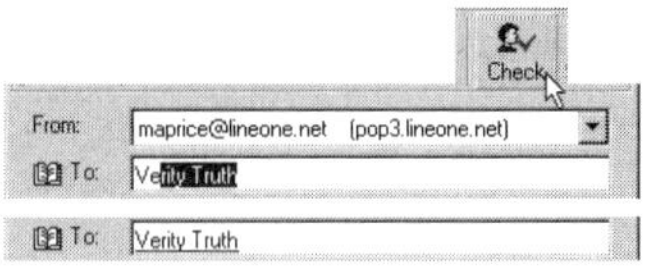

Extracting data

Avoid typing in contact details by using your incoming mail to supply them.

Every time you are sent or copied on an e-mail message from a new contact, use it to update the entries in your address book. Pick up the details of the other addressees as well as the sender.

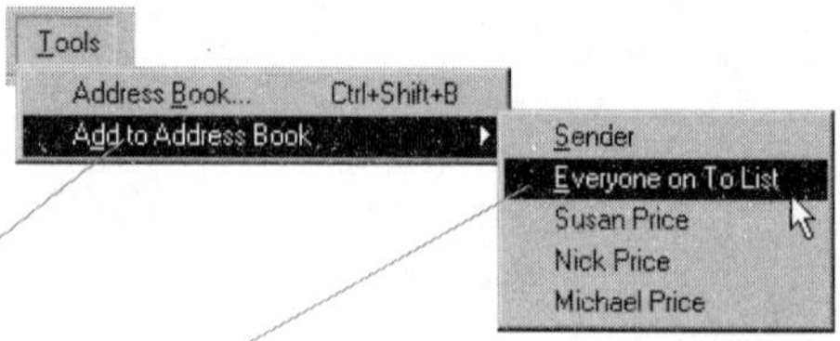

1 Click Tools on the Menu bar and select Add to Address Book.

2 Click Sender or the whole To list, or an individual addressee.

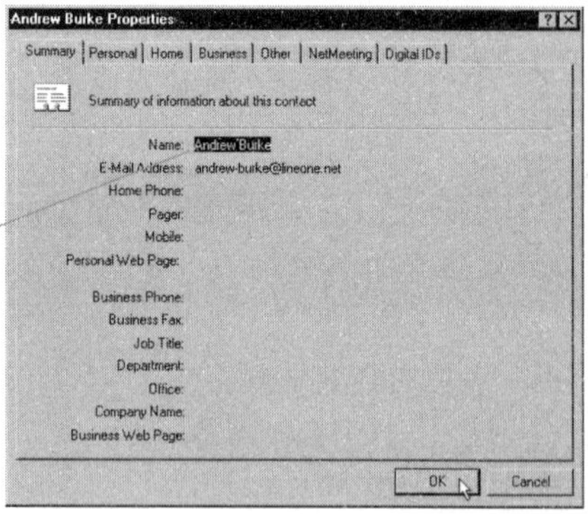

If you receive a vCard attached to the message, it has the details from the sender's own address book entry.

3 The Properties window is displayed with the available details filled in. Add any further data that you have available.

4 Repeat these steps to add the To and Cc other addressees. There's a check to avoid adding duplicates.

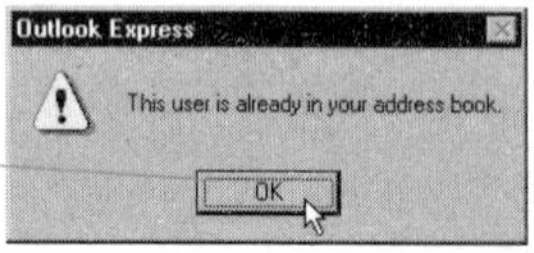

To automate this process, change the e-mail options so that e-mail addresses are added when you reply:

5 Select Tools, Options and the General tab. Check the box to automatically add people when replying.

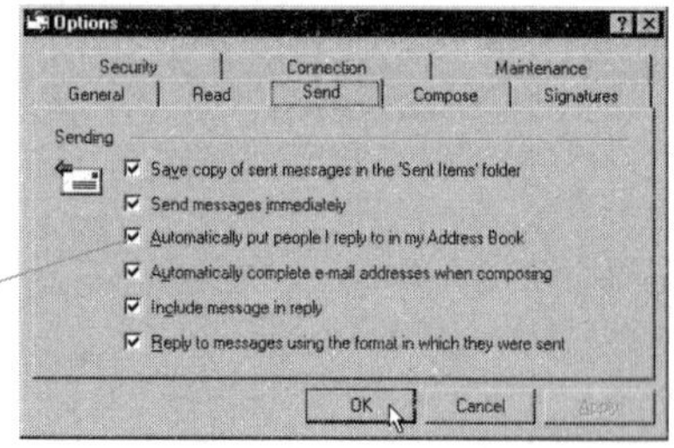

You may have existing name and address data in another Windows application, or in a file downloaded from the Internet. Bring the contents into your Outlook Express address book, using the file import facility.

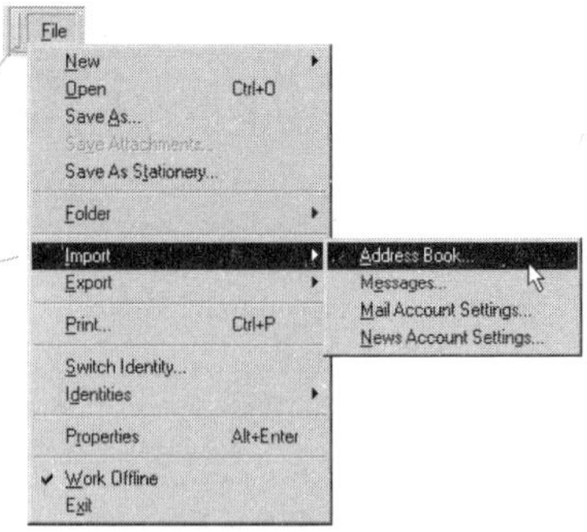

1 Select File from the Menu bar and choose Import and then Address Book.

Most applications let you extract data fields with commas between them, forming a comma delimited file which Outlook can interpret.

2 Import data directly from Eudora, Microsoft or Netscape address books. For other sources, use comma separated files.

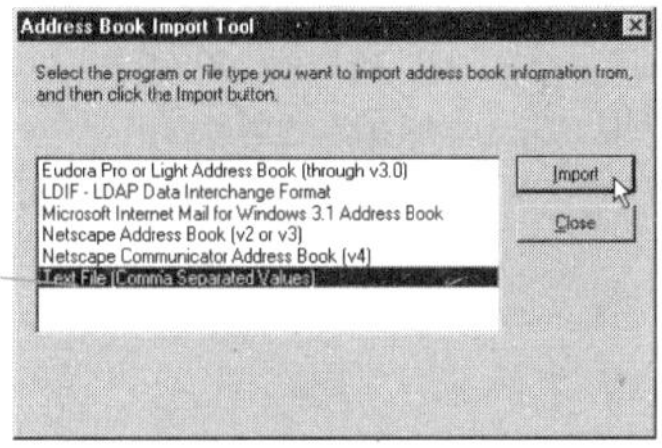

3 Tell Outlook Express how to store the data, by linking the input data field names with the associated Windows address book fields.

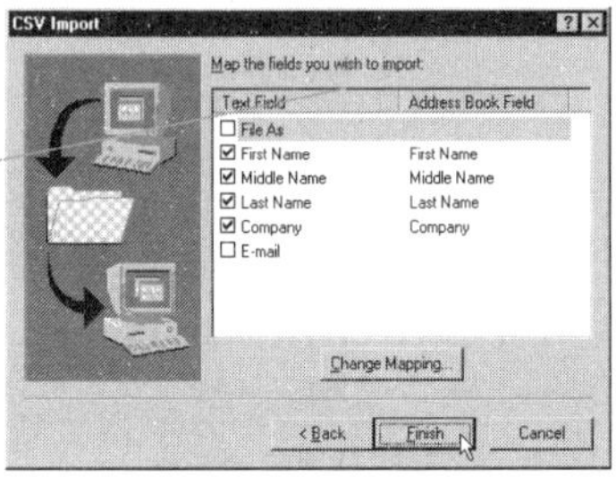

In the full Outlook you must make sure that the input fields have the same names as the folder fields, since mapping is not supported.

4 The records are stored in the address book. Outlook detects duplicate entries.

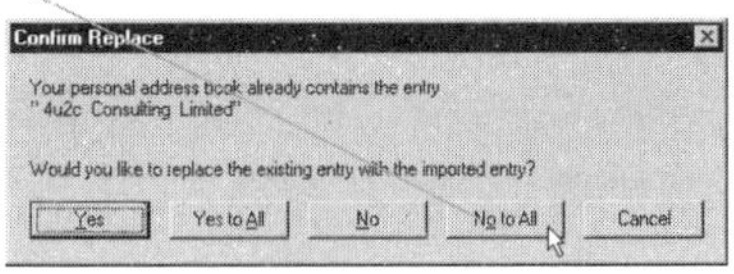

Select invalid or incomplete entries, and click Properties to correct any errors and to add any additional contact details that you may have available.

Finding people

Address books make it easy to send mail and e-mail messages, but you need the contact details in the first place to set up the entries in the book. If other sources fail, try the Find People function to search the Internet. This uses Directory Services tools at various Internet sites that look up names of people or organisations. A list of popular services is already defined in Outlook Accounts.

To search on the Internet:

Find People is not supported in the full Outlook, so you must use the Windows method.

1. In Outlook Express, select Edit from the Menu bar and click Find, People.

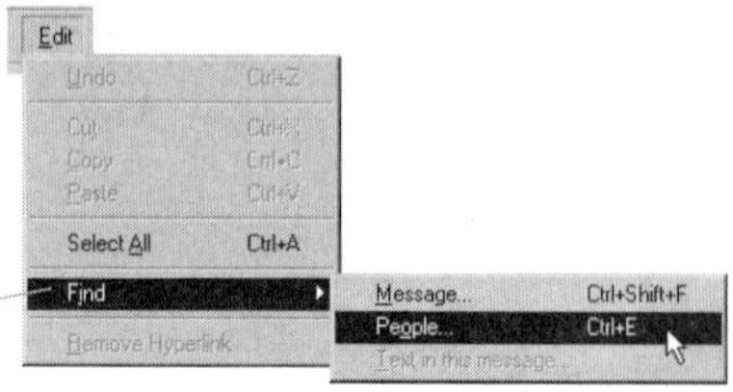

2. From Windows Desktop, select Start, then Find and then People.

3. Select the Directory Service Internet search facility that you want to try.

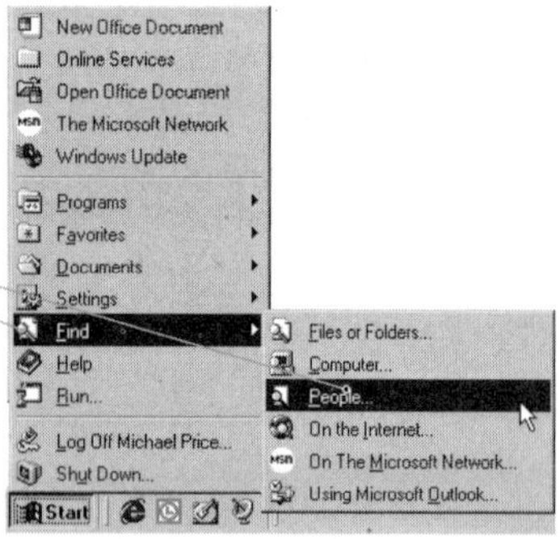

It may be better to connect to the web site before you press Find Now, since some services time out if there is a delay.

4. Enter the name or the e-mail address of the person whose details you need, and press Find Now.

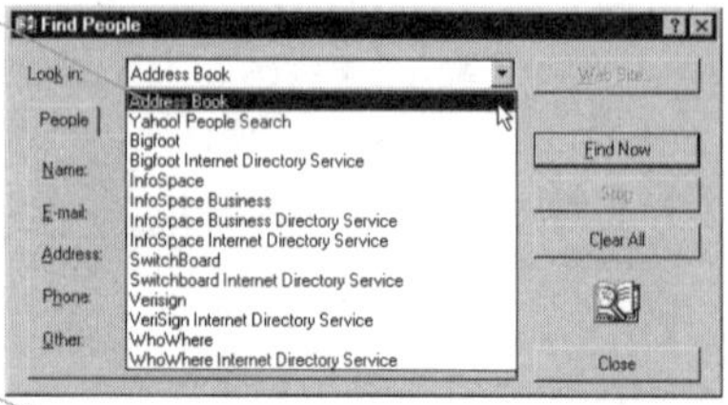

5. Allow the system to dial up to your ISP and pass the search details to the directory service, then wait for the results.

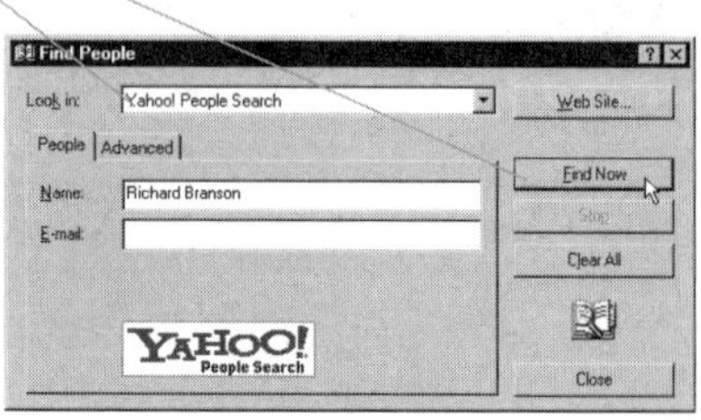

Try several different directory services to find the details you want.

The service looks for near misses as well as exact fits. If you get too many matches, switch to the web page to refine your search, or try the results from a different Internet directory service.

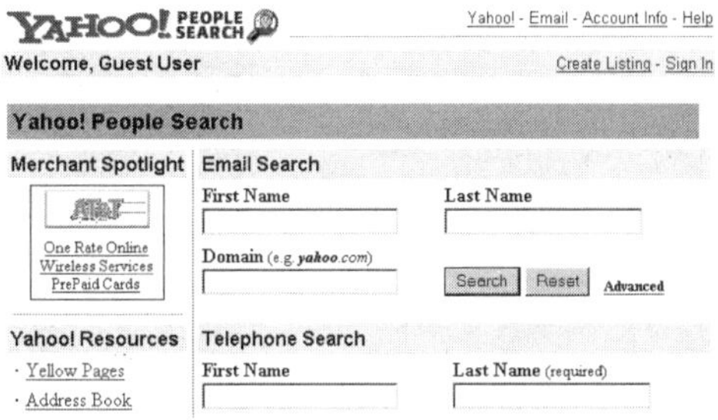

When you have a results list of reasonable size, look more closely at the ones that appear promising.

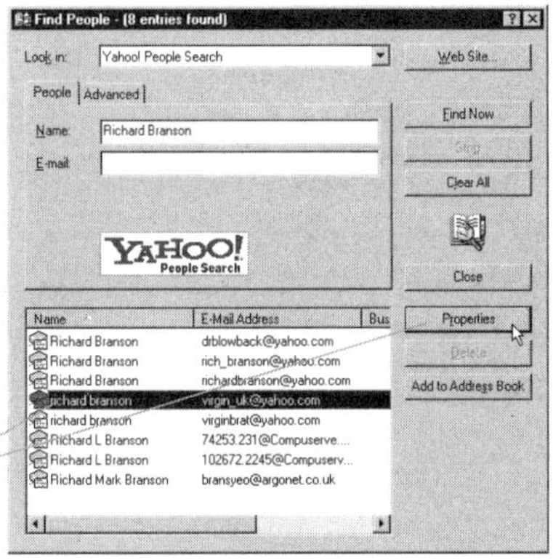

6 Choose an entry and press Properties to view the extra details available.

7 Press the Add to Address Book button for each entry that you want to take note of. Then press Close and disconnect from the Internet.

If there is a directory service that works well for you, make it an extension to your normal address book.

To use a directory service on a regular basis, select Tools, Accounts and choose the service. Open its Properties and check the box to use that service when sending mail.

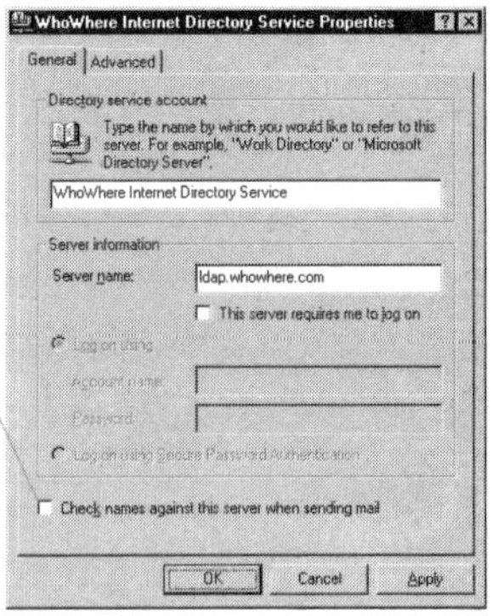

When Outlook checks names (see page 77) it will look in the address book first and then in any directory services you have selected. You'll need to be connected to the Internet at that point.

Distribution groups

When you have a large address book, and send lots of e-mail messages, you may find it easier to create groups of addresses and use these as distribution lists. To create a group in the Address Book:

1. Press the New button and click New Group.

You can add new contacts or change properties for existing contacts, while building your list.

2. Type a name for the group, and then Add names and e-mails.

3. Press Select Members to choose people from the address book.

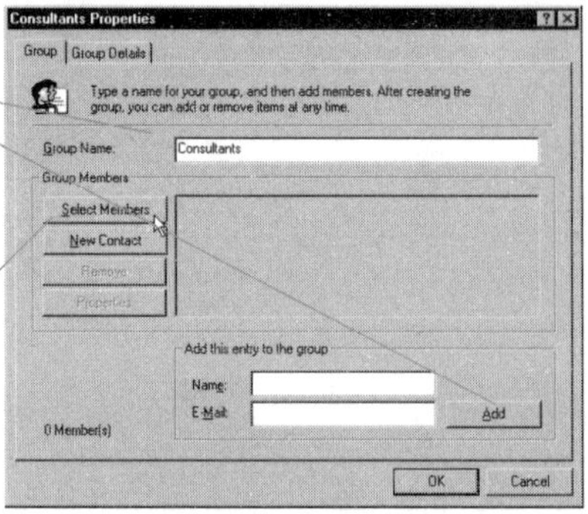

4. Click a name in the list and press Select to add it to the list.

5. To select several addresses at a time, hold down the Ctrl key as you choose names.

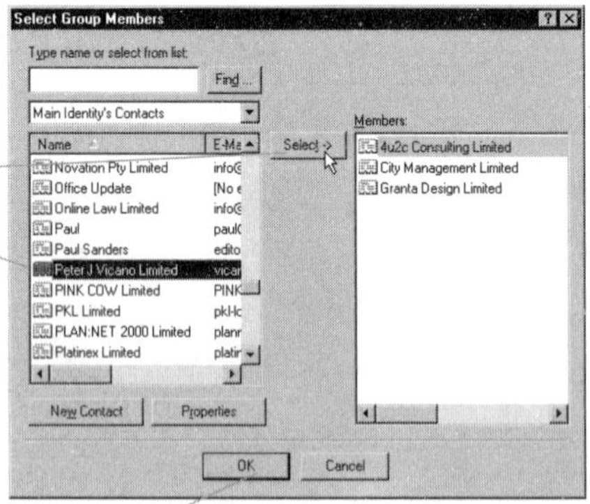

Changes to details for a name will apply to all the groups it belongs to.

6. Press OK to save the new distribution group.

Note that the same entry may appear in several different groups.

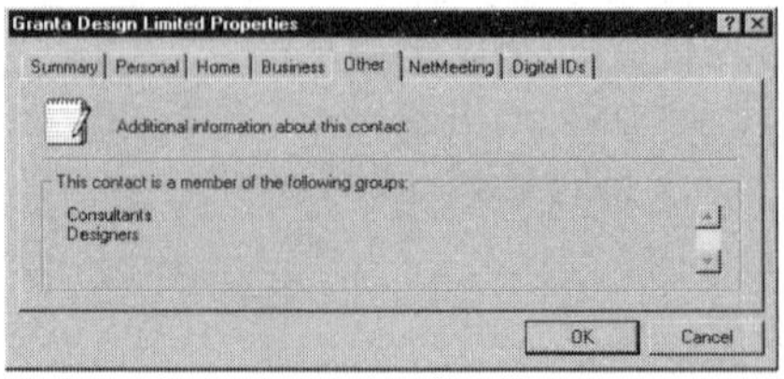

Group entries are shown in bold print, to distinguish distribution lists from ordinary entries.

To display the contents of the distribution list:

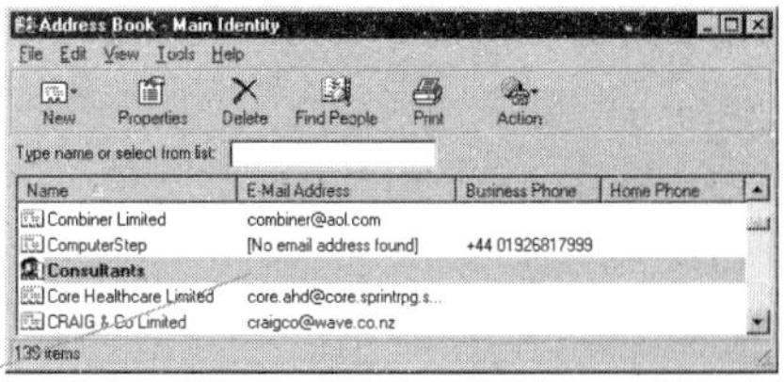

7 Double-click the group name to list the entries in the group, and add or remove members.

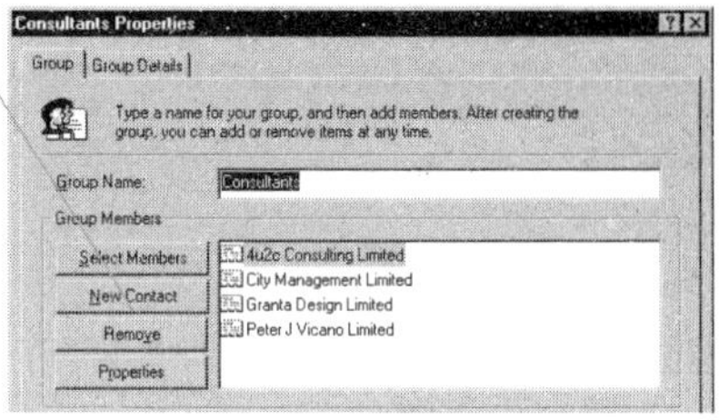

You can display your address book in group view:

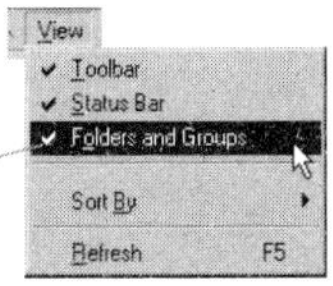

1 Open the Address Book, select View from the Menu bar and click Folders and Groups.

When you delete a name from the address book, it will also be removed from any groups that it belonged to.

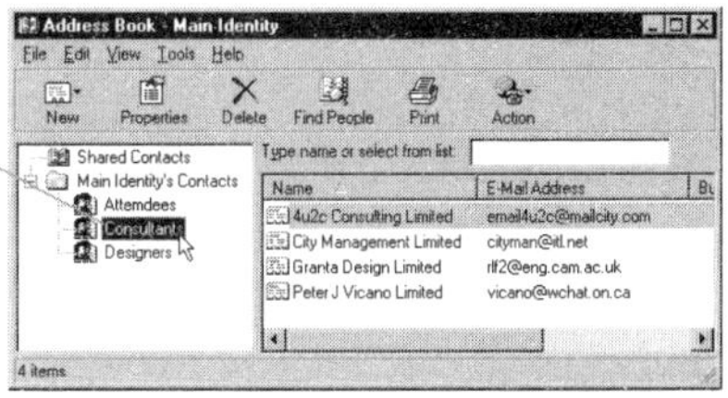

2 Selecting the group name will display its contents.

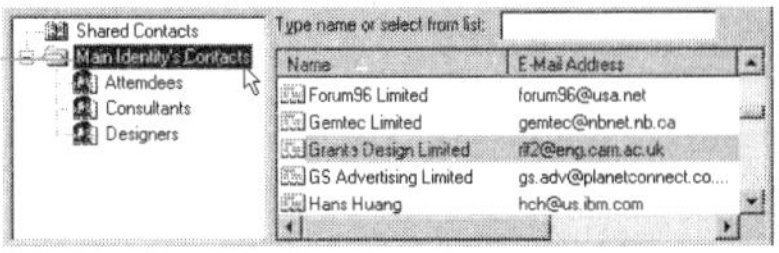

3 Select the main contacts list for individual entries.

Use the group names in the To, Cc and Bcc boxes just as you use ordinary names, and mix single and group entries as required. The group names are shown in bold in the message boxes, to remind you that they represent several recipients.

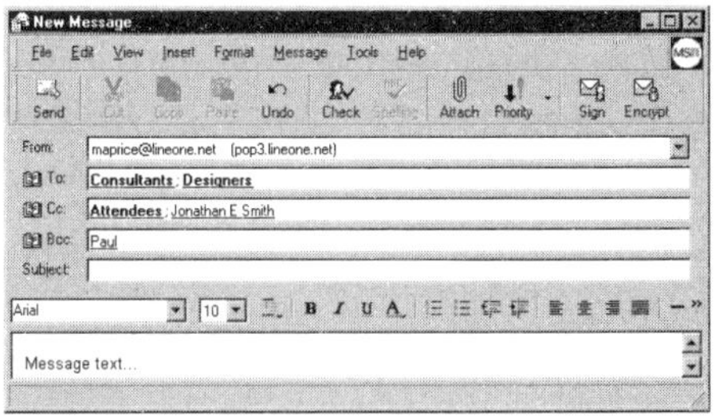

Outlook Contacts list

There are two ways to look up name and address details in Outlook: Windows address book and Contacts Manager.

When you upgrade to Outlook, the address book from your original e-mail software is converted into a Contacts list, and there is a new Contacts function. However, you will still find an Address Book entry on the toolbar. You can use either function to view or change the contact details:

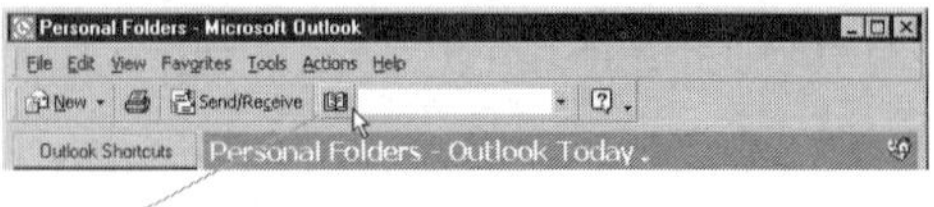

1 Press the button on the toolbar to open the address book.

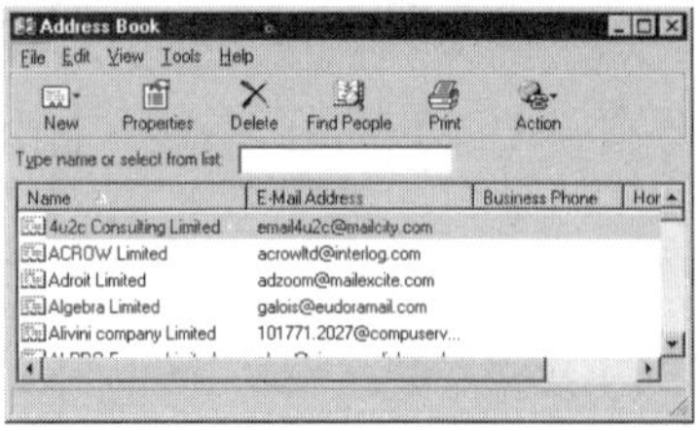

2 Use the Address Book as in Outlook Express to add and change contacts.

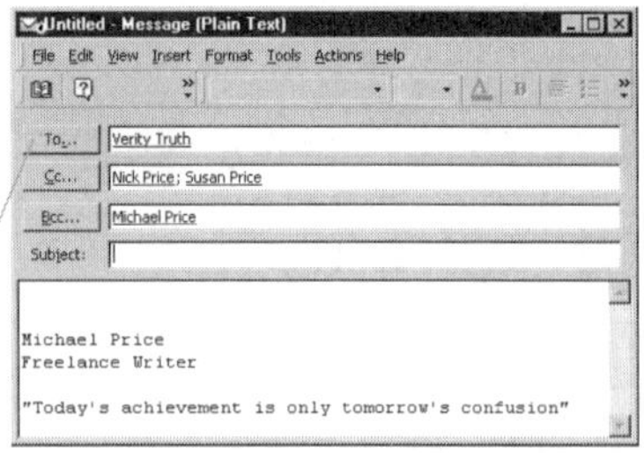

3 The To, Cc and Bcc buttons still open the address book for you to select names when composing messages.

Although this looks different, it is just another way of viewing the same set of data.

You can also access the contacts details using the Contacts Manager to display and process the details:

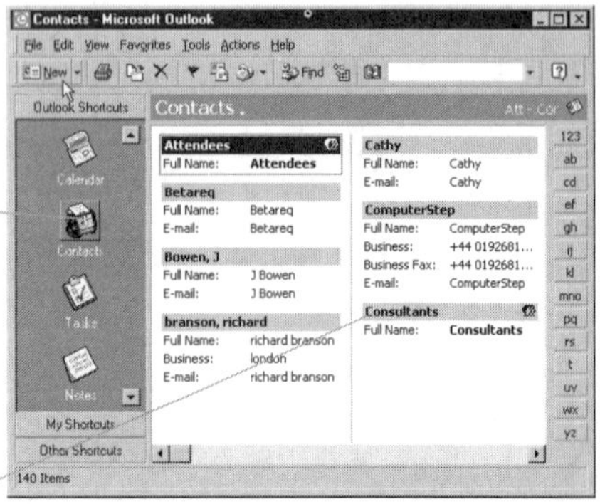

4 Select the Contacts function from the Outlook bar.

5 Press New Contacts button to add entries, or double-click an entry to open and update it.

By default, the entries in the Contacts list are displayed in the Contacts function as address cards, sequenced by the File As field (last name, first name).

Check on page 88 for more ways of organising your Contacts list.

Change the level of detail, or have the entries presented as lists arranged in various ways, using the View facility:

1 Click Contacts on the Outlook bar to open the Contacts Manager.

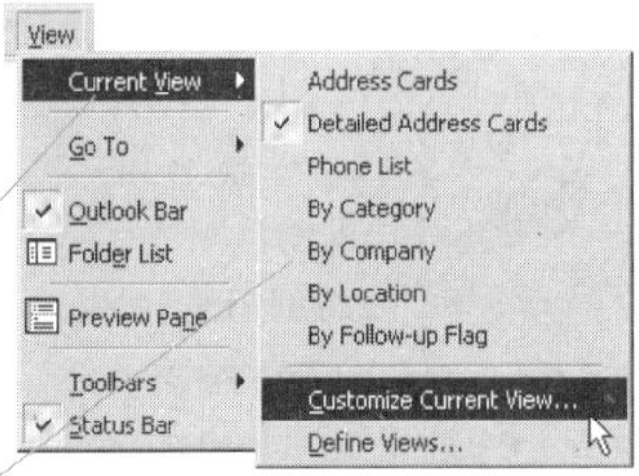

2 Select View from the Menu bar and click Current View.

3 Choose one of the views offered. There are two card views and five list views.

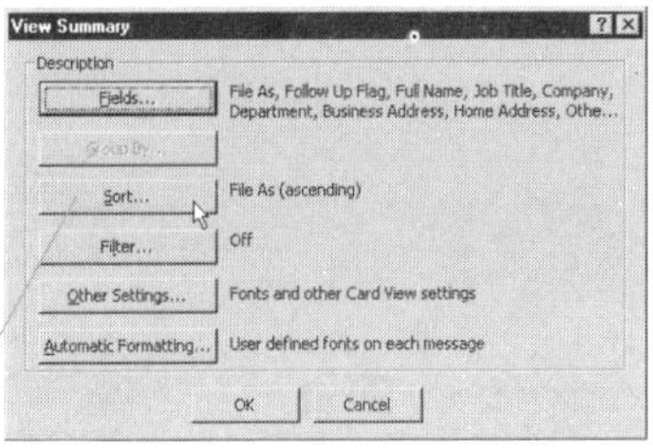

4 Click Customise Current View to review and change the fields, filters and sort options used.

You can select any field to sort the items in your desired sequence.

5 For example, click Sort and change the sort field and sequence to First Name, Ascending.

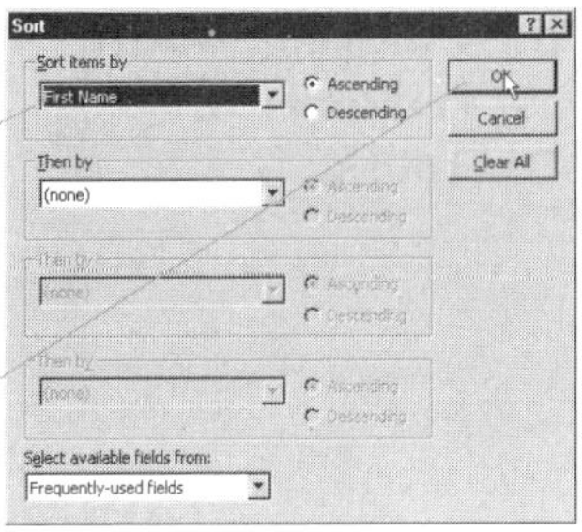

6 Press OK to complete and apply the changes.

New Contacts

Outlook tries to format and restructure the data to reduce the amount you need to enter.

1 Open the Contacts folder, and press the New Contacts button on the toolbar.

2 Enter the full name (ie, first middle last), job title, and company name for the contact.

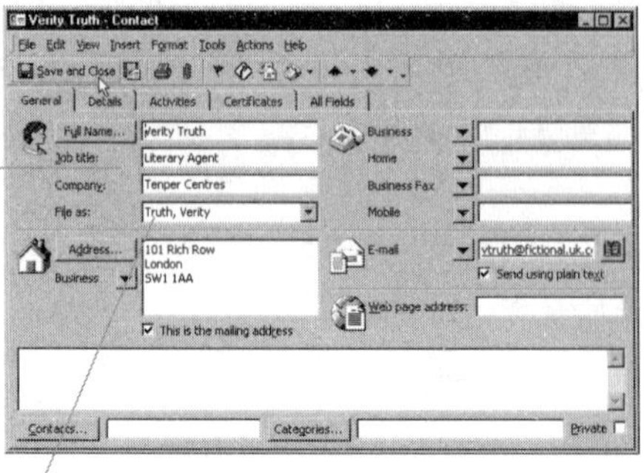

Note that you can mark particular contacts as private, to separate them from your business entries.

3 Outlook fills in the 'File as' entry (ie, last, first middle).

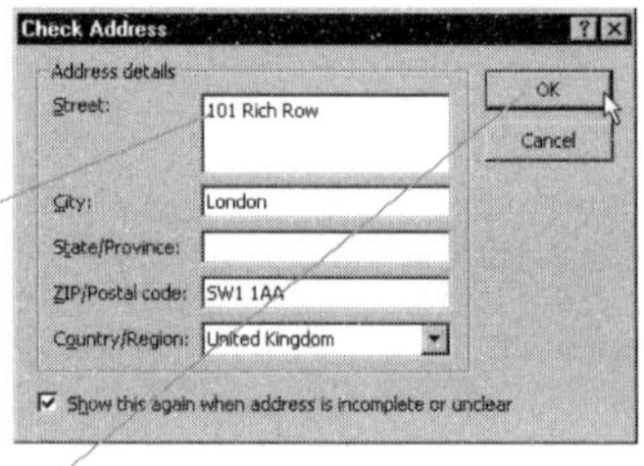

4 Type in the full address, then press Full Address to see how Outlook has interpreted the parts of the address. Make any corrections needed. Press OK.

The contact you have added can be accessed from the Address Book as well as from Contacts.

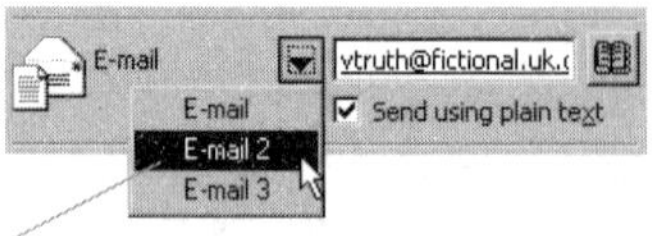

5 Enter the e-mail address. Click the arrow to get spaces for any additional e-mail addresses.

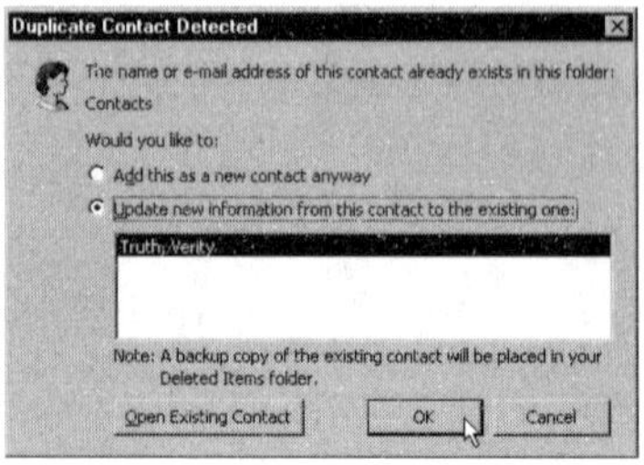

Fill in the entries for the phone numbers. You can select from a long list of descriptive titles. Choose the Details tab to enter other information such as department, manager's name, birth date or spouse name.
Press Save and Close to enter the details into the contacts list. Duplicate names are detected, and you can update the current entry, or add a new entry.

Pick up contact details from incoming mail.

The distribution fields on incoming messages can be used to update your contact list in Outlook, but the process is not quite as well structured as the Windows address book process (see page 75). To extract the e-mail details:

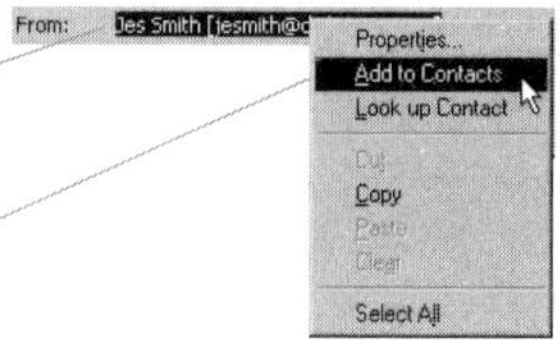

1 Open the message and right-click one of the e-mail addresses.

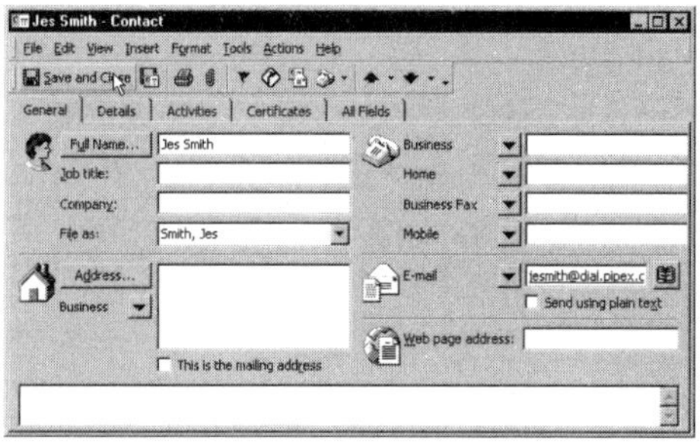

2 Select Add to Contacts to create an entry. Add other details such as phone numbers if available.

3 Select Look up Contact, if you think you might already have this address.

4 Repeat for all other e-mail addresses in the message.

An easier approach is to add e-mail addresses automatically when you reply to messages.

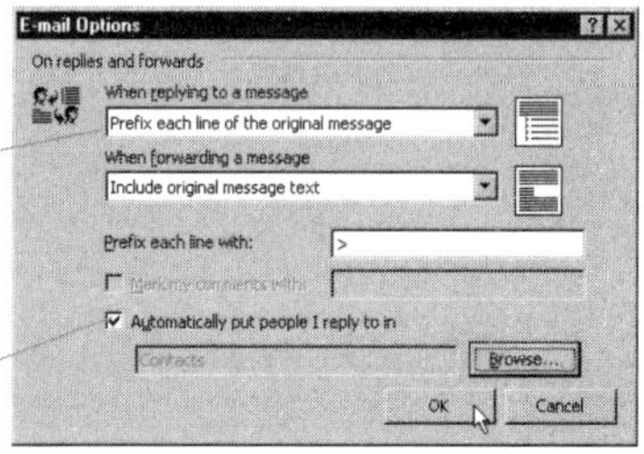

5 Select Tools, Options and press the E-mail Options button. Check the box to automatically add people you reply to.

Organising Contacts

Outlook helps you to associate groups of related items, of the same or different types, that belong to the same project. It does this with categories, which are keywords or phrases that you select from a master list. There are twenty general categories in the list supplied with Outlook, but you can add your own as required.

1. Open Contacts, and then select View, Current View, By Category.

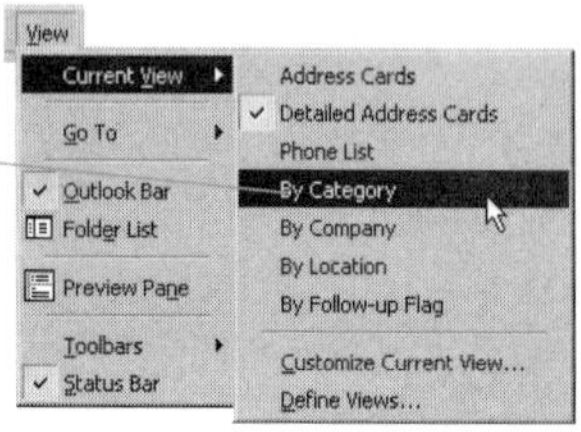

2. Press the Organize button and select Using Categories.

3. Select the contacts to add to a Category.

4. Create a new Category.

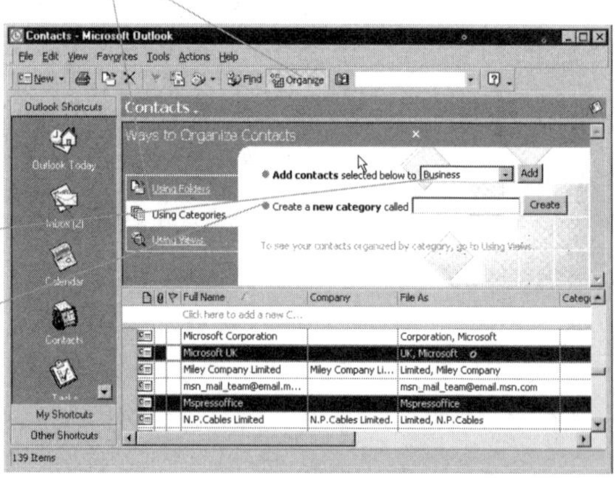

5. Press Organize again to return to the Contacts view.

Address book groups (see page 82) are known as personal distribution lists in Outlook 2000.

You can assign other Outlook items such as messages and tasks to the same categories as the associated contacts. This will allow you to search for items of all types that belong together, and view or print them as a group.

Distribution lists can still be created, but these cannot be associated with other types of Outlook items.

Phone directory

You can decide which fields you want to see in the phone list view of Contacts.

The Contacts folder Phone List view acts as a phone directory, showing all your contacts with their business, fax, home and mobile numbers.

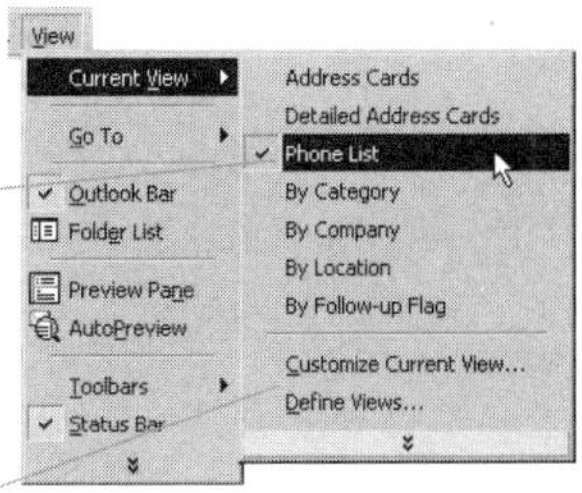

1 Select Contacts, View, Current View, Phone list.

Customise the view to add other phone number fields:

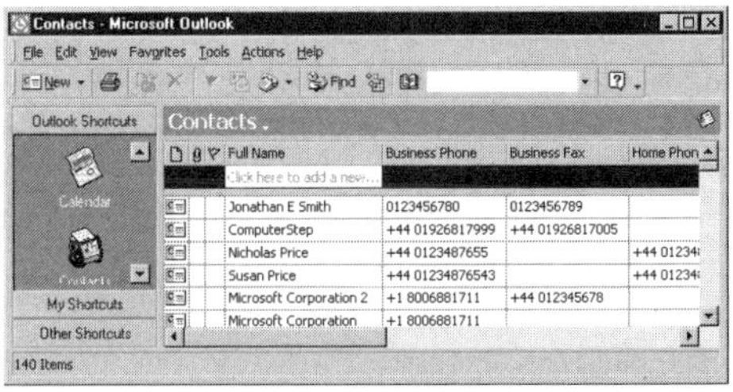

2 Select View, Current View, Customize Current View.

3 Press Fields on the View summary to change the selection.

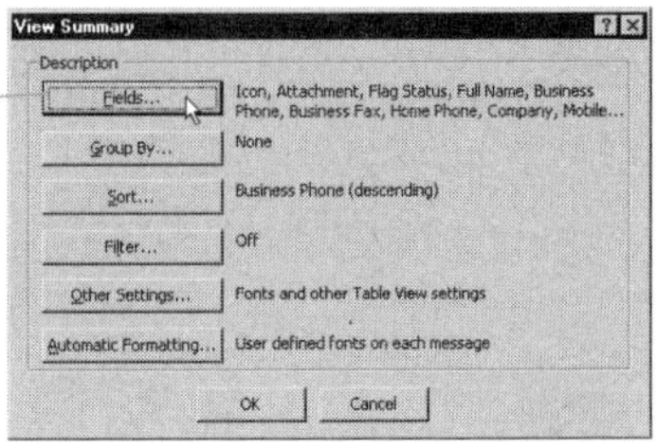

4 Pick 'Phone number fields' from the 'Select available fields from' option.

Select and drag the field to reposition it in the list, or press Move Up or Move Down.

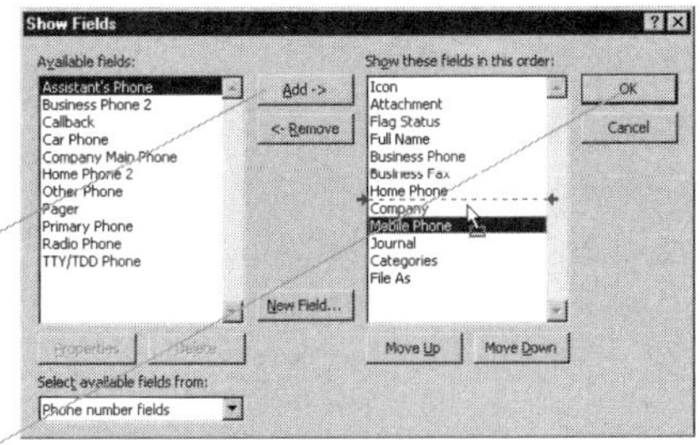

5 Press Add and Remove to revise the selection of phone number fields.

6 When the list is complete, press OK.

Phone dialer

Outlook will place voice calls for you, and keep track of phone numbers and duration.

With a modem attached to your PC, Outlook will dial a phone number from the Contacts list, or any number that you specify. For frequent calls, create a speed dial list, or select a number from the list of recent calls.

To call the number specified in a Contacts entry:

1 Open Contacts and select the entry you want to call.

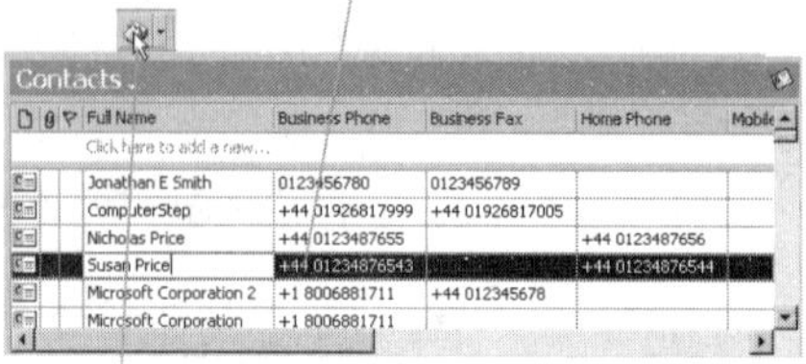

Click the Create Journal Entry box to automatically time a call and make notes in Outlook while you talk.

2 Press the Autodialer button on the Contacts toolbar.

3 To call now, choose the phone number, and press Start Call.

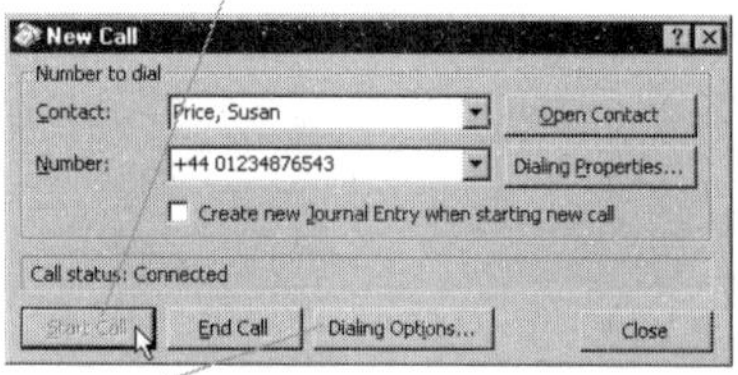

4 To add the number to the speed dial list press Dialing Options.

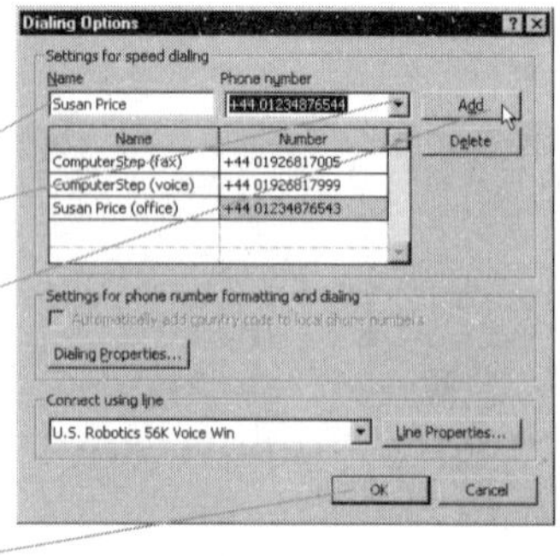

Edit the name field in the autodial list to clarify the type of number (eg, Fax or Home).

5 Enter each name, select the number and press Add.

6 Press OK to save the list

Click the Autodialer down-arrow, select Speed Dial and pick the phone number, or click Redial and select a recently called number.

Mapping contacts

The Street Map function in Address Finder is for US addresses, but it shows high level maps for places worldwide.

If you have a mailing address for a contact, you can view a map of the area:

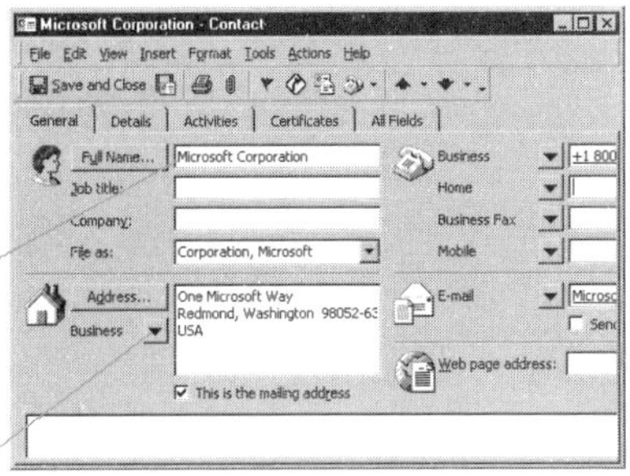

1 Select Contacts and open the contact entry whose address you wish to map.

2 Select the type of address Business, Home, etc.).

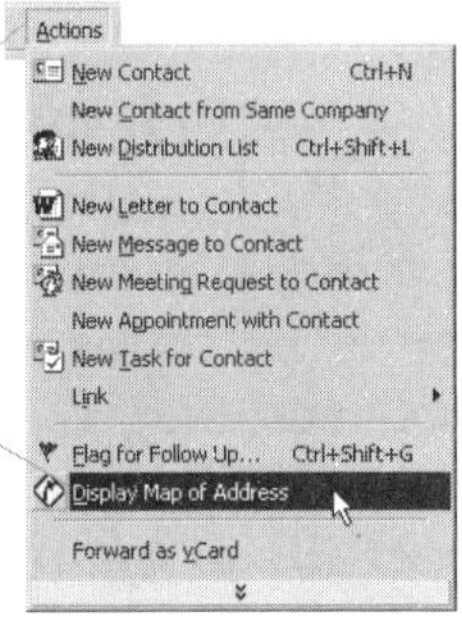

3 Choose Actions from the Menu bar, and click Display Map of Address.

4 You must be connected to the Internet to find the maps.

Make sure that your zip code is specified as five digits. If you don't have the zip code, you'll have to select the right state or country from the results.

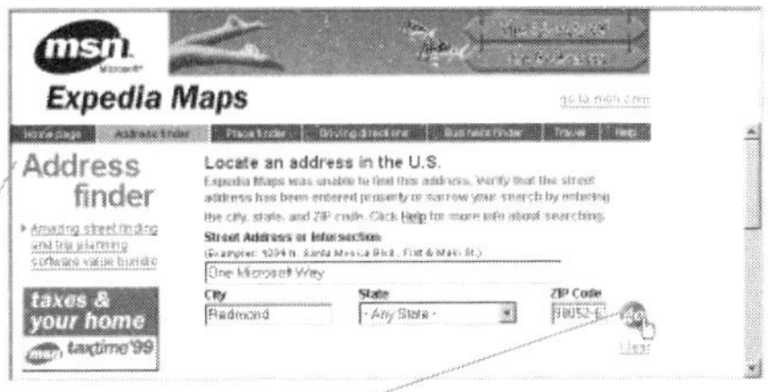

5 Your Web browser opens at the Expedia Maps page, with the criteria for the search.

6 Adjust the entries and press Go to display the map.

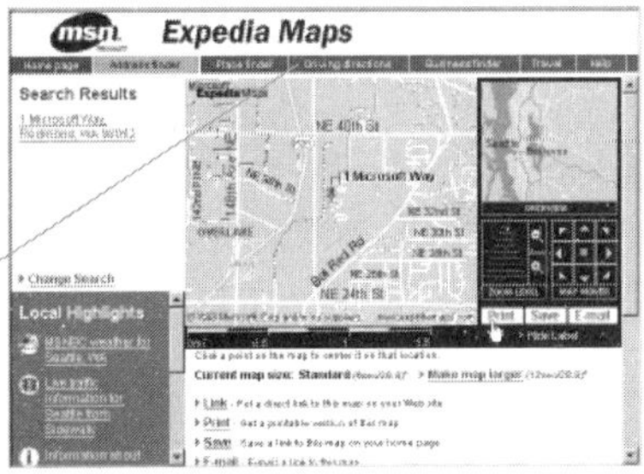

7 There are options such as driving directions and city plans, which apply to US locations only.

Electronic business cards

Outlook supports the vCard standard for exchanging personal data. This is an electronic business card attached to e-mail messages, and used to update address book and contact lists. To create a vCard to attach to your signature:

1. Select Tools from Menu bar, then Options, and click the Mail Format tab.

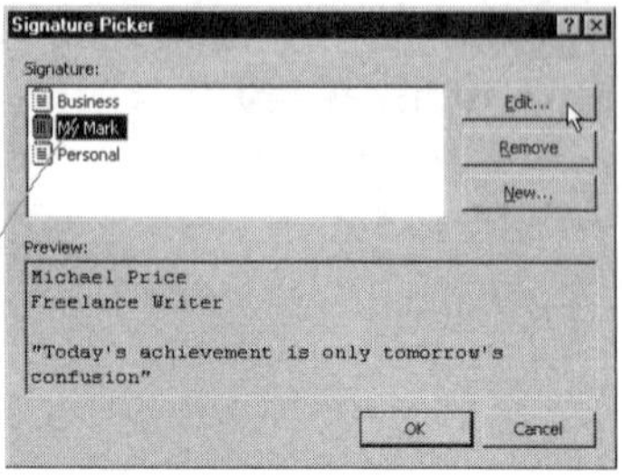

2. Press Signature Picker to display your list of signatures, and choose the one to edit.

Define multiple signature files and vCards – eg, to provide personal details or business details.

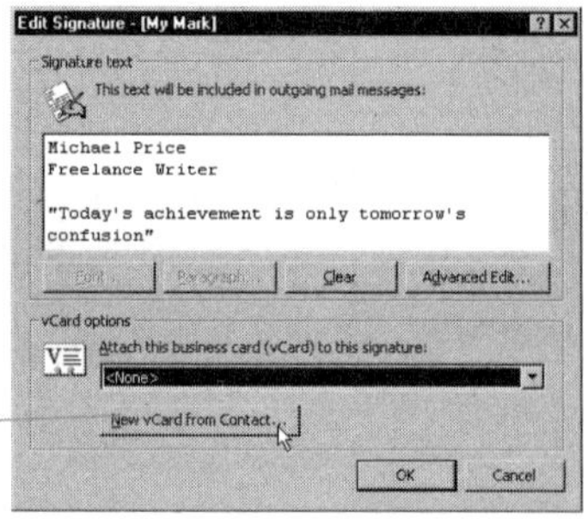

3. Click the down-arrow to select from a list of vCards, then press Select New vCard from Contact.

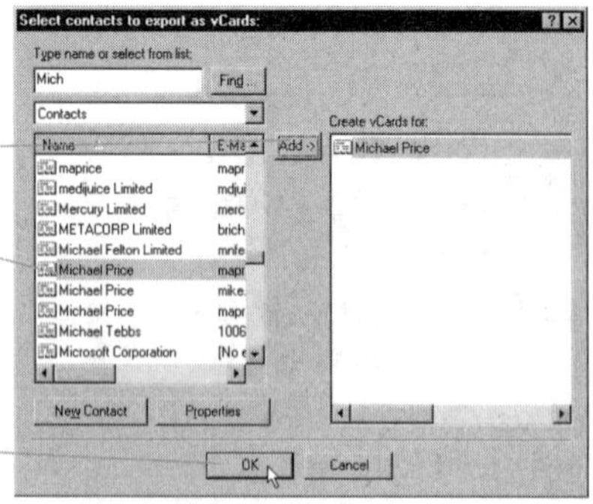

4. Locate your own entry in Contacts and press the Add button.
5. Click OK to create the vCard, then save your changed signature file.

This process creates a plain text vCard file with the same name as the Contact entry you chose, but with .vcf as the file type. It is stored in the same folder as your signatures.

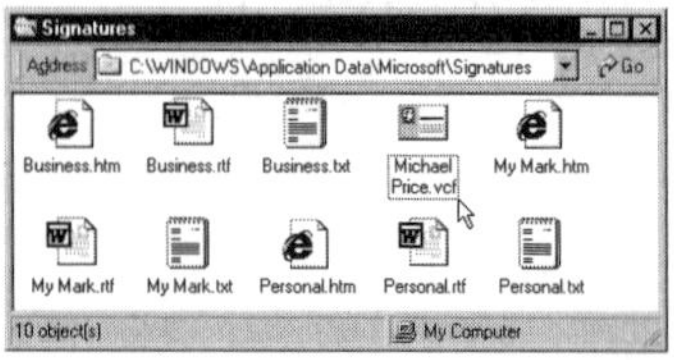

vCards allow you and your contacts to update address list information automatically.

When you create a message, your vCard is inserted as a text file attachment.

1. Automatic signature text.
2. Attached vCard text file.

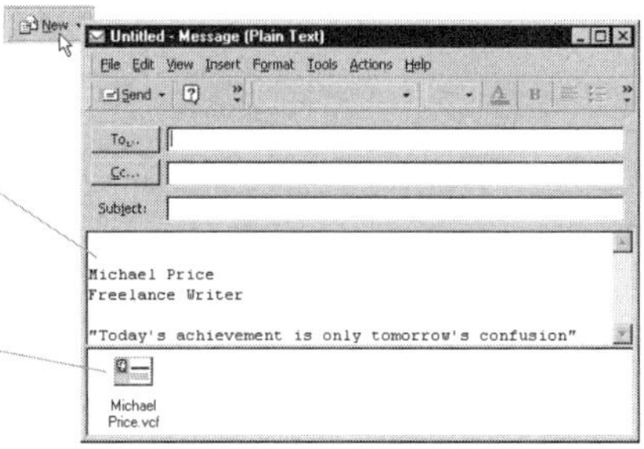

When the message arrives at its destination, your contact details can be added to the addressee's Contact folder or address book.

Similarly, when you receive e-mails with vCard files attached, you can add their contents to your own Contacts folder.

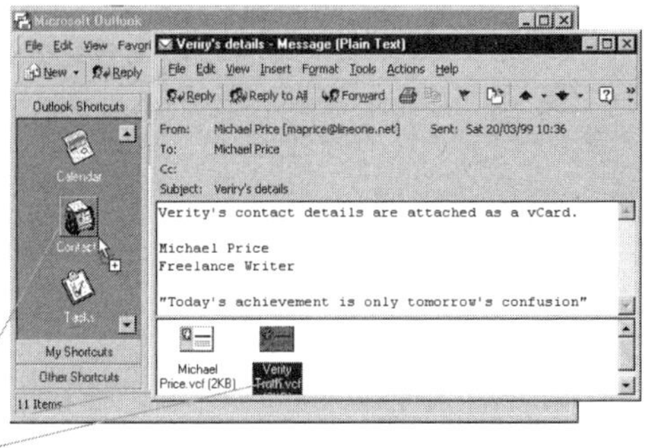

3. Open the message with the vCard attachment.
4. Select and drag the vCard, to the Contacts shortcut on the Outlook bar, or right-click and select Open from the menu.

Double click the vCard to open it or save it to your hard disk, as with other file attachments.

5. Amend or extend the contact data as appropriate.
6. Press Save and Close to enter the data into your Contacts list.

Mail merge with Contacts

You can send form letters or e-mails to all the contacts in your list, or a selected subset.

The Contacts list will help you generate form letters or mailing labels in Word, by exporting the details to a data file.

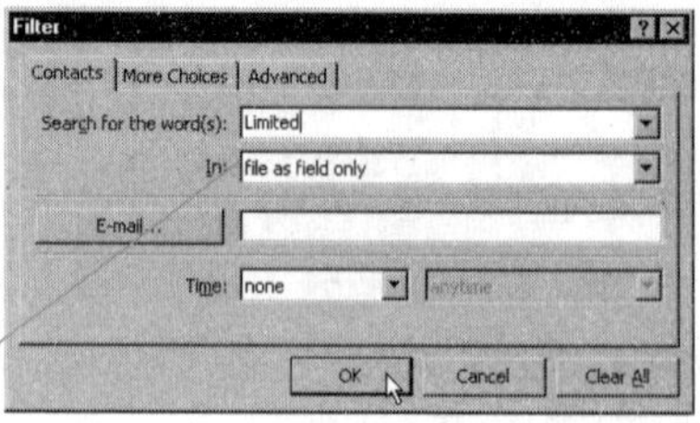

1. Customise the current view and define a filter to identify the target contacts.

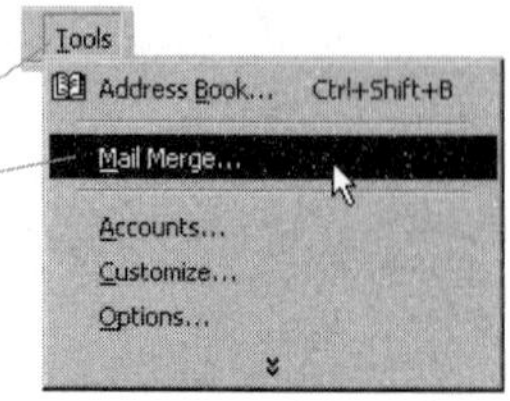

2. Select Tools from the menu bar and click Mail Merge.

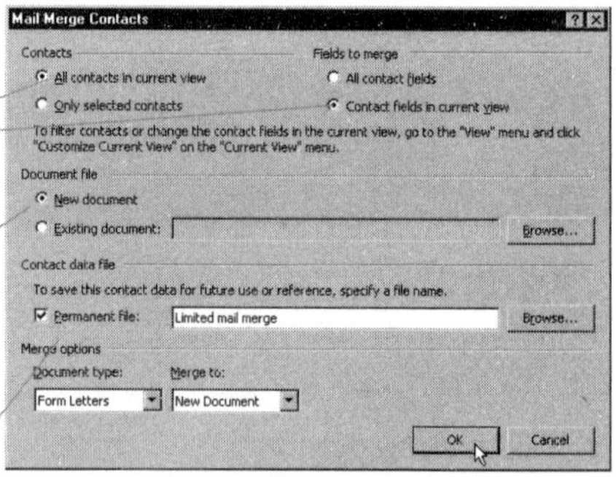

3. Pick All contacts in current list, and Fields from current view. Name the form letter document, or specify a New Document.

Choose the Comma Separated Values file type to use the exported data in most Windows applications.

4. Choose to save the extracted data in a permanent file, if you want to reuse the list.

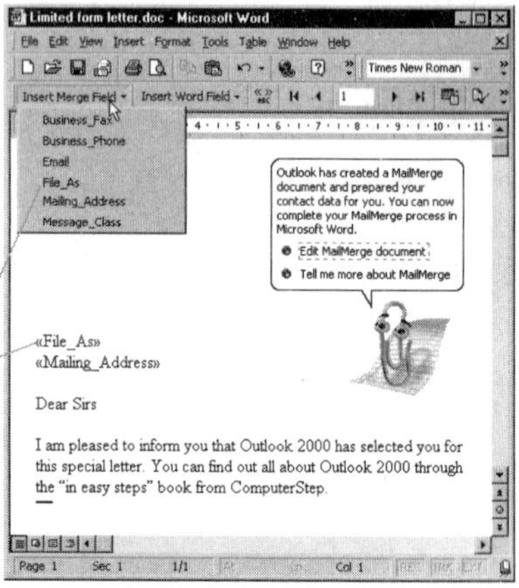

5. Click OK, and the Word mail merge wizard starts. You can create your form letter using fields from the list as variables, and generate the letters required.

Organising messages

This chapter takes an in-depth look at e-mail productivity features such as previews, filters and rules to help you organise and structure the messages as the volume grows, using backups and archives for older items.

Covers

Chapter Six

Adding new e-mail accounts

This is for Outlook with Internet Mail Only (IMO).

You'll need the server names, the e-mail id or name and the password, plus any special Internet settings specified by your ISP.

There are many situations where you have multiple e-mail ids. You may sign up with several ISPs, or your ISP may offer extra ids for a shared connection.

You can manage each e-mail address separately, logging on to the appropriate ISP, or you can have Outlook handle all the e-mail accounts in one folder. To tell Outlook the details of the additional accounts:

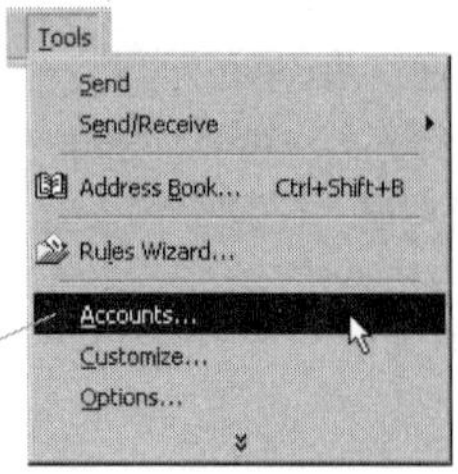

1 Select Tools from the Menu bar, and then Accounts.

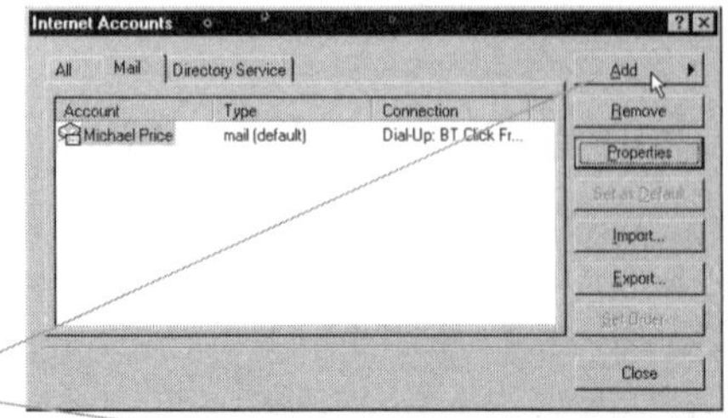

2 Press Add, and then select Mail.

3 Type the account owner's name as it should appear on e-mails.

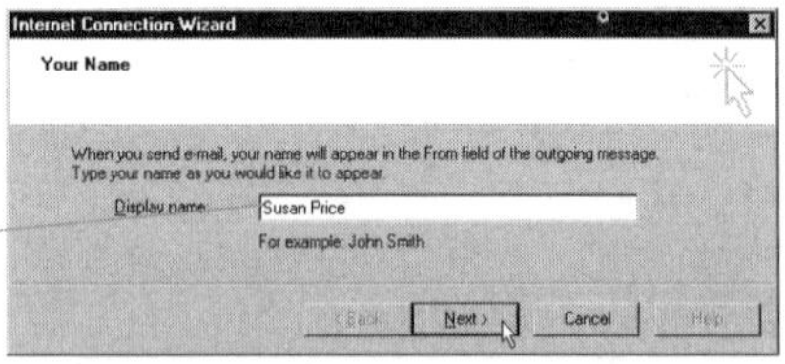

4 Type the e-mail address for the account.

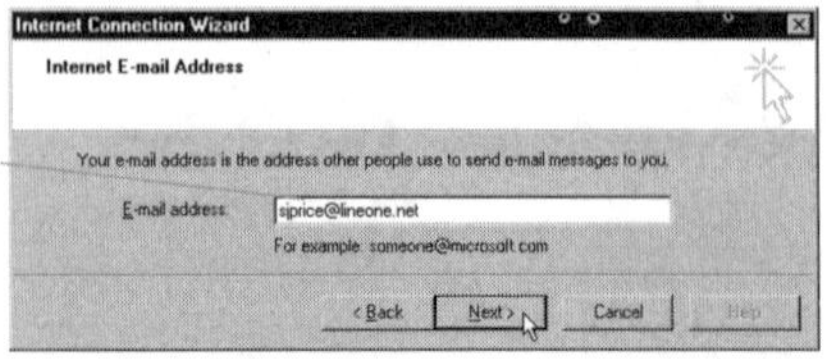

5 Select the incoming mail server type (POP3 or IMAP).

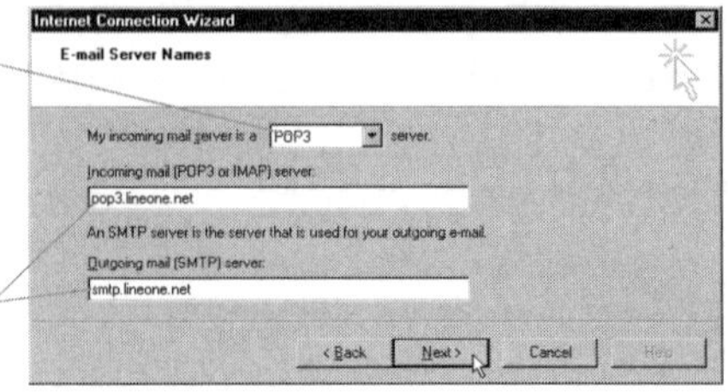

6 Enter the incoming and outgoing mail server names or numeric IP addresses.

The Internet Connection Wizard guides you through the steps.

7 Enter the account name and password. Select Secure Password Authentication (SPA) if advised to do so by your ISP.

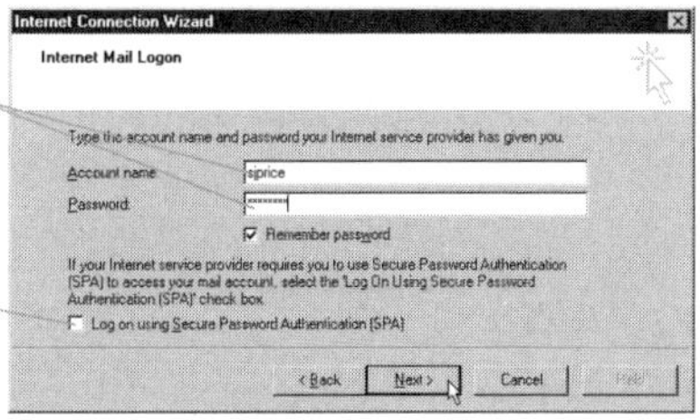

8 Choose your connection type (your phone line for dial connections).

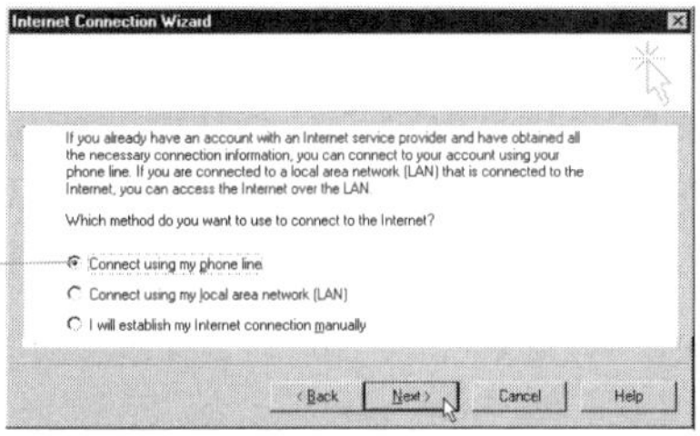

9 Select to use an existing networking connection, choose one if there are several, and press Next.

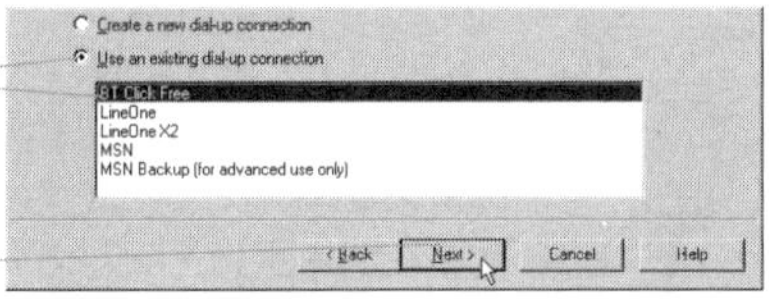

The account will be added to your list of mail services. Repeat the process to all the accounts that you need to access through the same Internet connection.

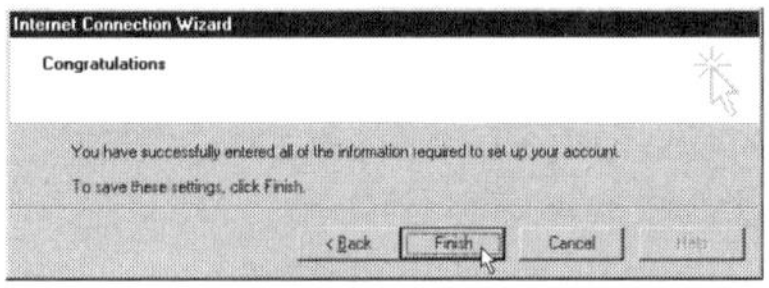

1 Open Accounts and click Properties to supply a unique self-explanatory name for each of the accounts.

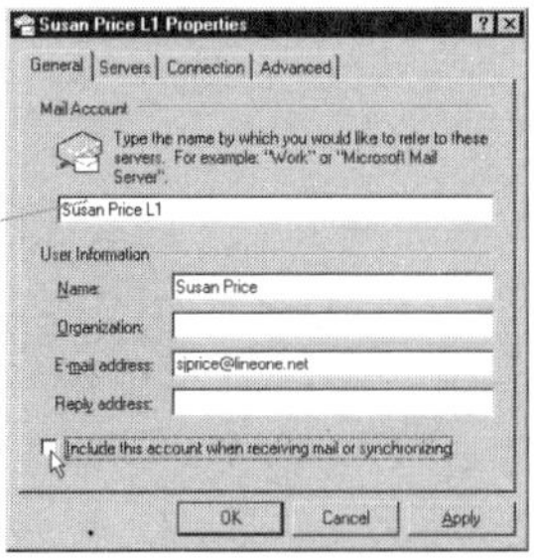

The accounts can be located at other ISPs, and may be for different people, but they will all share the same set of Outlook mail folders. Use filters if you want to receive incoming mail in separate folders for each account (see page 102).

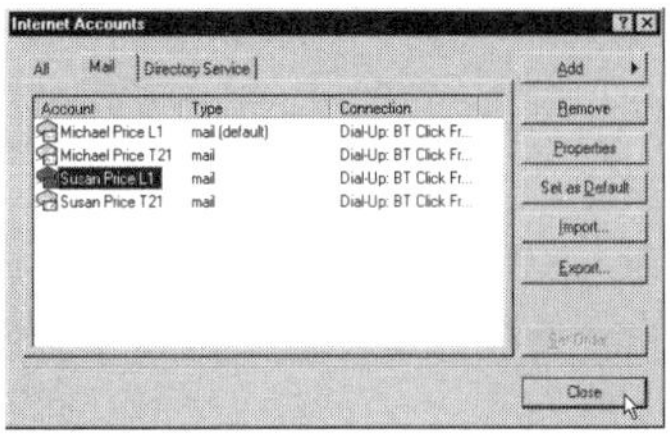

Receiving mail

If there are multiple e-mail accounts defined, you will normally receive messages for all the accounts, each time you issue a request for mail:

Outlook dials your default Internet account and collects mail across the network from the other mail servers.

1 Press the Send and Receive button on the toolbar, and Outlook connects to the Internet. It empties the Outbox and then collects waiting mail.

You may be able to read mail, but leave it on the server for later collection or deletion (see page 108 for details).

2 Press Details to see what is happening behind the scenes.

3 Check the box to disconnect from the Internet on completion.

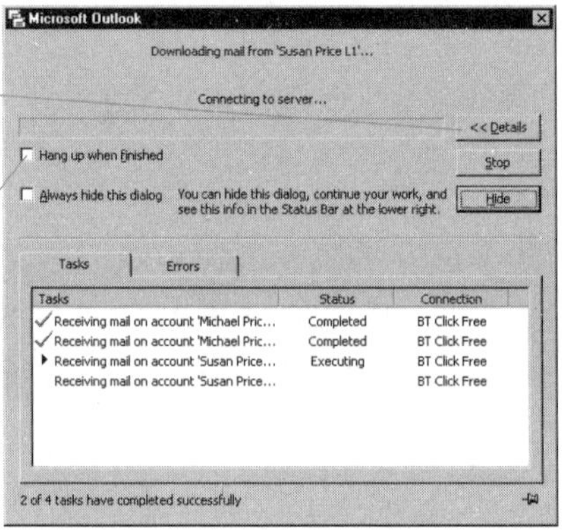

There is no need to access all the e-mail accounts if you just want to process the mail for a particular account or user:

Mail for the chosen account will be processed. No other mail is processed.

4 Select Tools from the Menu bar, then Send and Receive, and then choose the specific account.

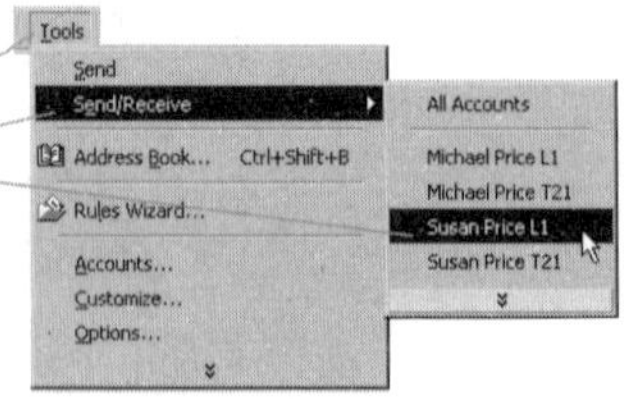

5 Select File from the Menu bar, then Send Using. Choose an account and send waiting mail without receiving any mail.

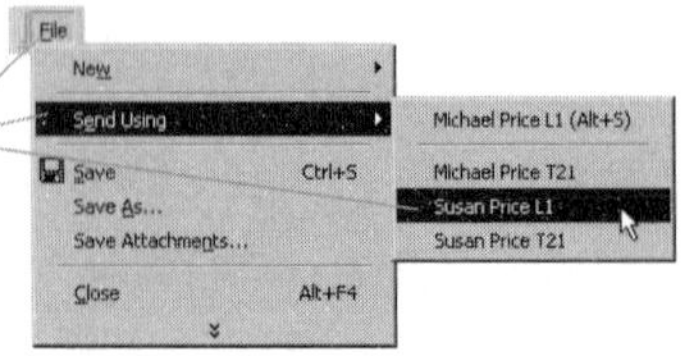

Newsletters are e-mail messages sent out on a regular basis. See Chapter Seven for details of Newsgroups, interactive discussion groups based on e-mail.

You may wonder how web sites such as the WinFiles Shareware facility can afford to run, since there is no charge for access. The answer is your e-mail account id. This is a key asset, and most of the web pages you visit will do everything possible to encourage you to leave your e-mail address and other details. One method commonly employed is to offer you a regular and useful newsletter.

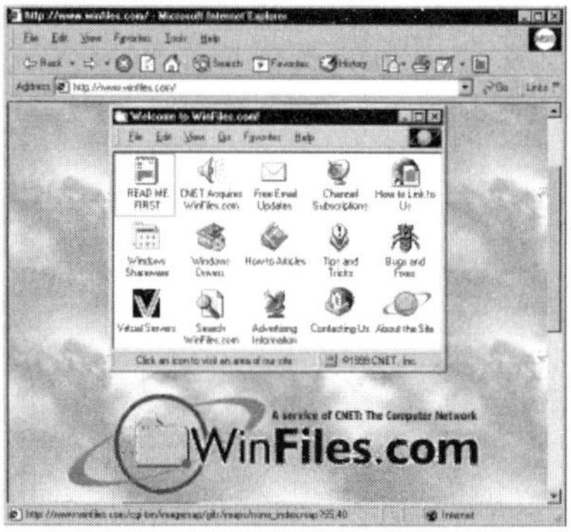

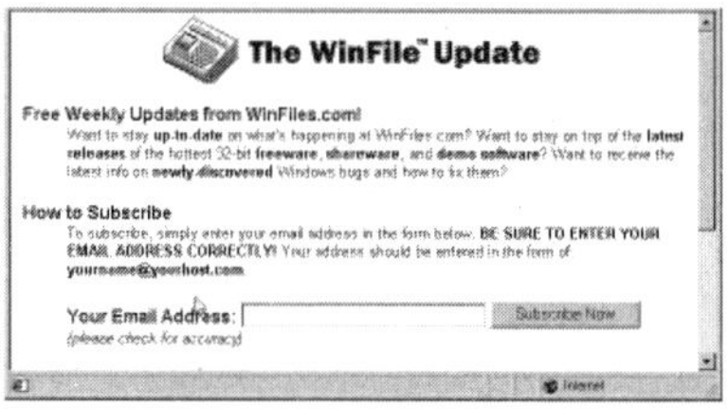

The WinFiles Update for example is a weekly newsletter giving you current news, and details of the latest shareware applications.

The main purpose of newsletters may be for advertising, but they can still be very valuable, as long as you are selective.

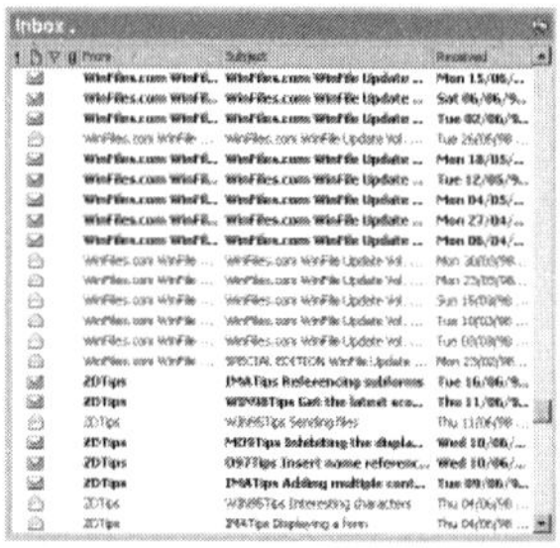

There are similar e-mail newsletters offered by most software vendors. They are not unsolicited mail, since you have to request them. However, they can soon fill up your Inbox.

The suppliers usually make it easy to discontinue a subscription that you find is no longer of interest, or to change your details if you acquire a new e-mail address.

To make it easy to work with your mail, you will need ways to manage your Inbox, to sort out the categories of messages, keeping what's important and disposing of unnecessary items, as discussed on the following pages.

Managing the Inbox

With a large contacts list, multiple e-mail addresses and with newsletters and other communications from web-based vendors, you'll soon find your Inbox with a huge list of messages.

Outlook offers numerous ways to alleviate this problem, including views, filters and folders, but the simplest method is to sort the messages into order by table heading:

1 Click the header to sort in ascending order (eg, click From to sort by sender).

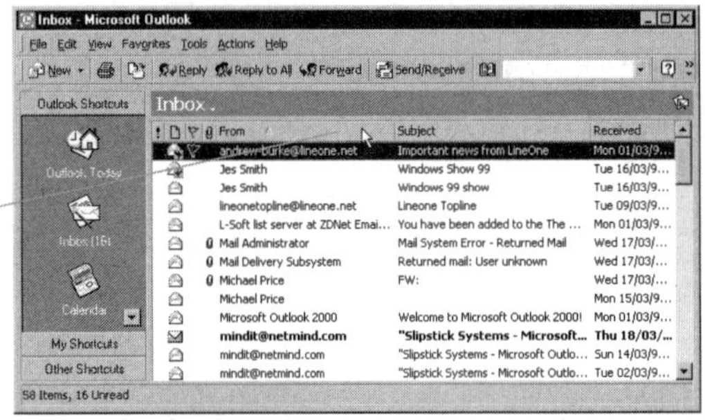

2 Click the same header again to reverse the sequence.

Sort will ignore the RE and FW prefixes in the Subject field when sequencing.

3 Hold down Shift, and click another field for a second level of sort (eg, Subject, to sort by topic within sender).

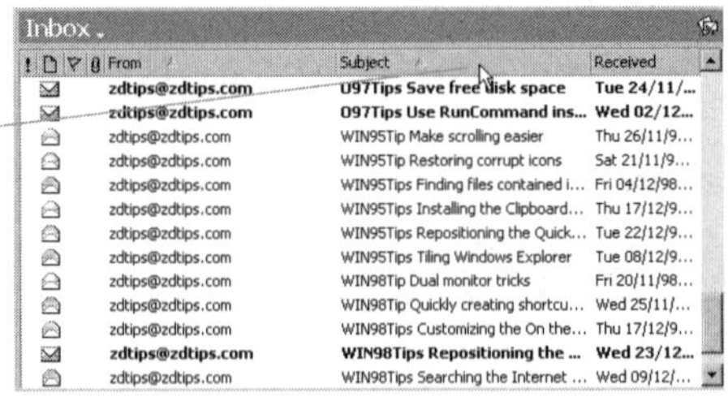

To make changes to the sorting options for more than two fields:

4 Select View from the Menu bar, and click Current View, Customise Current View.

5 Press the Sort button and choose up to four fields. Select (none) to clear a level.

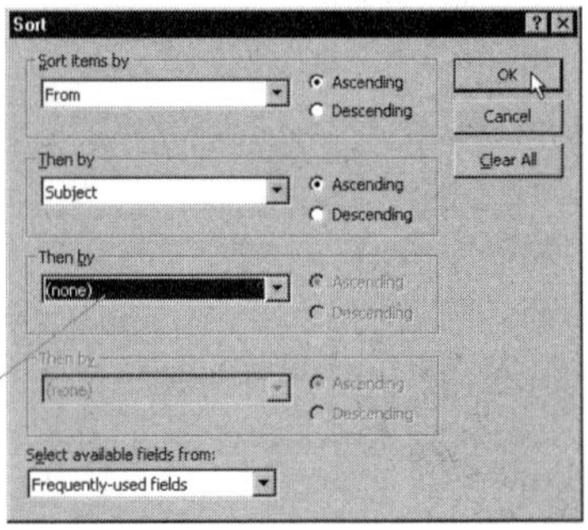

There are a number of different views predefined for the Inbox. The views group the messages in various different ways, by age, status or content. They may restrict the amount of detail shown, but the underlying data is unchanged. To choose a new view:

View Unread Messages only to check your outstanding mail.

1. Select View from Menu bar and then Current View.

2. Click on any one of the views offered (eg, By sender).

The Inbox displays the new view as soon as it is selected.

3. Click the [+] to expand the group. Click the [-] to collapse the group.

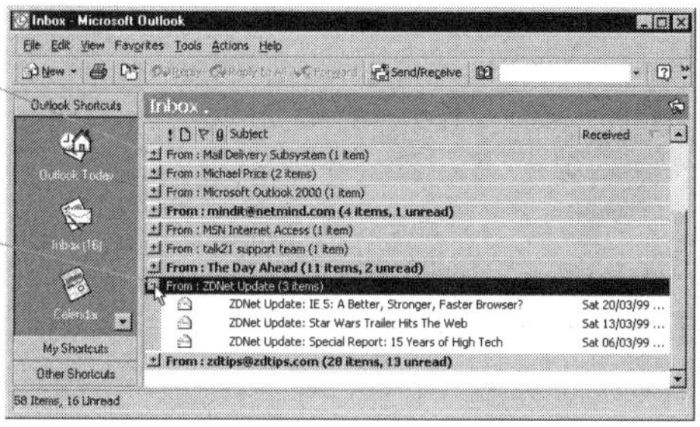

All the views except Message Timeline work with the same set of fields: importance, message type, attachment indicator, flag, sender, recipient, subject, date sent, and date received.

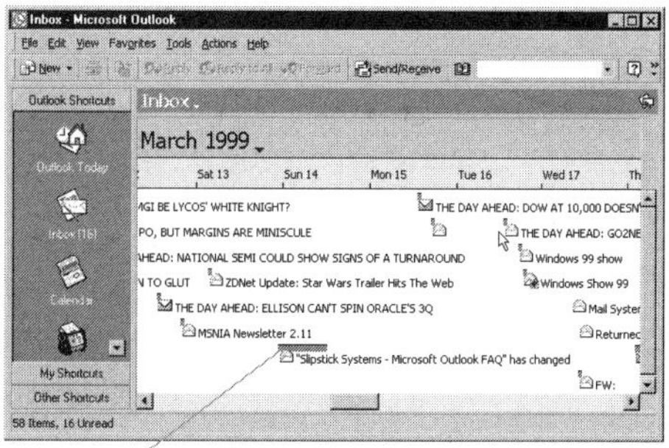

In Message Timeline view, there are fewer fields. Each item is shown as an icon at the message date, with the subject title. When the date received is different from the date sent, it shows a horizontal bar which therefore identifies the delay in message transmission.

Filtering

You can restrict the messages displayed in your Inbox by specifying values for fields.

Filters can be applied to any of Outlook's folders, as well as to the Inbox as shown here.

1. Select View, Current View, Customize Current View, and then click Filter.

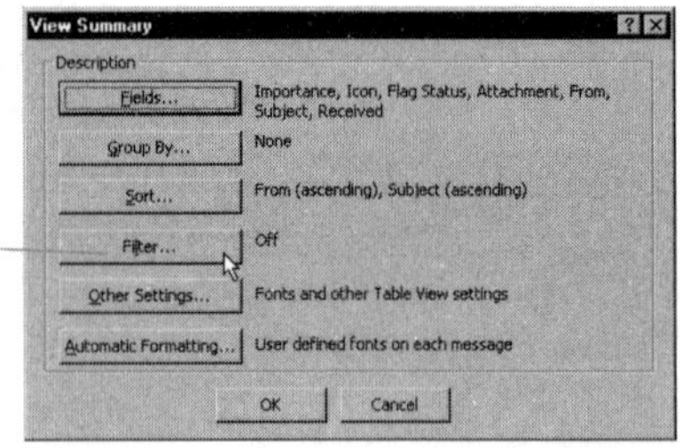

2. Specify the word or phrase to search for – eg, Outlook.
3. Specify where to look – eg, in subject and text of message.

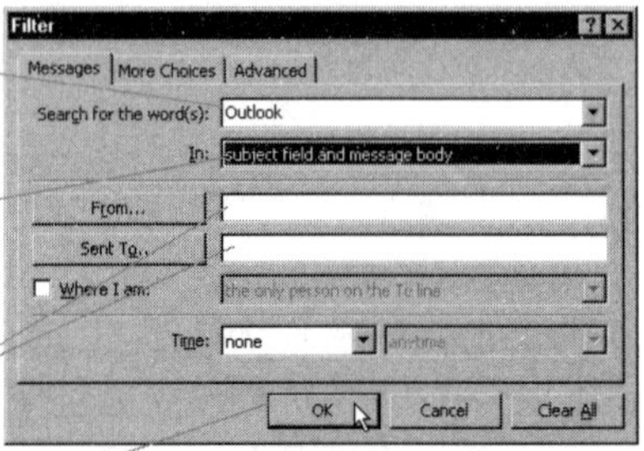

4. Enter details for From or Sent To fields, if needed.
5. Press OK to apply the filter.
6. Note the Filter Applied on the status bar.

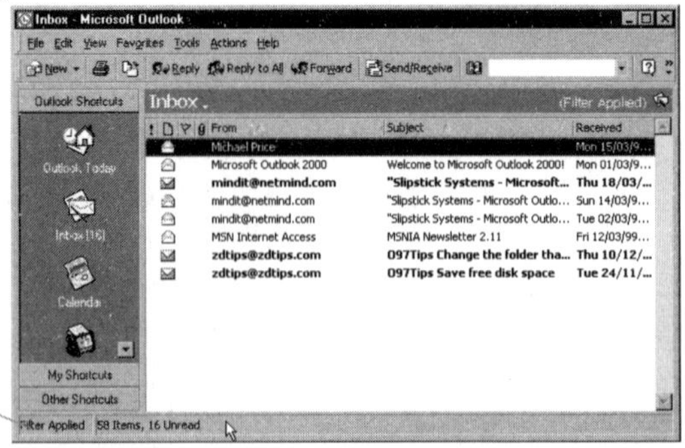

The Sent To field isolates messages for a specific e-mail address, when you have multiple accounts.

In the illustration, 8 messages out of a total of 58 Inbox messages are displayed, these being all the messages that refer to the Outlook topic.

The More Choices and the Advanced tabs allow you to add further criteria and check the values of additional fields. When your filter includes several criteria, only those messages that meet all of the criteria will appear.

Previews

Another way to manage large numbers of messages is to use previews to make it easier to spot important items without having to open them.

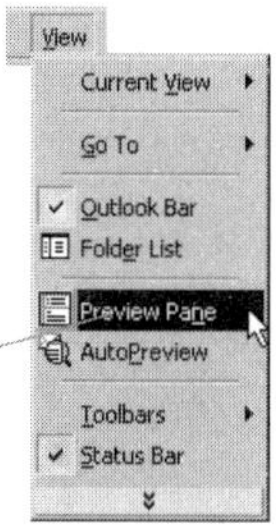

1 Select View from the Menu bar and then Preview Pane.

You can scroll the message preview to see more of its contents.

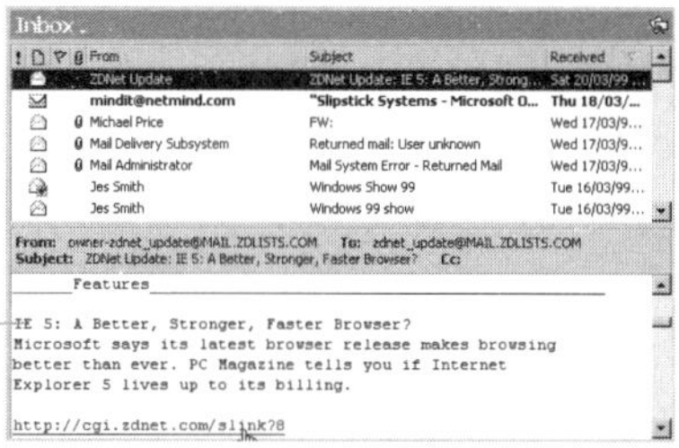

2 The current message contents are shown in the lower half of the Inbox viewer.

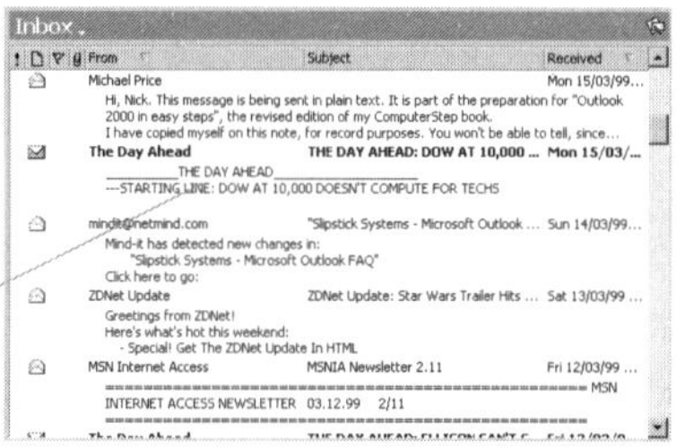

3 Select View from the Menu bar and then AutoPreview.

4 The first few lines of each message are shown.

You may not want to take up display space for messages that you have already seen. You can select a view that limits the messages previewed.

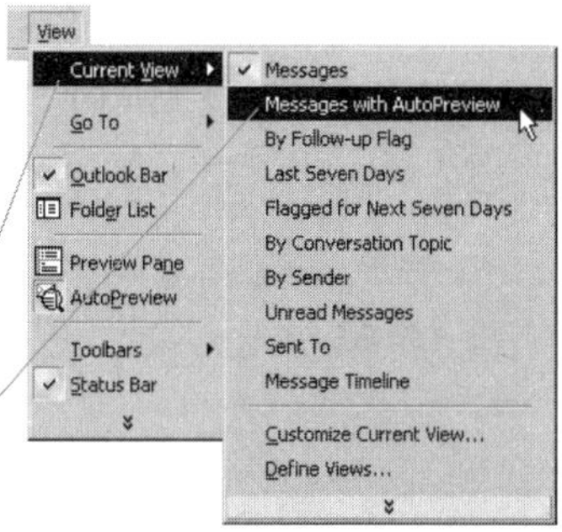

5 Select View, Current view, then Messages with Auto Preview.

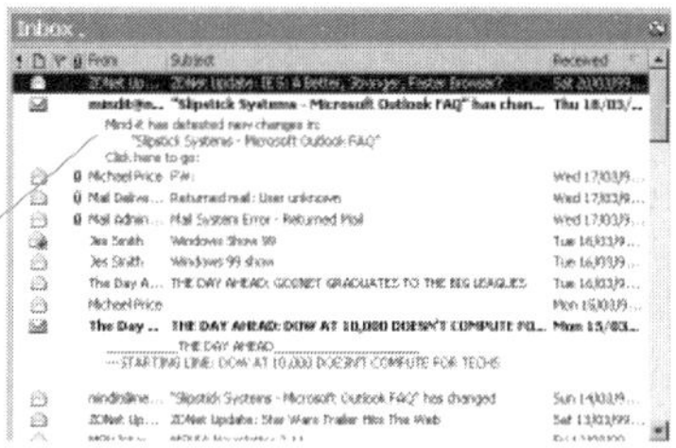

6 The first few lines of each unread message are shown.

Adding folders

If it becomes too time-consuming to manage all your messages in the Inbox, you can add more folders and divide up your messages. To create a new folder for mail:

This field is preset to the type you are currently viewing, but you can select any type.

1 Select File from the menu bar, and click New, Folder.

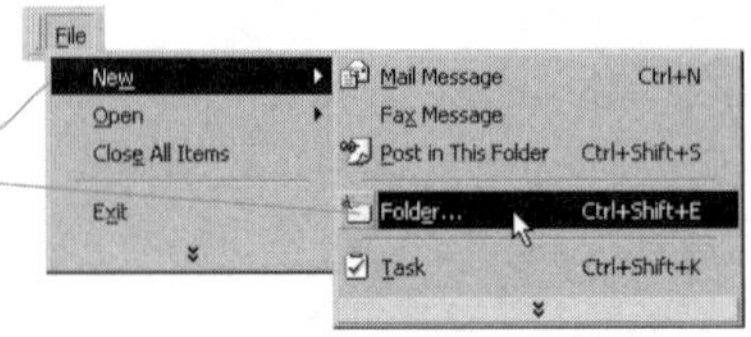

2 Enter the name for your new mail folder – eg, Tips.

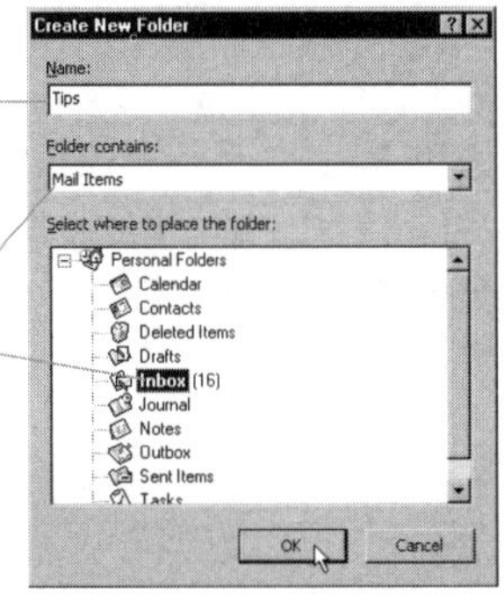

3 Select the type, and the position where the new folder should be created – eg, Inbox.

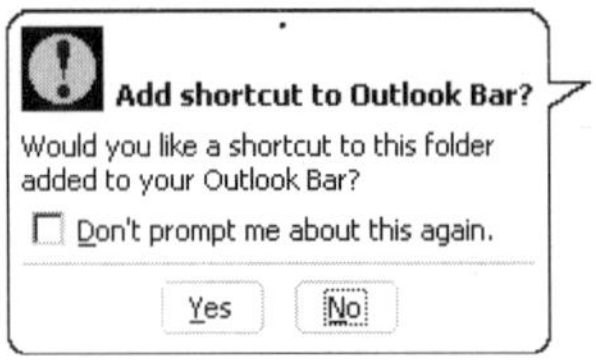

4 Add the folder to your Outlook shortcut bar, if you wish,

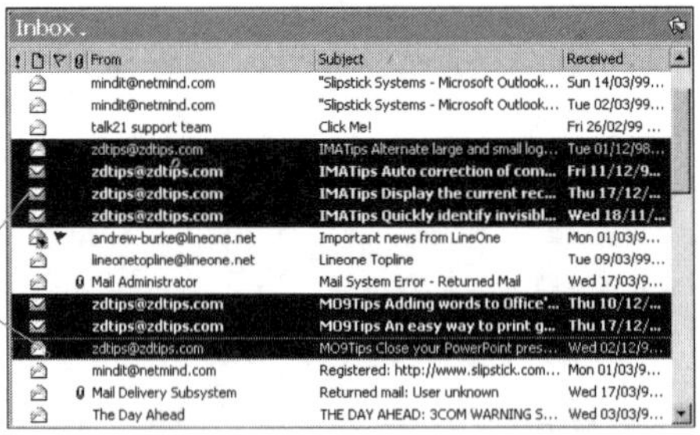

Use a filter or a view to select the mail you want.

5 Select the messages that you want to move to the new folder.

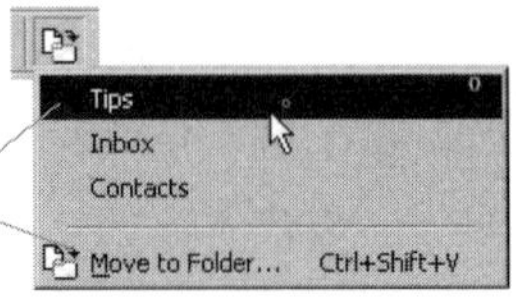

6 Select the Move button and click the folder name on the list, or press the Move to Folder button.

Outlook builds a list of folders recently used.

Access the new folder using the Outlook bar shortcut, or open the folder list and select the folder name.

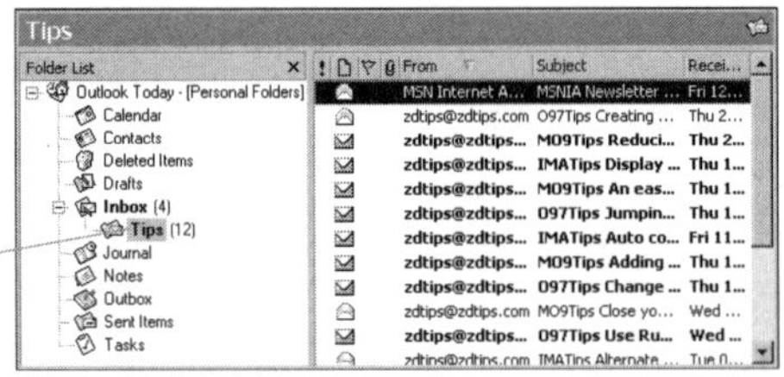

Organising

This is the long term solution, that automates the moves you make.

There are many ways to identify messages that you want to move. See page 106 for examples.

You can move messages from a particular sender to another folder, but you'll have to repeat the exercise if more arrive from the same sender. The solution is to tell Outlook how you decide which messages to move, and let it make the move for you when the messages appear.

1. Select an example message from the Inbox, and press Organize on the toolbar.

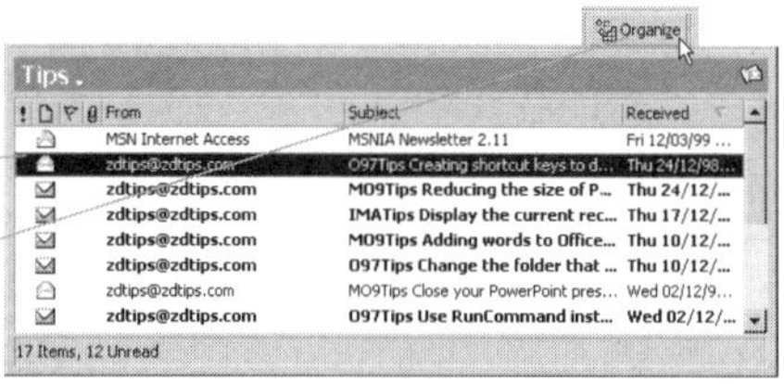

2. Choose From, to redirect messages by the Sender.

3. Specify the target folder and press Create to generate the rule.

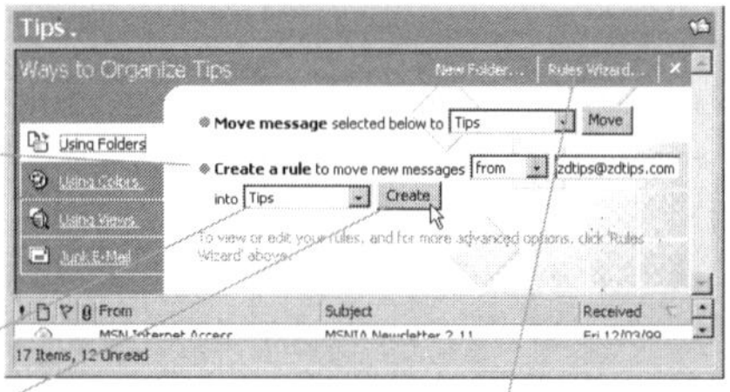

4. Specify whether you want to apply the rule to existing messages in the Inbox.

5. Click Rules Wizard to see the rule that now applies.

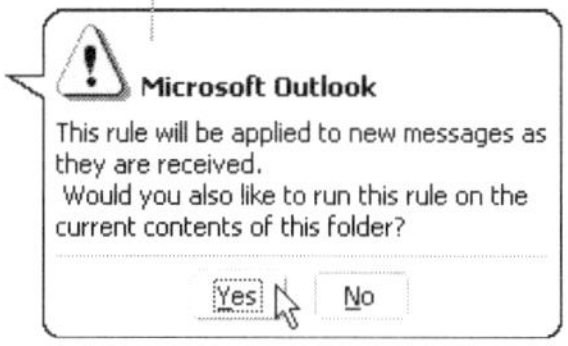

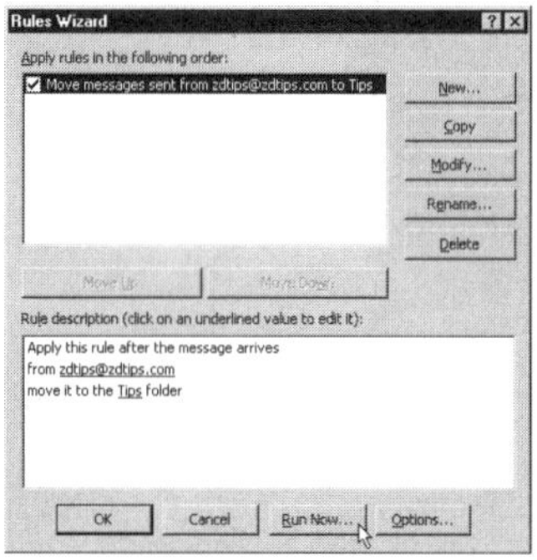

All future messages that fit the criteria will be handled by the Rules Wizard, and will be moved immediately to the target folder when they arrive on your system.

Applying rules

When the e-mail address alone is not enough to identify the messages, you must define the rule in more detail. For example, to collect all the messages for a special topic:

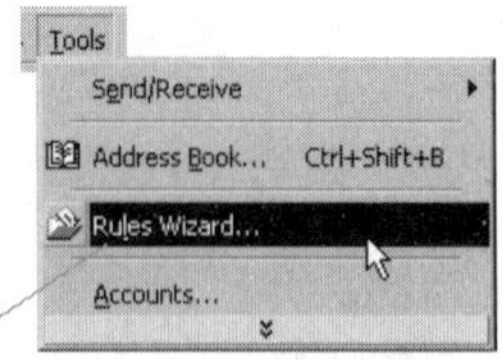

The wizard gives a list of possible things to check for. You can amend your choices later if you find you need to be more specific.

1 Open Rules Wizard and click New to create a rule.

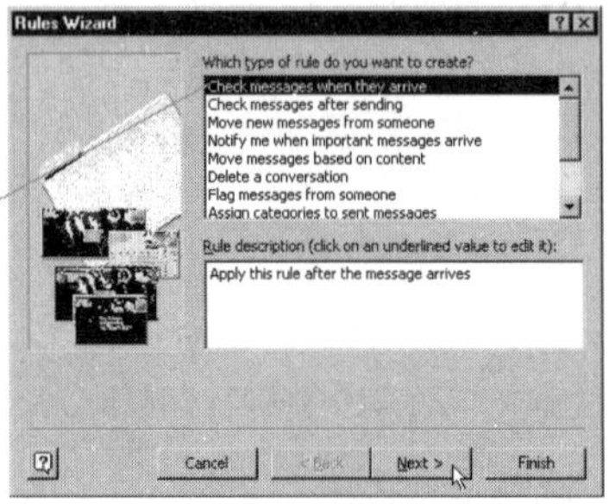

2 Choose to check messages when they arrive.

Rules with multiple words or phrases cannot be used with previous versions of Outlook.

3 Check for specific words in the message subject or the text – eg, look for Outlook 2000, Office 2000 etc.

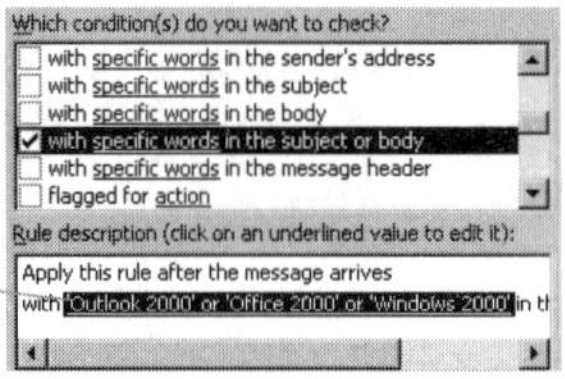

4 Tell the wizard to move the message to a specified mail folder – eg, About 2K folder.

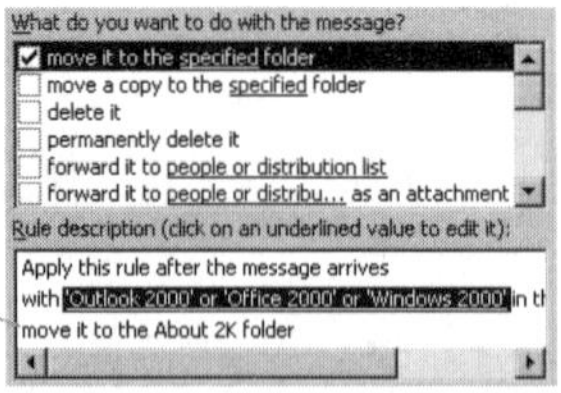

5 Specify exception conditions under which it wouldn't be appropriate to move the message.

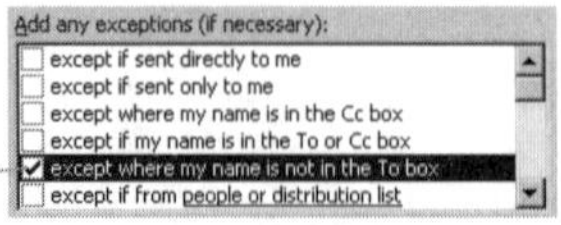

Change the order by moving rules up or down in the list.

6 You can apply the rule to the current or future entries in the Inbox folder.
The new rule is added to the beginning of the list.

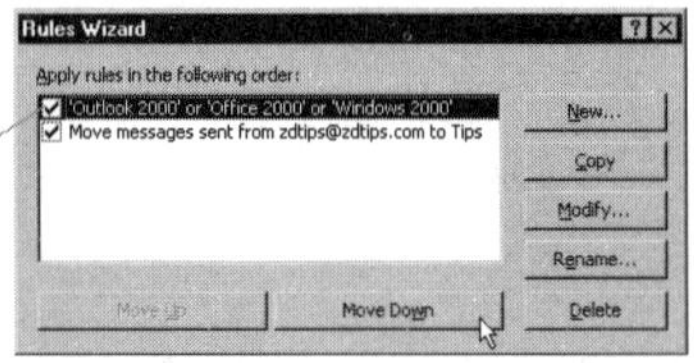

The list of terms that Outlook uses are listed in the file called Filters.txt.

There is a growing business in using e-mail messages as a direct marketing tool. If you do not wish to receive such mail, Outlook can search for common phrases to detect them and move them to a junk e-mail folder (or your Deleted Items folder). Outlook can take similar action for messages with adult content, if you find unsolicited mail in your Inbox.

1. Open Inbox and select Organise and then click on Junk E-Mail.

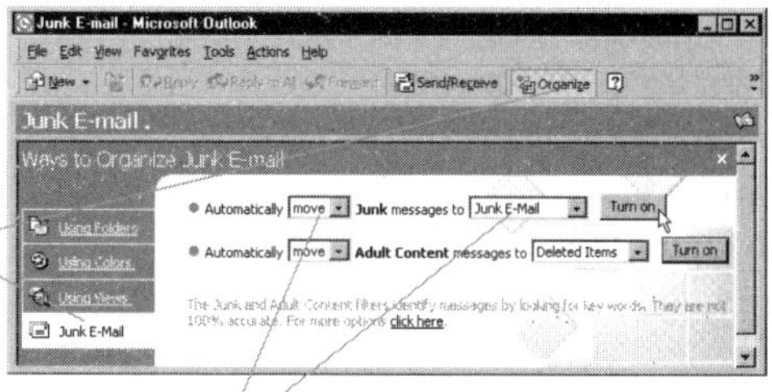

2. Select the Move action, and the folder name and Turn on checking.

3. Add similar settings for adult content.

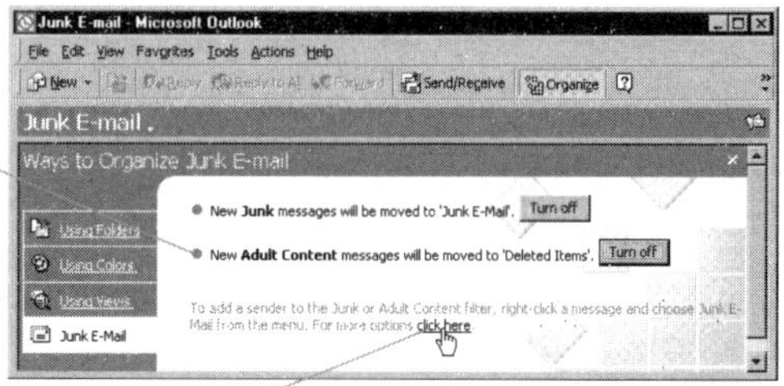

4. Add specific senders to the filter, and view or edit the list of addresses.

If junk mail is a problem for you, there is add-on software that provides much more rigorous checks.

The checks are added as rules and will appear in the list managed by the Rules Wizard.

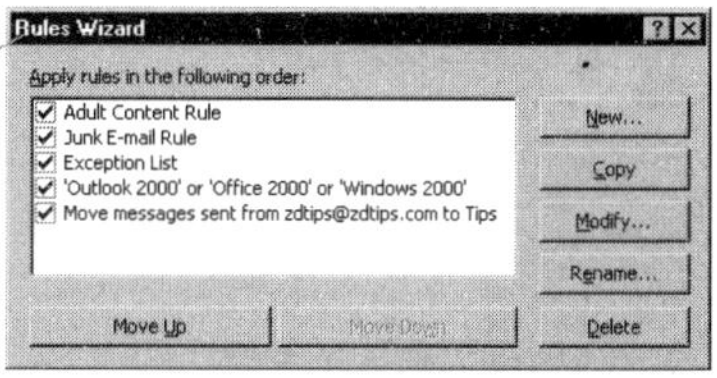

Check the Outlook Web site for updates to the filters and suggestions for preventing unwanted mail in your Inbox.

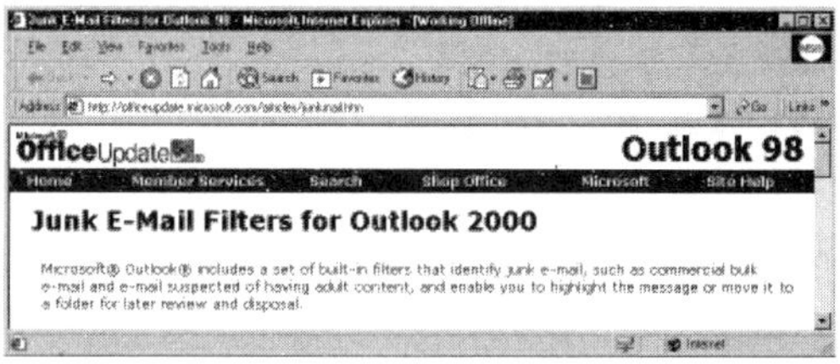

Leaving mail on the server

Your ISP may not allow you to save messages on the server. If so, you will see a message box telling you this, when you access your mail with the new setting.

If you sometimes read your mail from more than one PC, you could end up with your mail spread across several mail boxes. While you can export mail from one system to another, a much simpler option is to leave your mail on the server unless you are connecting via your main system.

You can store mail on either a POP3 or an IMAP server. Start Outlook on the system where you want to review mail without removing it from the server.

1. Select Tools on the Menu bar and click Accounts.

2. Select the account concerned, press Properties and select the Advanced tab.

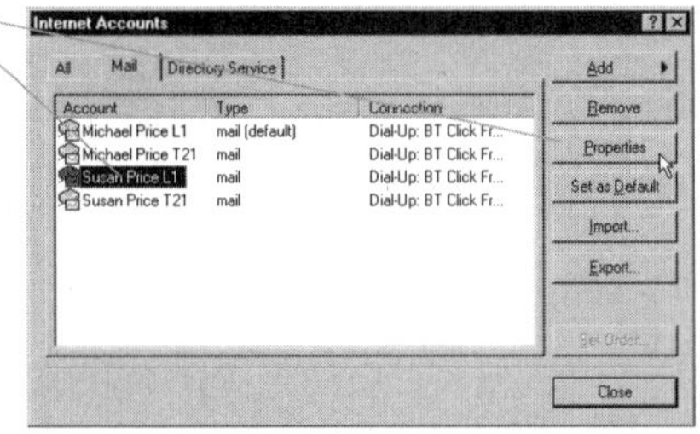

If you have an IMAP server, you should enter in the Root Folder Path.

3. If you have a POP3 mail server, click to Leave a copy of messages on server.

4. If appropriate, specify the number of days after which the messages can be removed from the server. Press OK and Close.

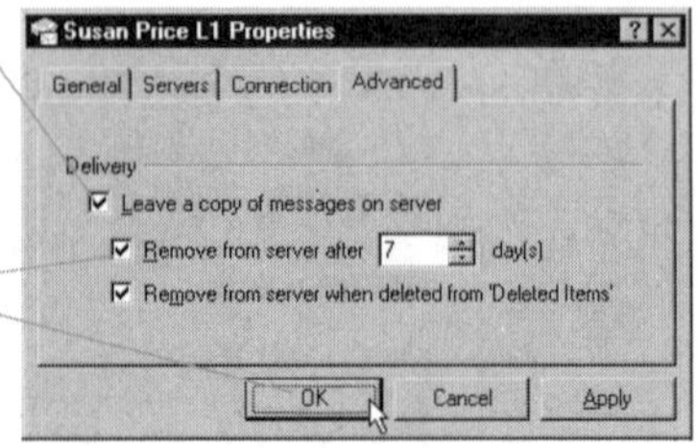

This action could be very useful when you access your mail from a laptop and from a desktop PC.

Messages will still be downloaded for viewing, but will also left on the server. If you sign on using a different PC where this setting has not been selected, the messages will be read and then removed.

Outlook folder files

Knowing Outlook's way of storing its folders makes it easier to manage them and keep your system efficient.

If you know the file type, you can locate the Outlook folders using the Find command.

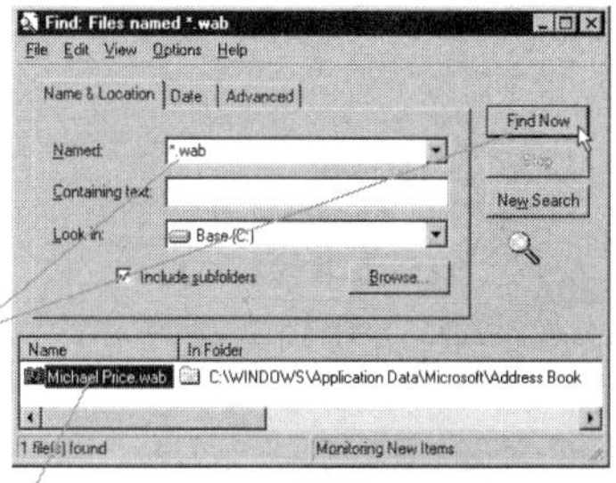

1. Enter the file type e.g. *.wab, and press Find Now to search the C: drive.

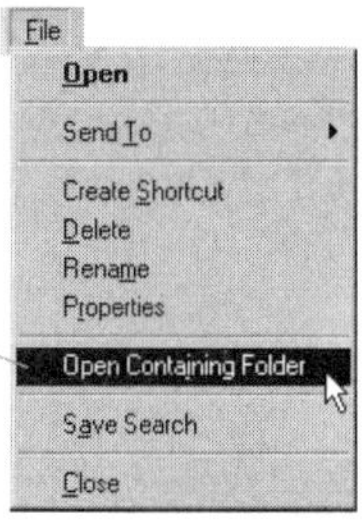

2. Select a file name and click File, Open Containing folder.

The Windows Address Book is file type .WAB. You can open this using the Windows Address Book viewer Wab.exe, or by selecting Find, People from the Start menu.

Outlook Express folders are in separate files of type .DBX. They can be copied for backup, using normal Windows functions, but they can only be opened using Outlook Express itself.

You won't see the individual Outlook 2000 folder names in Windows Explorer or My Computer.

Outlook 2000 stores all its folders inside one single file of type .PST. The Outlook Contacts list is also included inside this file, even though you can access Contacts through the Windows address book and the Find People command. You can copy the whole file for backup or to transfer a copy to another computer. To view the component folders and their contents, you must run Outlook.

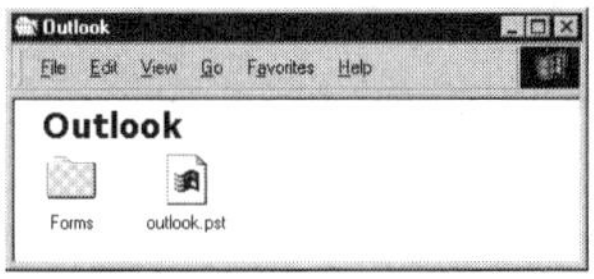

To copy individual folders, use the Archive function within Outlook (see page 112).

Saving space

Delete messages that you no longer need, to prevent the mail folders becoming too large: To delete messages:

Hold down Shift to select a range of messages or Ctrl to select groups of messages when clicking on them.

1. Open the Inbox and pick messages to delete.

2. Press the Delete button (or the Del key).

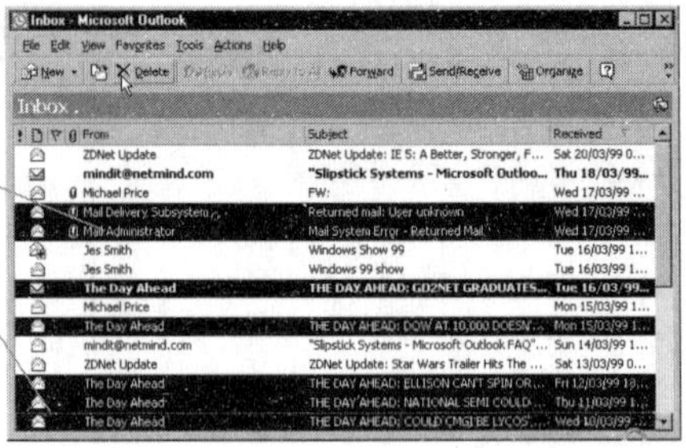

A quick way to recover a message is to Drag it from Deleted Items onto the target folder, in the Folders List or the Outlook bar.

3. To retrieve messages deleted in error, open Deleted Items and select the messages.

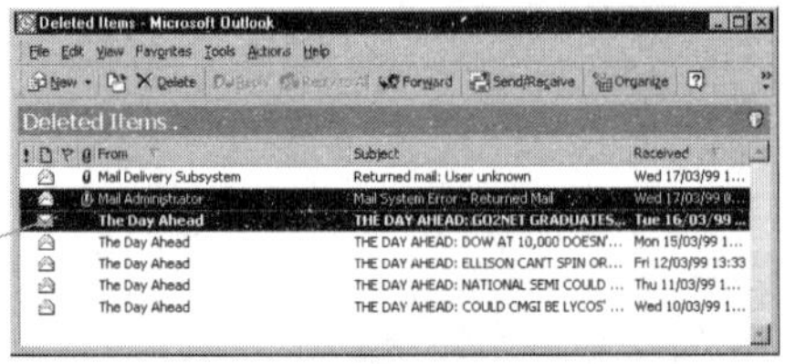

4. Press the Move to Folder button and choose the Inbox.

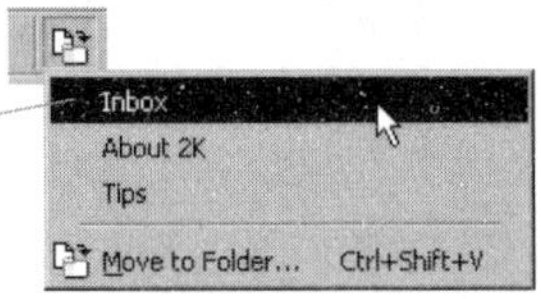

Free up the disk space used by clearing the contents of the Deleted Items folder:

5. Select Tools from the Menu bar, and click Empty "Deleted Items" Folder.

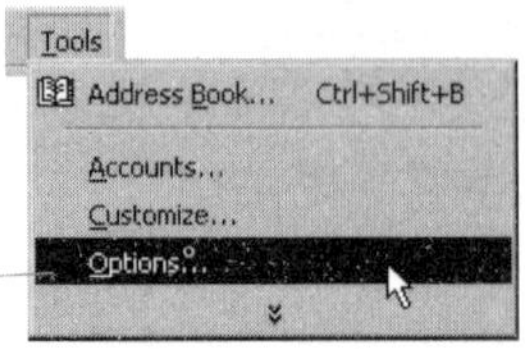

Choose to clear all the items from the Deleted folder when you close Outlook.

6. Select File, Options and the Other tab.

7. Select the box to clear the Deleted Items folder on exit from Outlook.

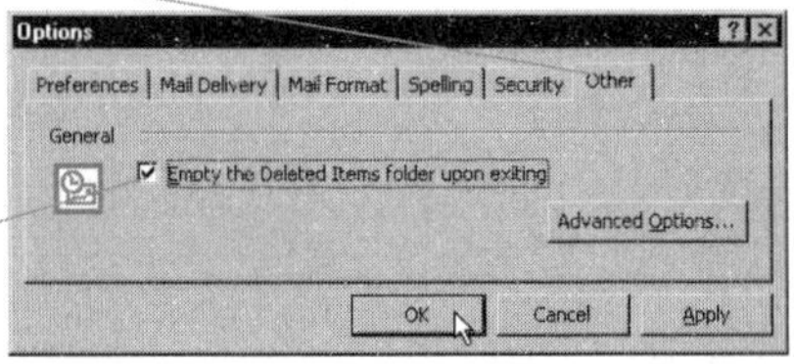

Outlook Express folders are separate, so you can compact them individually.

Deleting messages may not immediately free disk space, even when you clear the Deleted Items folder. You may need to run the Compact process to eliminate the deleted item space from the mail folders and make it available for other files.

1. Open the folder list and select the mail folder to compact.

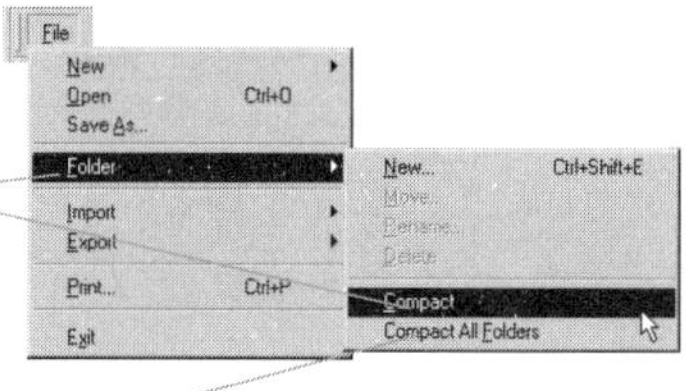

2. Click File, and Compact to process the selected folder.

3. Choose Compact All Folders to process them all at once.

Outlook 2000 will compact its folders automatically, with a background task.

With Outlook 2000, you do not normally need to compact the folders, but you can check to see how much space is allocated to the individual mail folders:

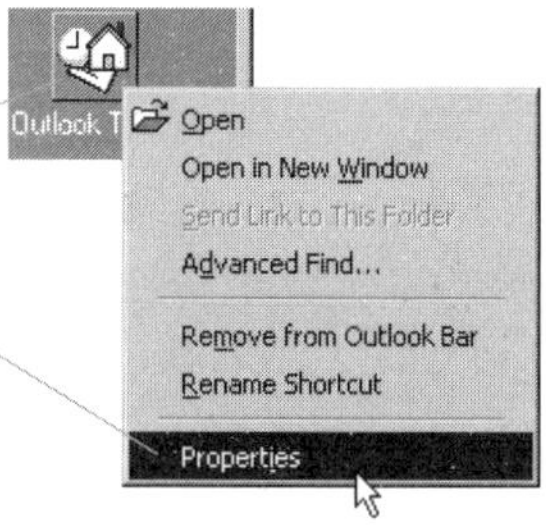

4. Right-click Outlook Today on the Outlook bar and select Properties.

5. Press the Folder Size button to show the total and compressed sizes of the folders.

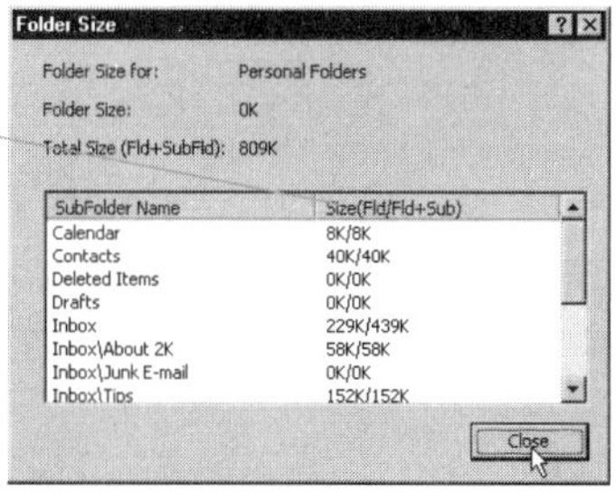

6. To manually compact the folders, select Properties, Advanced, Compact Now.

Exporting and archiving

Share message folders even if you are not on a network by exporting copies to a removable disk.

Export the contents of Outlook message folders to a personal folder file for backup, or to a Comma Separated Values file type to use in Windows applications.

1 Select File from Menu bar, and click Import and Export.

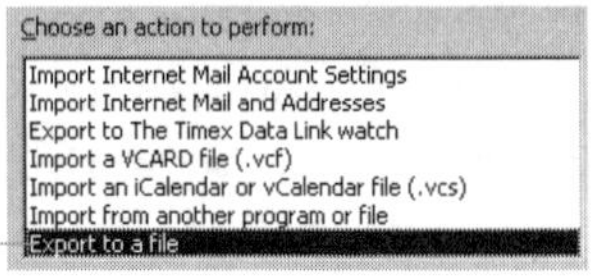

2 Choose the action – eg, export to a file and select the file type. Choose Personal folder file (.pst) to create a backup.

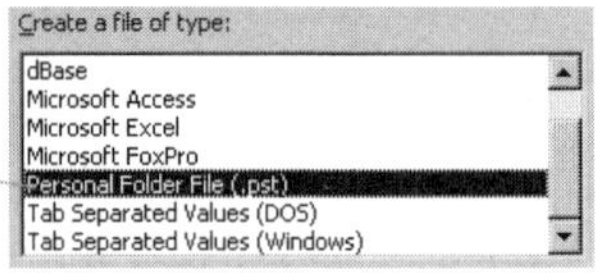

3 Select the folder to export from – eg, Inbox. You can include subfolders or apply filters to select a subset of messages.

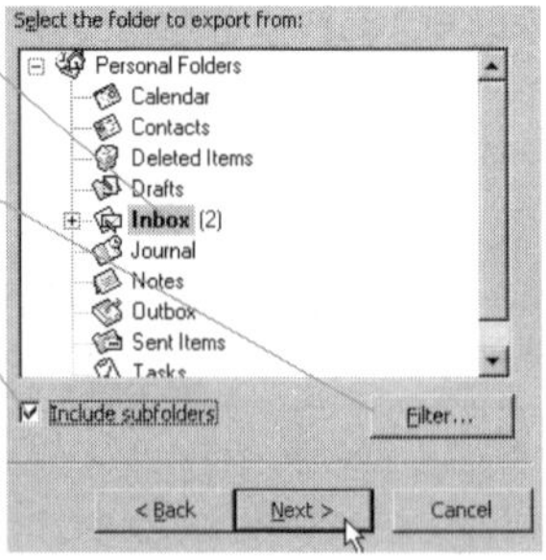

4 Specify the location and name for the file, and the action to take with duplicate messages.

5 The contents of the selected folders are transferred to the selected file type.

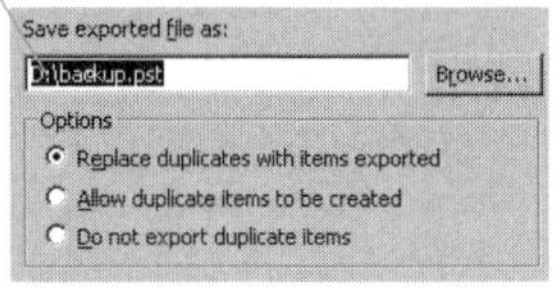

6 Select File, Import and Export also, to import any copies of folders that you may receive, or to restore a folder backup.

Outlook can archive any item in an e-mail folder, including attachments such as documents and spreadsheets.

You may have messages in your folders that you need for historical reasons, but don't require regular access. To manually transfer these items to a storage file:

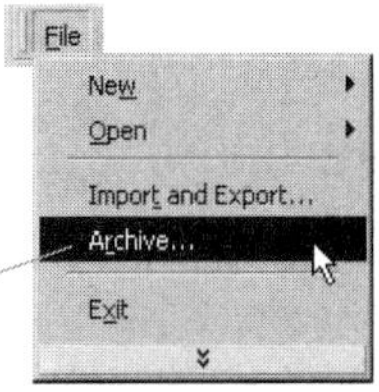

1. Select File and then click Archive.

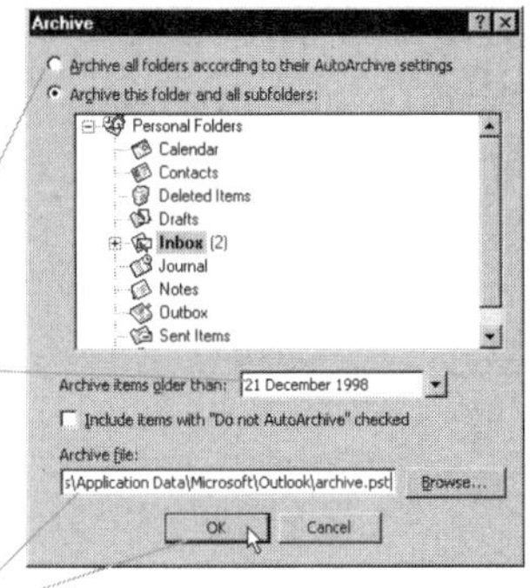

2. Choose to Archive all folders, or just the selected folder and its subfolders, and set the age for identifying archive items.

The existing folder structure is maintained in the archive file.

3. Specify the archive file and press OK to launch the process.

To have items automatically transferred, use the AutoArchive. To turn this on:

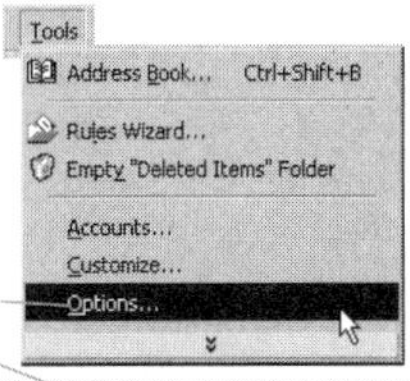

4. Select Tools, Options, and the Other tab, then click AutoArchive.

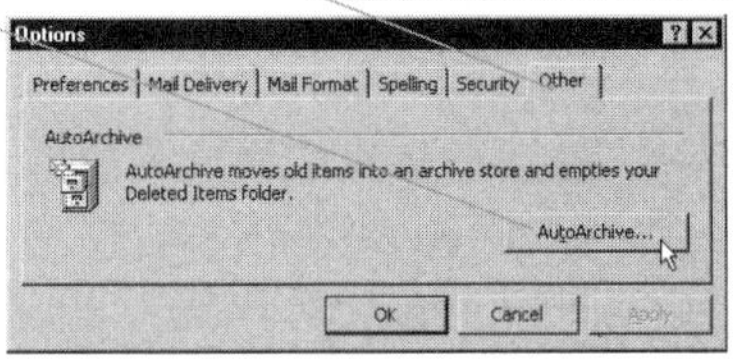

5. Specify the frequency for running AutoArchive, and request to be notified.

Archiving won't save space on the hard drive unless you can specify a different drive. A removable Zip drive would be ideal.

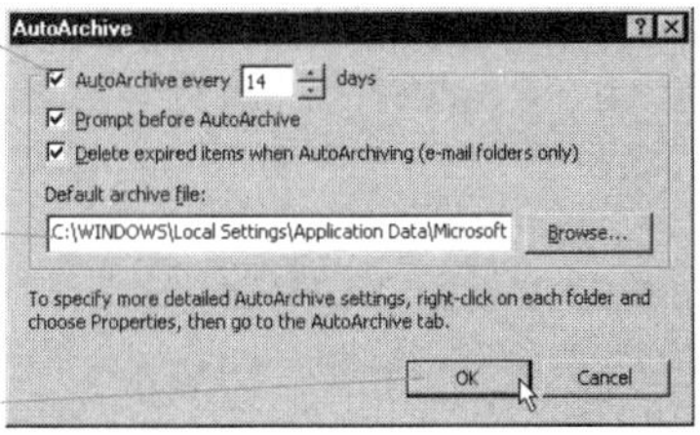

6. Enter the folder and file name for the archive file.

7. Click OK to record the settings.

Working with archives

Calendar Journal and Task folders are preset to 6 months, Sent and Deleted to 2 months. Inbox, Notes, Contacts, and Drafts are not preset.

You must set the AutoArchive properties individually for each of the folders that have items you want to archive:

1 Select View, Folder List to show the Outlook folders, right-click a folder, and select Properties.

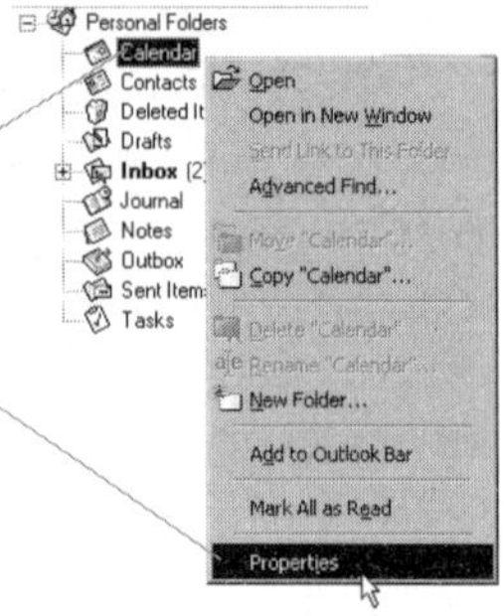

2 Click the AutoArchive tab and check the settings for age, target drive and file name.

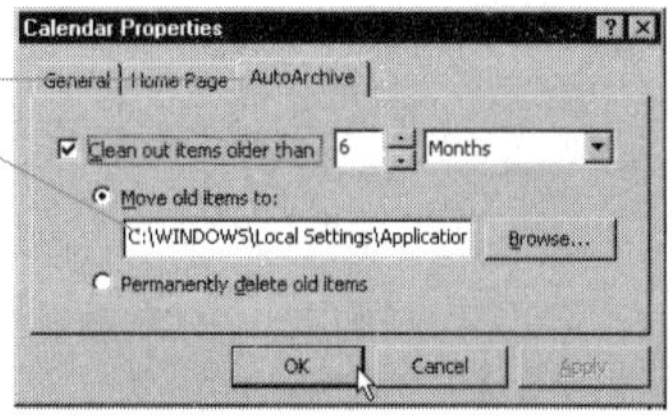

3 For folders such as Deleted Items, you can specify an automatic delete for old items.

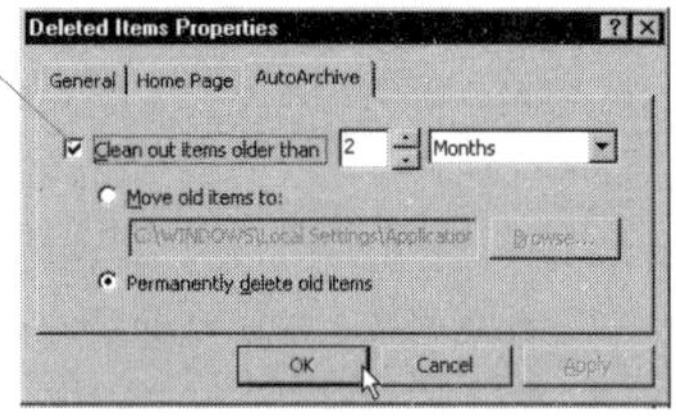

4 Repeat these steps for each of the folders to be archived.

When the archiving completes, the items are removed from their folders. If this results in empty folders these remain in the list, ready for future use.

When the due date and time for the archive arrives, and you start Outlook, you will receive a warning that archiving will take place. You can postpone the archive if you wish, or press Yes to allow the process to complete.

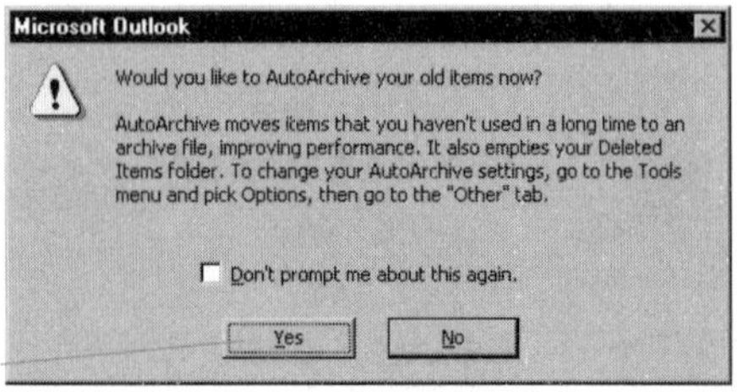

Archiving happens in the background, but you can check and control the operation from the notes on the Outlook Status bar.

You can view the contents of the mail folders stored within your archive folder.

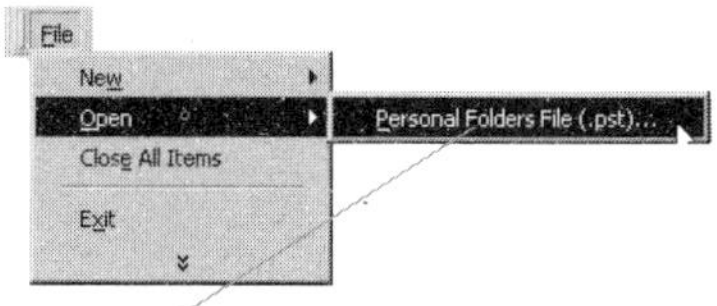

Use Find to locate the .PST archive folder files, as shown on page 109.

1 Select File, Open and then click Personal Folders File (.pst).

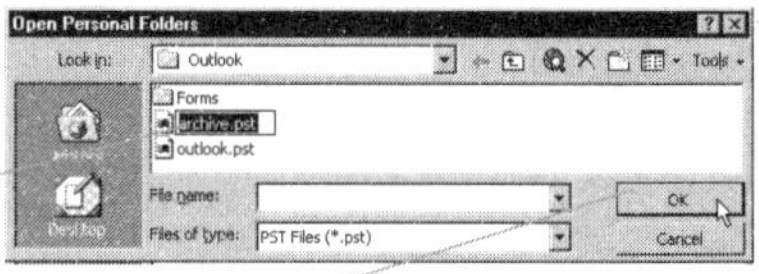

2 Locate the archive folder you want to review.

3 Click OK to open the archive.

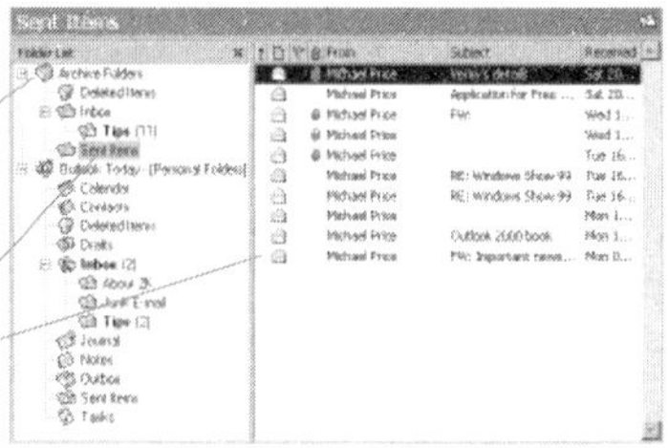

You can transfer individual Outlook items between the archive folder and your personal folder.

4 Click [+] to expand the archive folder and select a mail folder to explore.

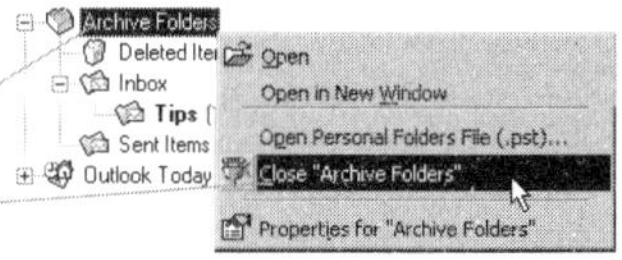

5 Right-click the folder name to close the archive folder.

To recover the full contents of the archived folders, import the archive as a file and move the items in bulk back to the folders that they originally came from.

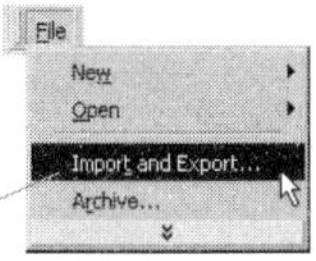

The Import wizard guides you through recovery of the whole archive, or individual folders.

6 Select File, Import and Export, and Import from another program or file.

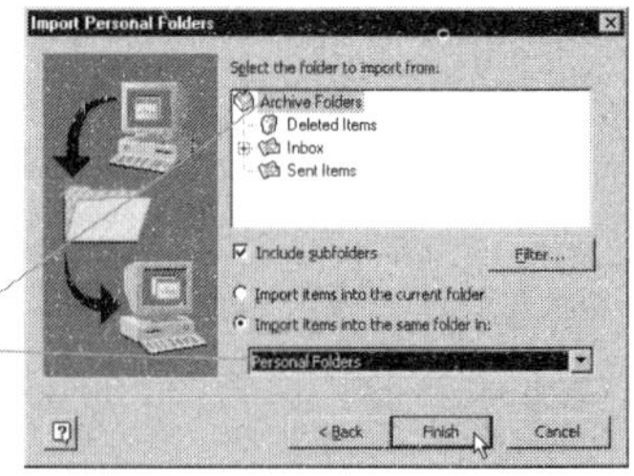

7 Specify the source and target folders to restore.

Searching for messages

With subfolders and archives, it may be hard to remember where you stored particular messages or other Outlook items, so you need a search facility.

To locate items in the current folder or its subfolders, use the Find command:

HOT TIP **Search subjects or click the box to search all the text as well.**

1 Click the Find button, enter word search text and press Find Now.

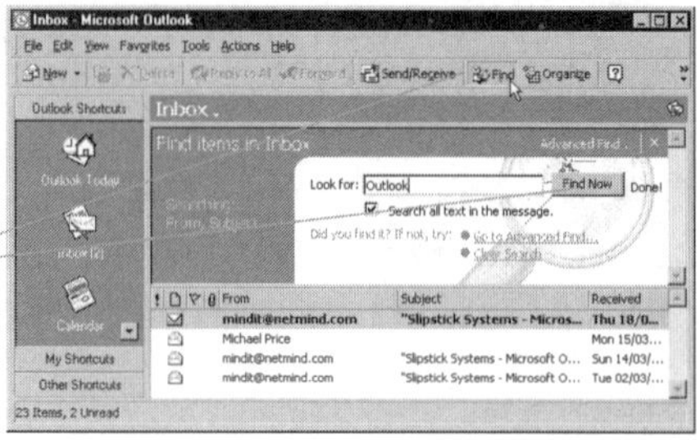

2 Reselect Find to finish.

If there are too many matches (or too few), try the Advanced find which searches across multiple folders, and allows more criteria:

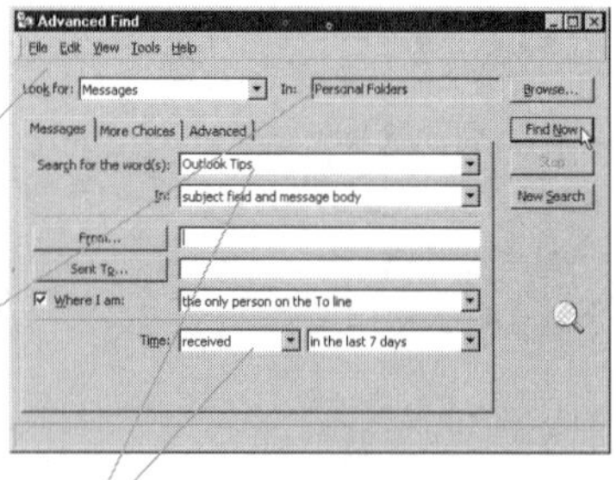

3 Click Advanced Find.

4 Choose the item type.

5 Pick the folders that you want to search in.

6 Enter search criteria.

You don't have to be running Outlook to search for items. Just select Start, Find, and then Using Microsoft Outlook, and you will go straight to Advanced Find.

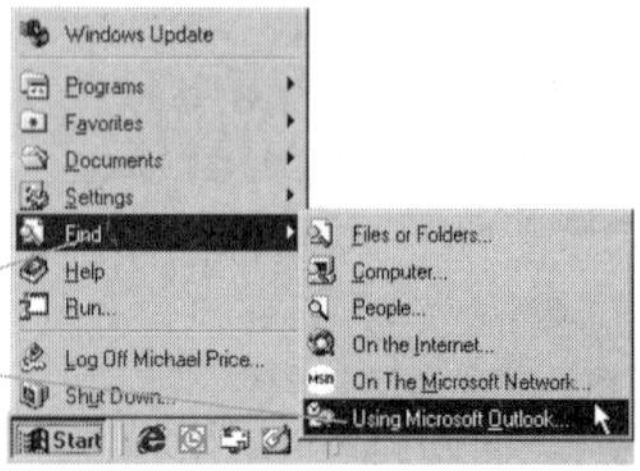

Newsgroups

This chapter looks at another way of communicating with others: using newsgroups. It discusses how to install a newsreader, access news servers, find and make use of groups that discuss the subjects that interest you, and how to add private newsgroups.

Covers

Chapter Seven

Newsgroups and newsreaders

There are many serious discussion groups that offer a high level of expertise in their particular subjects.

A newsgroup is like a public mail folder, which deals with one subject and contains messages and responses from anyone who happens to be interested in the topic concerned. The messages are stored on news servers, which may support thousands of such newsgroups. You need to be selective in your choice of groups to participate in. Some newsgroups are monitored, but most are not. Messages can be added and read by just about anyone who has access to the Internet, so the quality can be very variable.

Each ISP provides a mail server which contains copies of many though not necessarily all newsgroups, and these copies are updated regularly with the latest messages and responses. All you need to access the news server and its newsgroups is software called a newsreader.

The newsreader allows you to download and read news messages and to send replies to the newsgroups. Outlook Express has the newsreader function built in. When you install Outlook 2000, it sets up the newsreader from your previous e-mail system, or a news-only version of Outlook Express, to be used just for newsgroups.

Check to see that you have the newsreader installed:

Click the down arrow to extend the menu in case the entry is hidden.

Select View from the Menu bar, click Go To and look on the list for the News program entry.

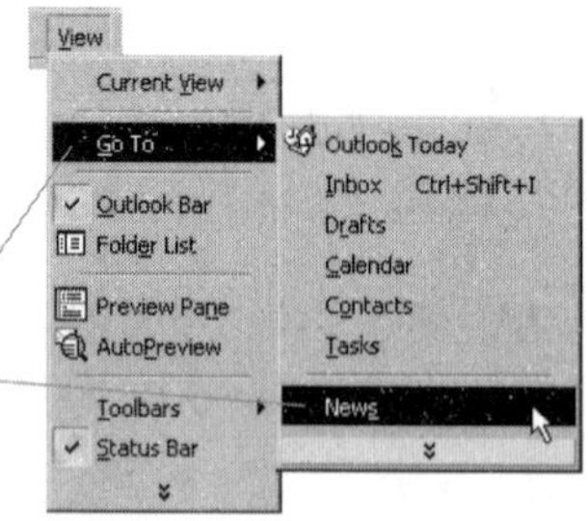

If you do not find the News option on your system you can install it from CD or the Web, as an additional component. Use the maintenance wizard for Internet Explorer 5 and select the Outlook Express Newsgroup reader.

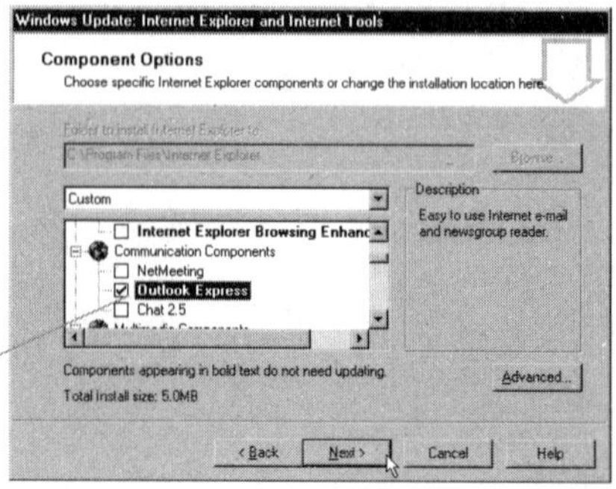

Starting the newsreader

Allow time for initial downloads on your first access to a news server or a newsgroup.

2 Select View, Go To, News, and Read News on the Outlook Newsreader.

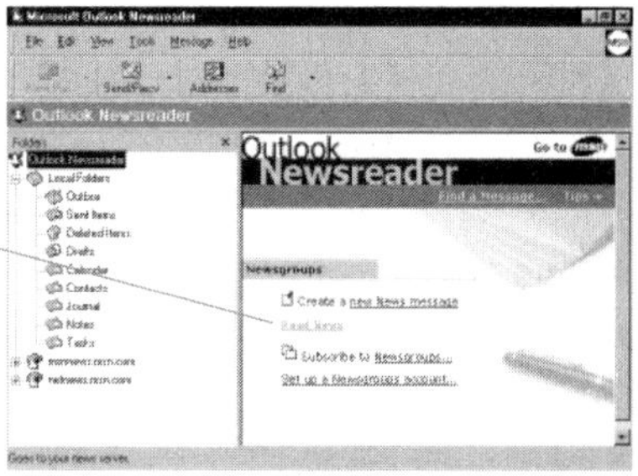

3 You are offered the list of groups to view, unless you have subscribed to a group already.

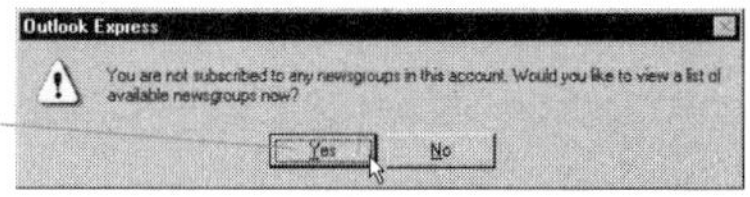

4 The first time, Outlook needs to connect to your ISP and download the current list.

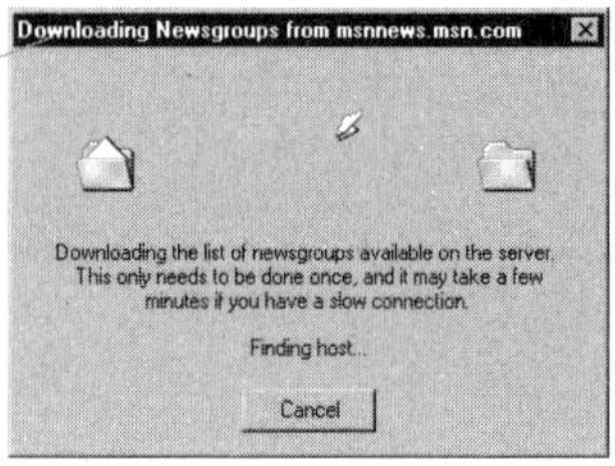

5 Repeat to download the lists for any other groups.

The names are displayed in the Newsgroups window. There could be 20,000 or more. Only the names are downloaded, so it does not take too long. To make it easier to locate a group that may interest you, type a relevant word in the box, and the list will immediately be limited to those groups that contain that word (or part word) in their titles. For example, to list discussion groups covering Outlook:

6 Type "Outlook" in the box.

7 Select an entry that interests you and press Go to.

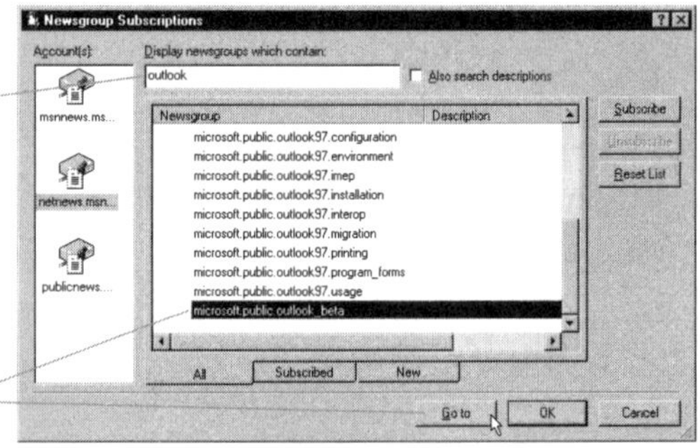

Viewing newsgroups

Connect to your ISP to download the list of messages for your chosen groups, and check the list of titles off-line.

When you Go To a newsgroup for the first time, you must connect to your ISP to download the list of headers (message titles). This may take several minutes, and must be repeated for each group that interests you. In the list:

1. Message titles are shown in bold, until you double-click to read the message (but only while connected).

2. Clicking [+] expands the list of related messages.

3. The header shows the sender, and the selected message is previewed.

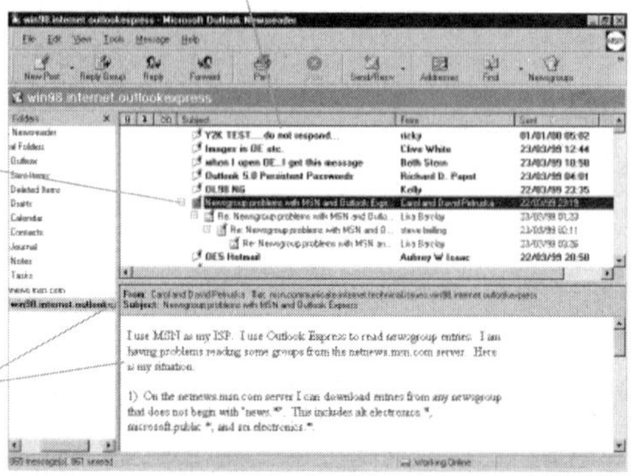

Messages and replies on a single topic are grouped to form a conversation thread.

Disconnect from the Internet to review the message lists for the chosen groups, and find the potentially interesting messages and threads to download later.

4. Pick sets of messages and select Tools from the Menu bar, Mark for Offline, Download Message Later or Download Conversation Later.

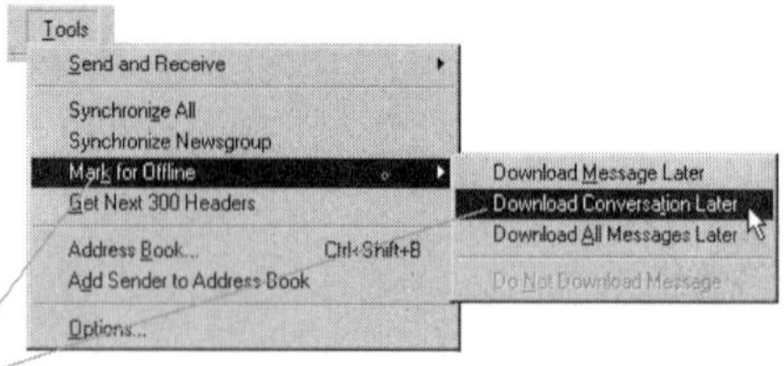

When you select a message, that is not yet downloaded, the preview pane indicates Message unavailable offline.

5. When you mark the main entry for a conversation, all of the related messages are marked as well.

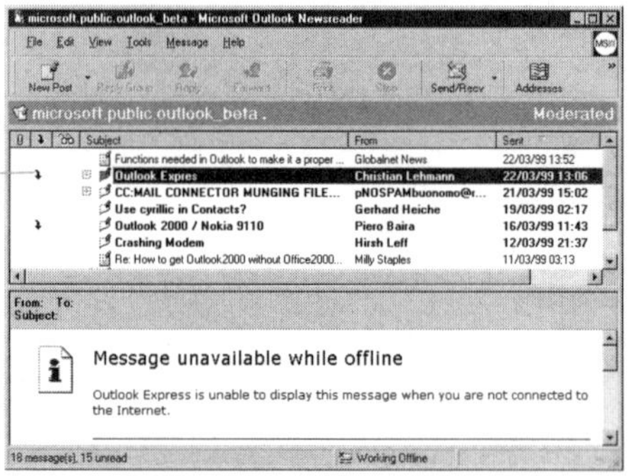

Reconnect to retrieve marked messages and threads, and to get message title headers added since your last connection, to update the list.

When you are ready to download the selected messages, you should connect to your ISP.

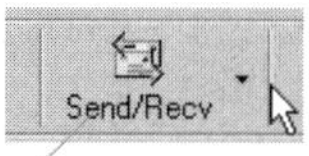

1 Click the Send/Receive button on the toolbar and confirm that you want to work online.

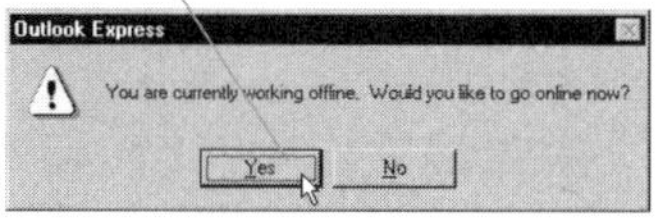

2 When connected, select Tools from the Menu bar, and then Synchronise Newsgroup.

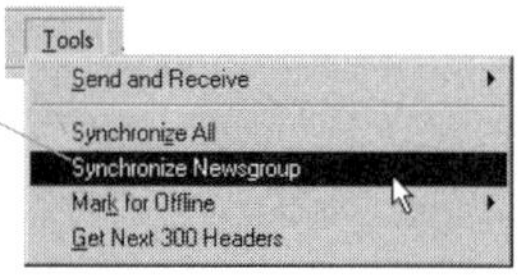

3 Select Get messages marked for download. You can also choose to download the titles or the full contents of new messages.

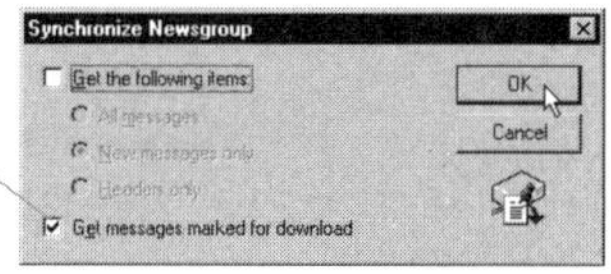

Disconnect to review the text of retrieved messages off-line, to minimise costs.

4 Select View, Current View, Show Downloaded Messages, to restrict the list to those messages.

In this view, all the displayed messages can be read off-line, since the headers and text have been downloaded.

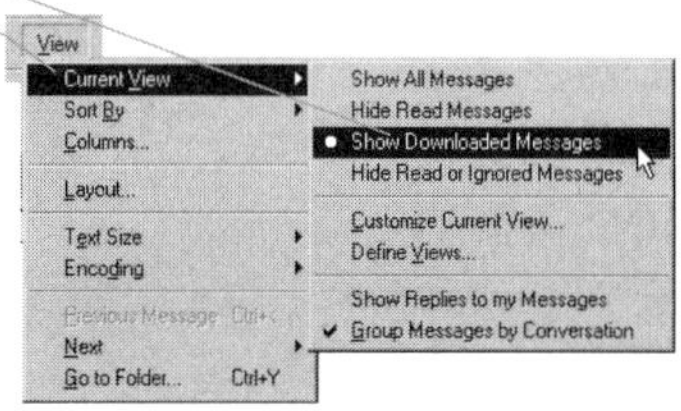

Check the newsgroup options to see what happens to the messages when you end the newsreader (see page 122).

5 Click on the message title to preview its contents.

6 Double-click the message title to view the full text.

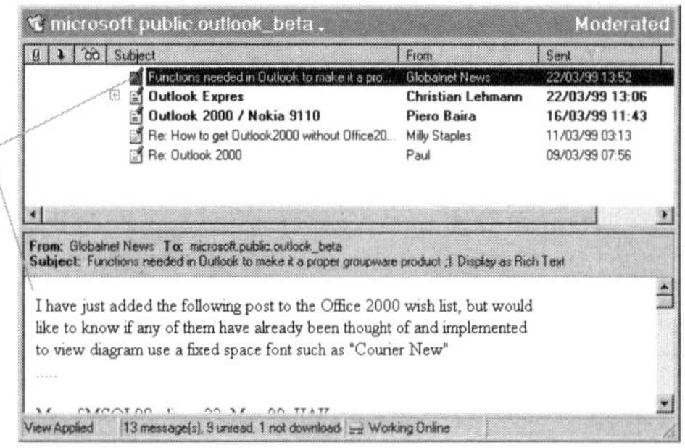

Newsgroup options

Adjust the preview options to prevent messages being downloaded or marked as read, just because you've paused at the title.

1. Select Tools from the Menu bar and then Options, and the Read tab.

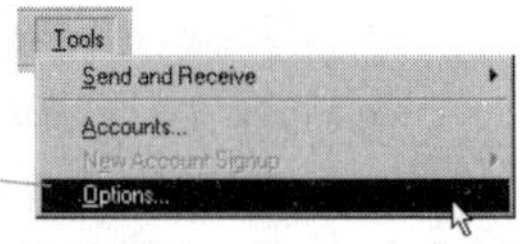

2. Messages will be automatically downloaded when selected, and marked as read after you've previewed them for 5 seconds.

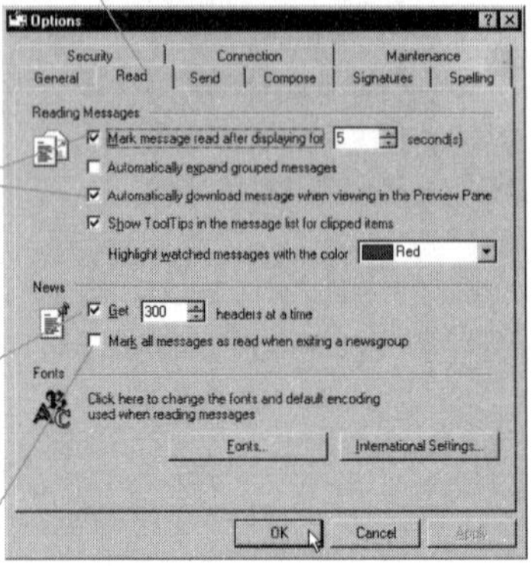

3. Limit the number of headers that get downloaded at a time.

4. If you Mark all Messages as Read when you exit, they may get deleted unseen.

If you find newsgroup messages disappear when you exit the newsreader, check the Advanced settings.

5. Select the Maintenance tab. Note that all messages are deleted five days after download.

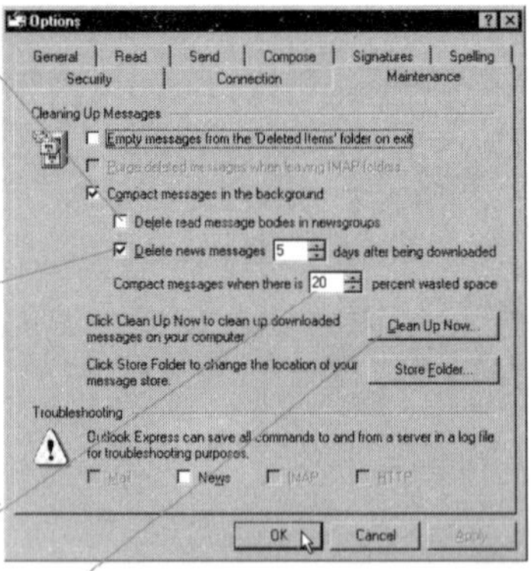

6. The folder will be compacted when the waste space reaches 20%, or the value you set.

7. Press Clean Up Now to see how large the newsgroup files have become, and see if action is needed. Press Close to end.

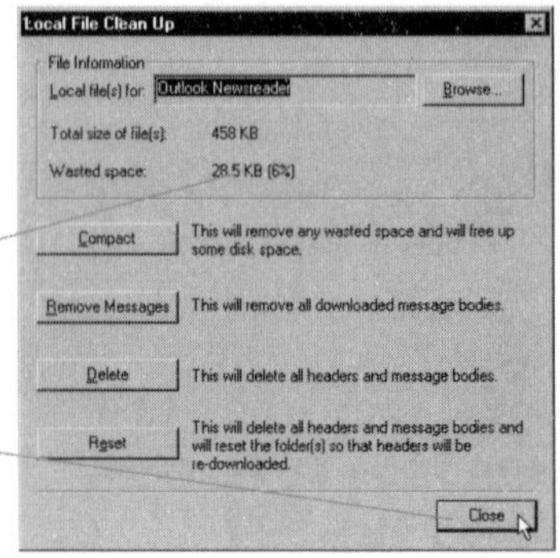

Filtering messages

Newsgroup messages sometimes get overly commercial or just plain distracting. You can avoid the majority of these with filters.

Newsgroups are organised by subject, but not everyone follows the rules, so you need filters to control the type of messages that you see:

1 Select Tools from the Menu bar and click Message Rules, News.

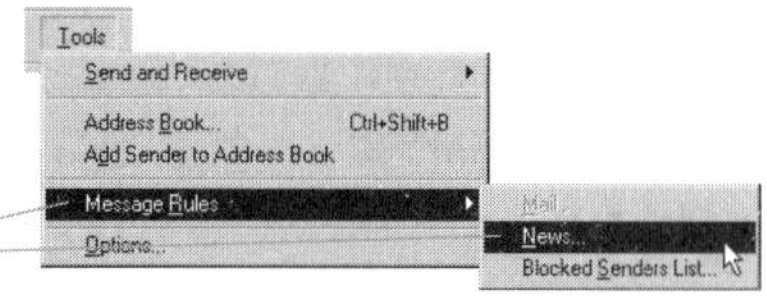

2 You can set criteria to say what messages are downloaded, and what messages are displayed.

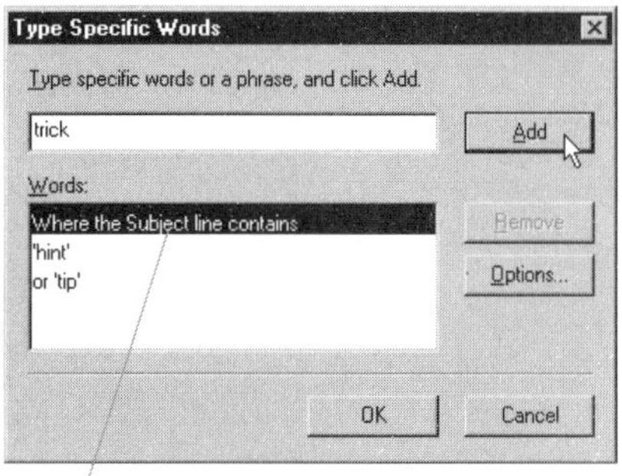

3 With this rule for example, messages with 'hint' or 'tip' in the title will be marked for download. Click the Contains item to add further words or phrases.

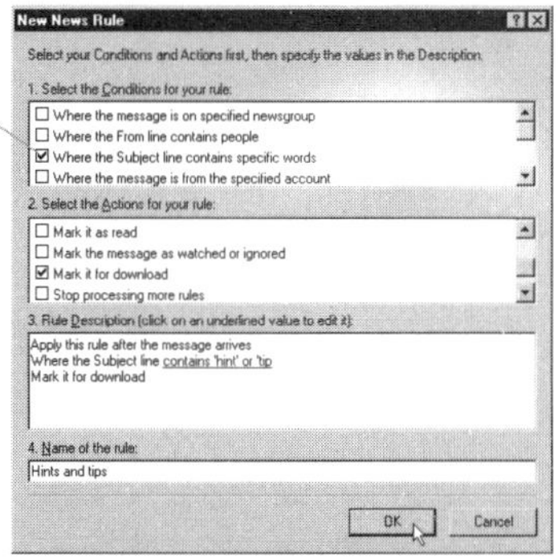

4 You can also exclude messages, by content, by sender, by size of the file or by the date the message was created.

5 Add additional rules to complete the criteria and adjust the sequence in which the rules are applied. Press OK to save the definition.

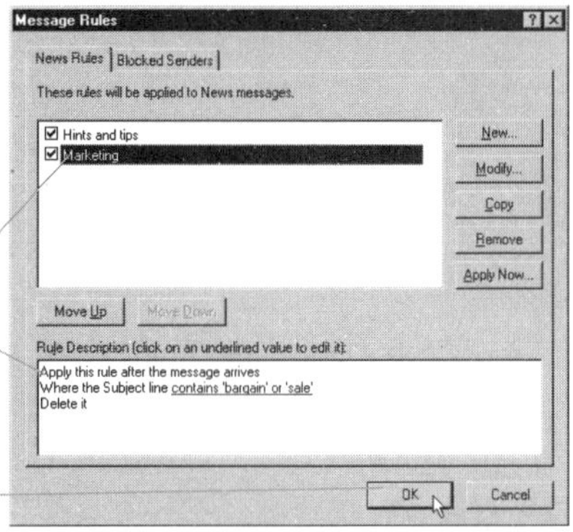

Subscribing to a newsgroup

It doesn't cost to subscribe, and it's easier to work with your favourite groups.

There are several ways to subscribe to a newsgroup, for example:

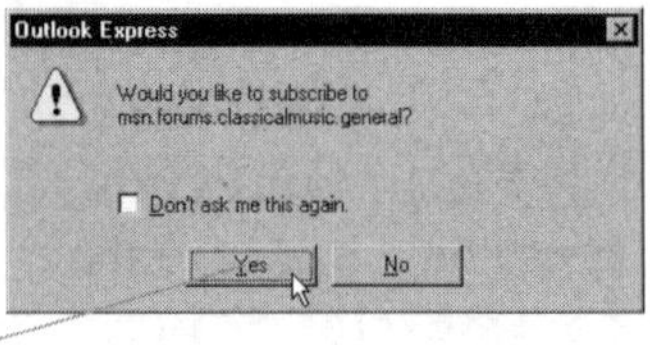

1 When you Go To a newsgroup, it offers a subscription.

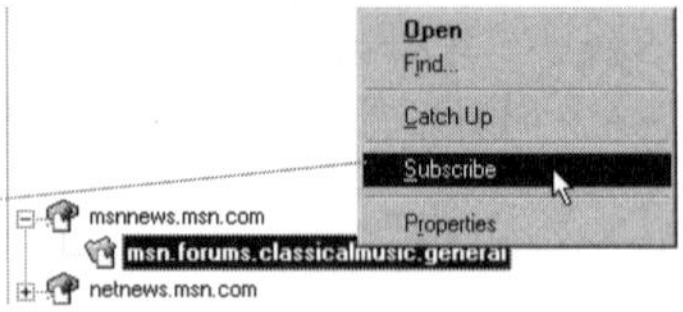

2 If you right-click the newsgroup in the Folders list, you can select Subscribe (or Unsubscribe).

When you start your news reader you can quickly display your list of subscribed newsgroups.

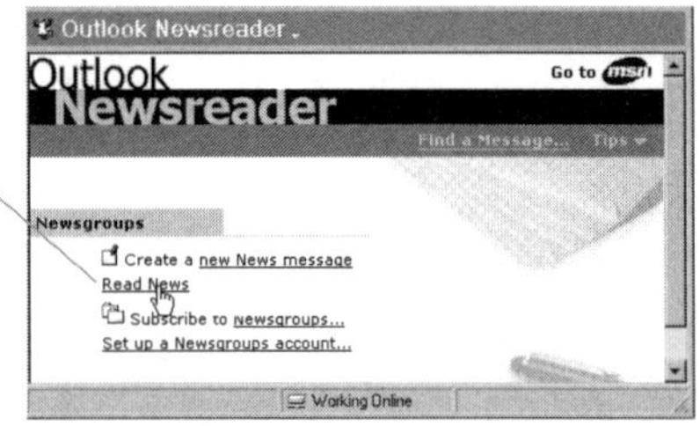

3 Click Read News on the main newsreader window.

4 Choose the news server from the folder bar, and double-click a name from the list of subscribed newsgroups.

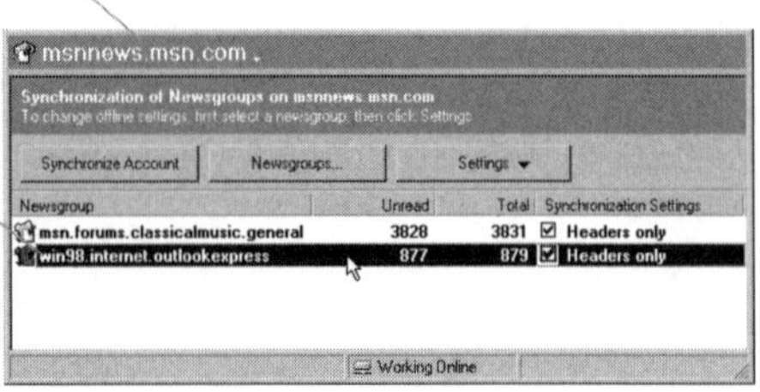

Your newsreader will normally start the dial up process to connect to the Internet. You can cancel this, but if you prefer to review the current contents before connecting, you can tell the newsreader that you want to work off-line:

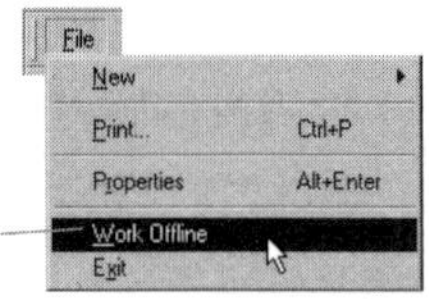

5 Select File from the Menu bar, and click Work Offline.

Updating your newsgroups

Define separate download settings for each of your newsgroup subscriptions.

1 Select the newsgroup from the list for the news server, right-click the newsgroup and click Settings.

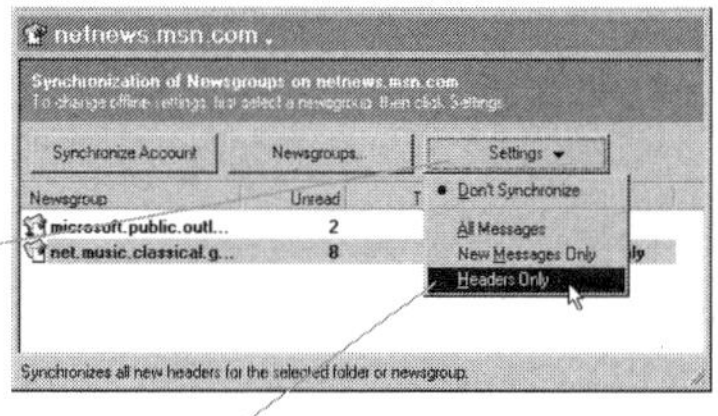

2 Specify Headers Only to have the titles of the latest messages downloaded.

Click the box on the progress bar to automatically hang up when download completes.

3 To update the headers, select Synchronise Account and the details specified in the settings for the newsgroup will be downloaded.

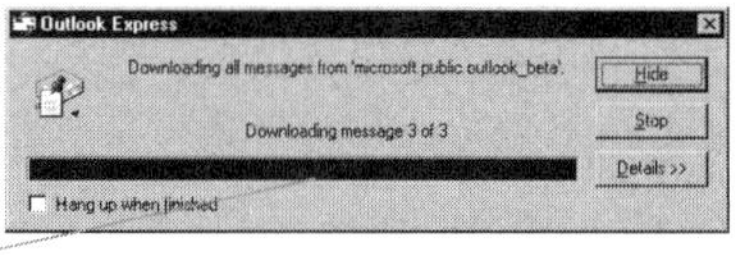

4 Review online, downloading message text as you browse, or disconnect from the Internet and review the headers off-line.

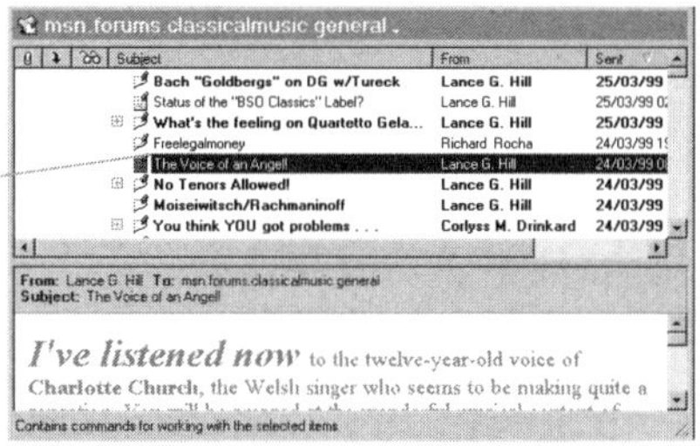

Sometimes you may get time-out errors on particular servers. If this happens often, try increasing the wait period.

Increasing time-out delay time may help resolve problems with particularly busy servers.

5 Right-click the server name, select Properties, Advanced tab.

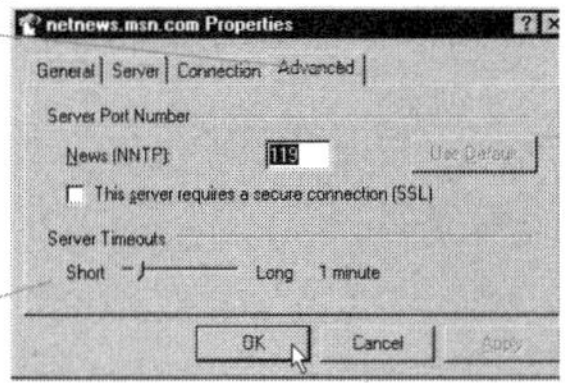

6 Move the slider for Server Timeouts to the right to increase it.

Posting a reply

Check the dates on messages before you decide to join in a conversation thread.

When you read messages in a newsgroup, you may feel tempted to add your own questions or comments. You can reply direct to the author, or you can add an entry to the newsgroup for everyone to see. In the jargon of newsgroups, this is called posting a reply.

1. Select the message that interests you and click Reply to Group.

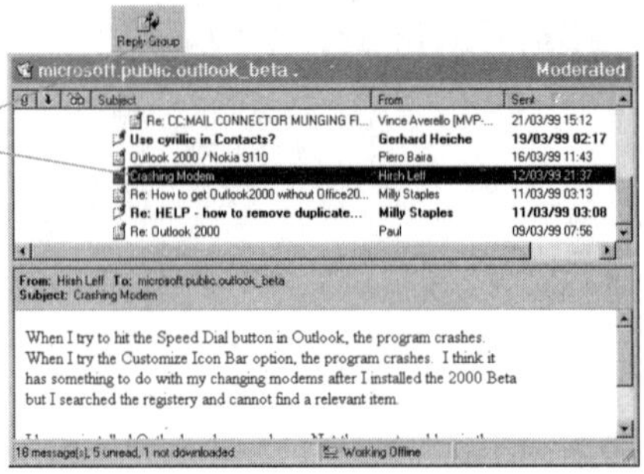

2. The Reply message picks up the group and the subject from the original.

3. Type in the text of your response, then click Post to send the reply.

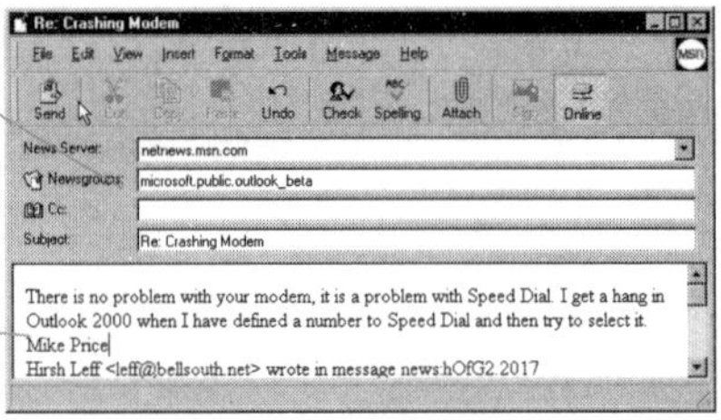

Send your reply as plain text, since not all newsgroup users are able to read HTML or rich text messages.

4. Your reply is stored in the Outbox, ready to be sent the next time you connect to the news server to update the newsgroups.

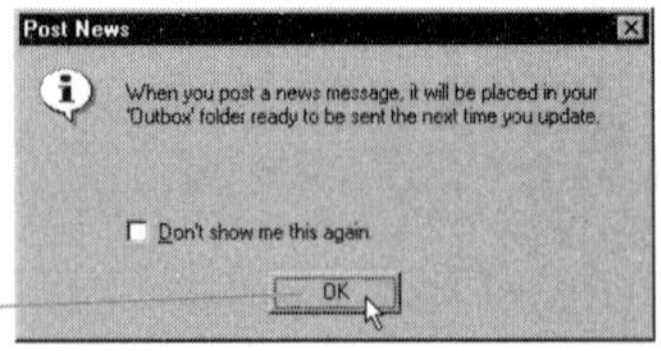

Your reply will be sent to the originating server for the group. It will take some time for the changes to appear on secondary servers, so you may not see it immediately on the news server that you are using.

After some time, perhaps a few minutes, the reply will be added to all copies of the newsgroup, including the copy on the news server that you access.

Be famous for five minutes, then your reply is superseded by the next message or the latest topic.

If you are still connected to the newsgroup at the time the message arrives, you will see the original message convert to a conversation thread as your message is appended. Your reply is now part of a thread on every copy of the newsgroup right across the Internet.

Some newsgroups are very active and get updated very frequently. The message files are trimmed from time to time, and after a while, perhaps just a few days, older messages will be dropped from the newsgroups.

To make sure that you do not miss out on further messages in a particular conversation thread:

Note that when you click in the Mark for Download column, the marker is toggled on or off.

1. Select Message from the Menu bar and click Watch Conversation, or click once in the Watch column.

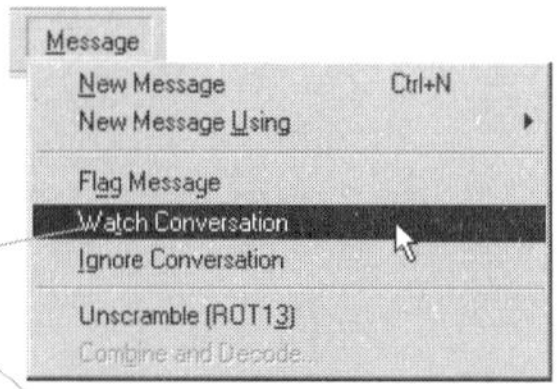

If there are conversations that you do not want to follow, you can avoid them being downloaded if you mark them to be ignored during updates:

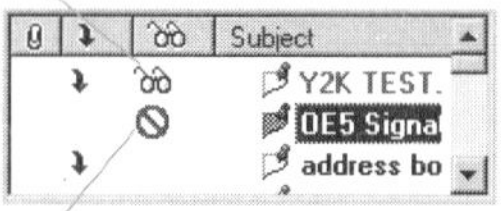

2. Click twice in the Watch column, or select Message from the Menu bar and click Ignore Conversation.

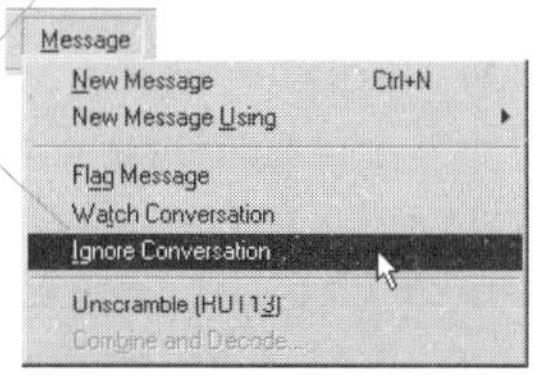

3. Select Tools from the Menu bar and click Synchronise Newsgroup.

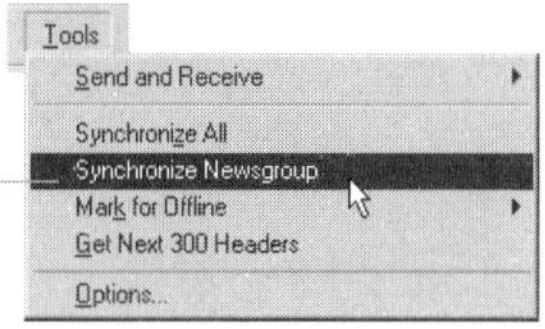

Updates to conversations that are being watched, plus updates to any messages marked for download, are retrieved from the server.

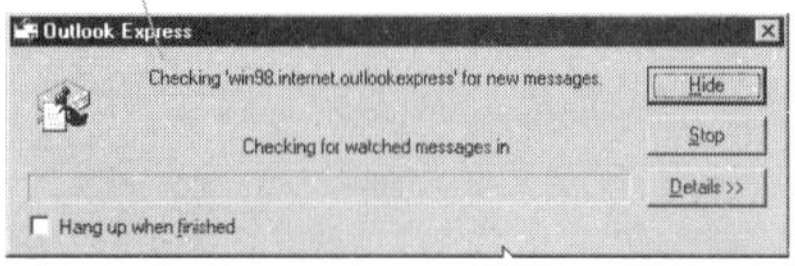

Private newsgroups

Private newsgroups allow you to share information with associates, making use of the Internet but retaining the privacy of the information.

Although most newsgroups are public and open to anyone who wants to read or post messages, there are some newsgroups that are private. They are accessed from dedicated news servers. Entry to these is by invitation only, and you will be given the news server name, the user account and a password in order to sign on.

Add the news server to your Outlook newsreader by selecting the Accounts function.

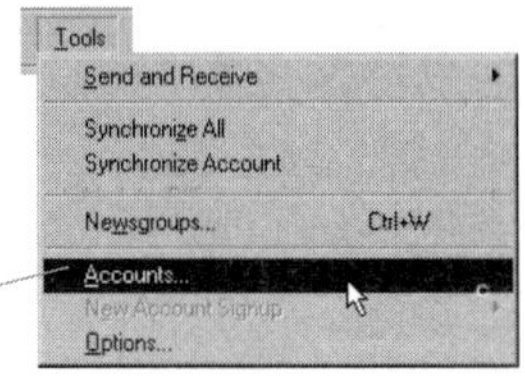

1. Select Tools from the Menu bar, click Accounts, select Add and then News to define a news server.

2. Follow the Internet Connection Wizard instructions to specify the news server properties.

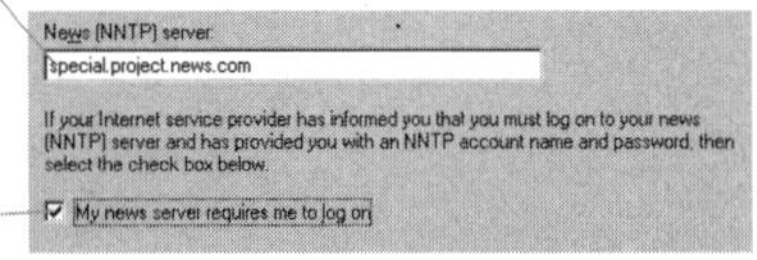

3. You'll need to specify logon information for using the private newsgroup.

There's another way to share private information over the Internet. See Net Folders, on page 178.

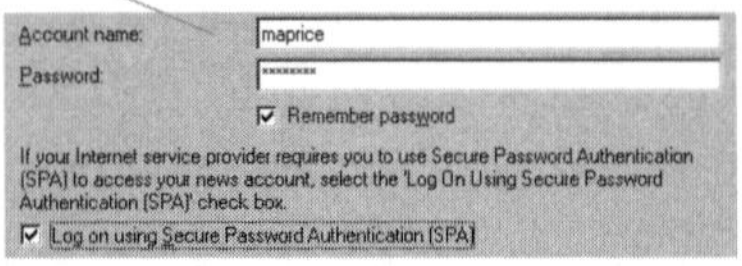

4. The news server is added to your list.

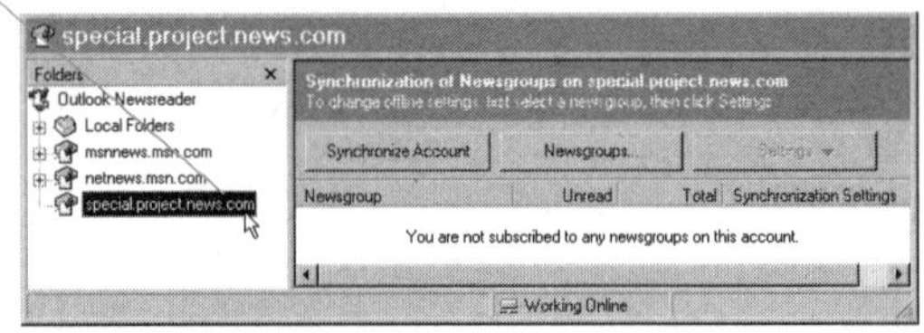

When you select the server, you will receive a list of the newsgroups that it contains, and can subscribe to the appropriate ones, just as with the public newsgroups.

Outlook Calendar

This chapter explores the Outlook Calendar, defining events, appointments and meetings. It also discusses using the calendar to help set up and manage projects and meetings, including virtual meetings across the Internet.

Covers

Chapter Eight

The Calendar

Outlook Express, needs a separate application such as Schedule+ for diary management.

The Calendar is a feature of Outlook that has no equivalent in Outlook Express. It is designed to keep track of activities and happenings. It gives you a high level overview of the week or month, but also maps the details by the day and the hour, so it is a diary as well as a calendar.

Outlook works with three types of item: appointments, meetings, and events. An appointment is an activity that involves just yourself. If you need to book resources or to invite other people, it becomes a meeting. Both types of activity are treated as busy and block off time in your calendar. If the activity extends for a whole day or more, it may be treated as an event. Events include such things as conferences, holidays and courses, or annual events like a birthday or anniversary. Events do not count as busy time, so meetings and appointments can be scheduled at the same time. To display the Calendar:

1. Click the Calendar icon on the Outlook bar, or click the link on Outlook Today.

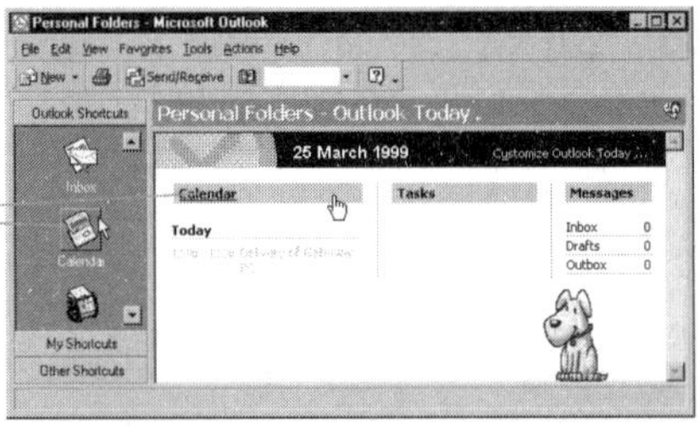

2. This shows Day view, but you can choose a week, a work week, or a month.

3. Calendar also shows the Date Navigator and the mini Task Pad area.

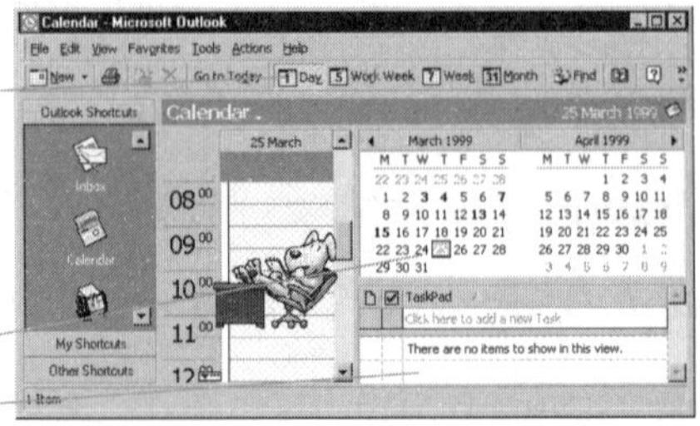

Outlook Calendar, unlike the planner or diary it emulates, has no holidays or special days ready entered.

As initially installed, the Calendar has no information to show you. However, you can enter events and define your free and busy time, to create exactly the type of calendar that works for you.

Adding an event

You'll probably want to start by transferring your pocket diary entries, putting down major events such as vacations and conferences or special events such as birthdays and anniversaries. To add an event to your Calendar:

You can create an event by double-clicking the date heading.

1. Open Calendar and select Actions from the Menu bar and create a New All Day Event.

2. Type the description for the event, enter the location, and specify the start date (and end date if different).

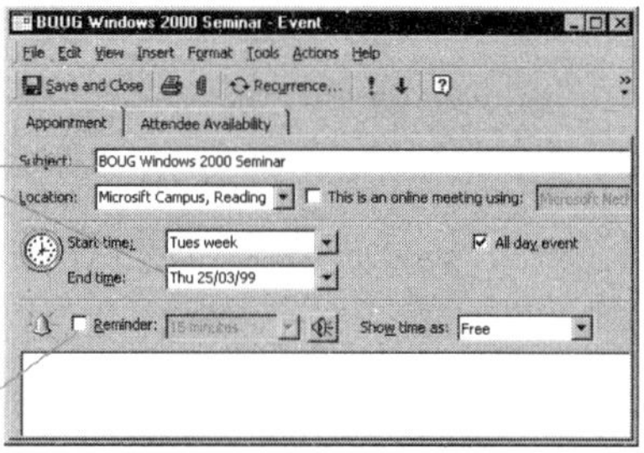

Outlook's autodate feature means you can put descriptions such as "next thurs" or "tues week" in the date fields, and they are converted to the standard form.

3. Click the box to request a reminder, minutes, hours or days before the event.

4. Show your time as Free, Tentative, Busy or Out of the Office, as applicable.

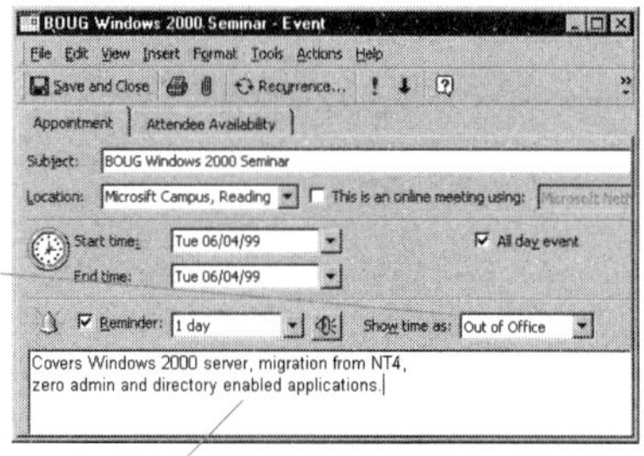

5. Add a comment or description. You can also set a high or low priority, as with e-mails.

All day events are assumed to run from midnight to midnight, and can be more than one day long.

6. Click Save and Close to record the name and duration of the event.

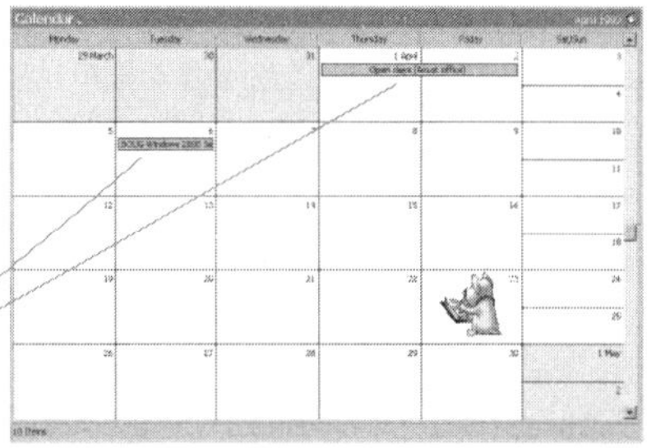

Adding national holidays

You can add all the national holidays for several years, in one block.

Adding entries one at a time can become tedious, so Outlook provides a way to add holidays en bloc. To add a set of national holidays to your Calendar:

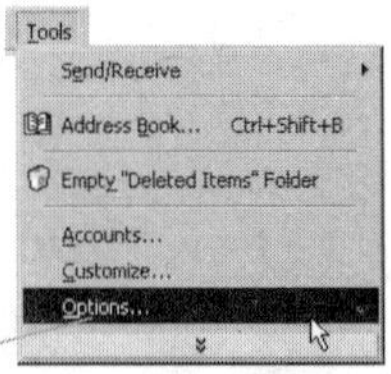

1. Select Tools from the Menu bar, and click Options, and then the Preferences tab.

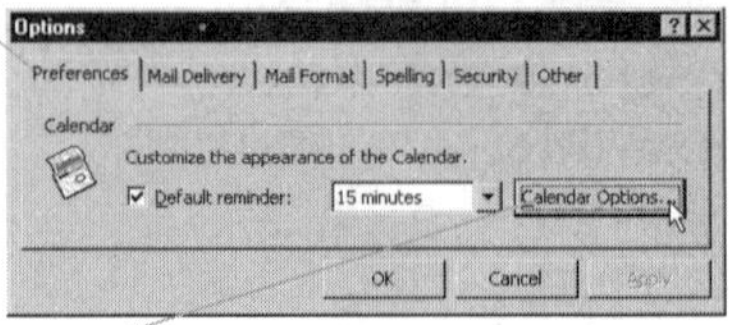

This screen also allows you to set the week to suit your work patterns.

2. Press the Calendar Options button, and then press Add Holidays.

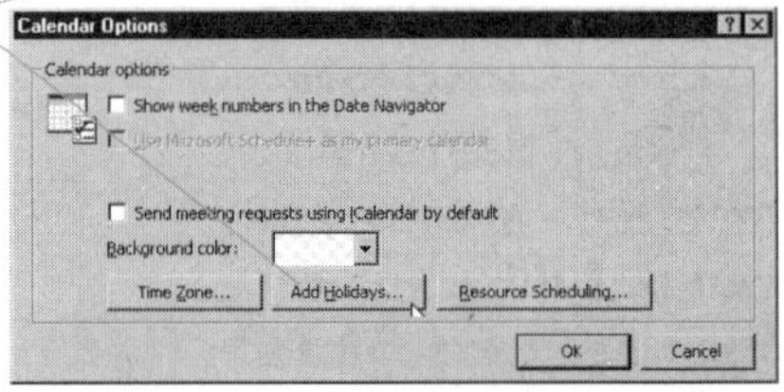

3. Choose one or more of the predefined groups of national and religious holidays, and click OK to apply the changes.

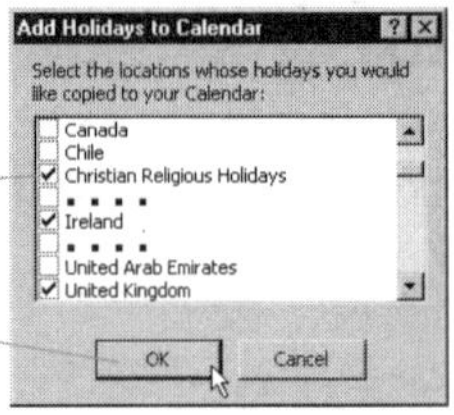

Modify the groups to cover more years and include additional events, or add your own groups. See page 134.

The holidays are added to the headers for the respective dates. They are shown as one-day events. Holidays are set for a range of five or so years.

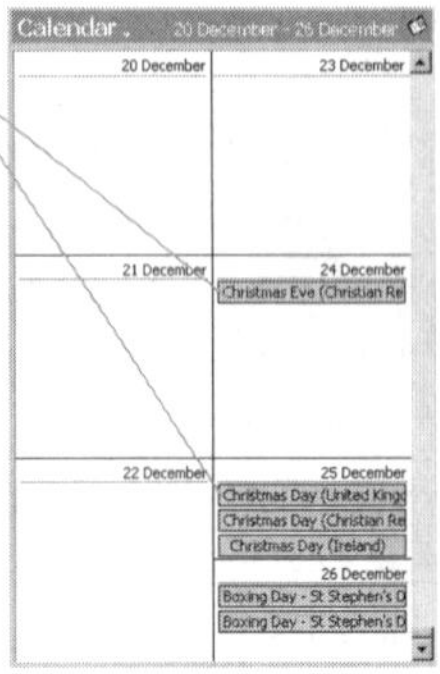

An alternative way to define holidays is to specify them as annually recurring events, as described on page 135.

Note that holidays such as Christmas Day are included in many of the national groups, and they will be duplicated if you select more than one group.

You can edit the events list to remove duplicate entries and other unnecessary items from the list.

Editing the events list

To check which holidays have been added to the Calendar, change the current view to display Events.

1. Open the Calendar, click View on the Menu bar and choose Current View, Events.

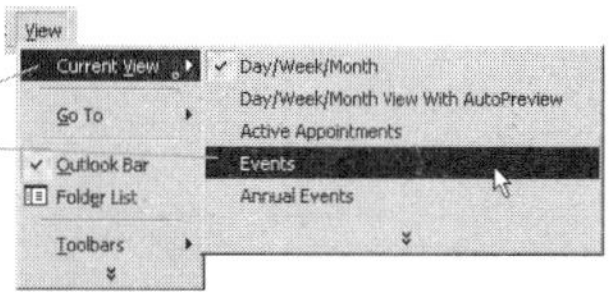

2. Select an event that is not required and click Delete.

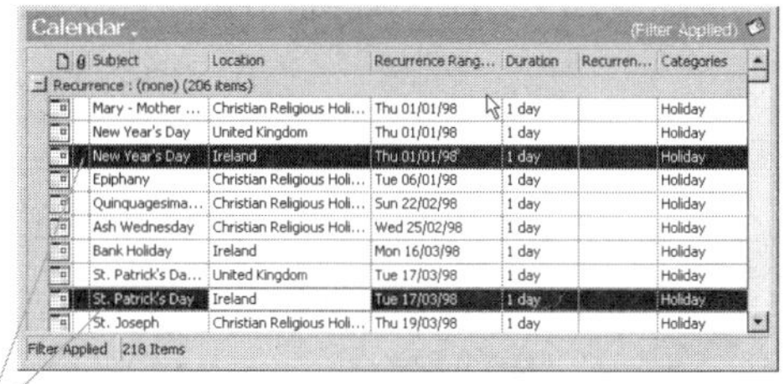

To remove or copy holidays, click the Subject heading to group similarly named events.

3. Hold down Shift to select a range, or Ctrl to select separate groups of events while left-clicking.

4. Select File, Copy and then File, Paste to make copies. Double-click the event to adjust the dates. E.g. add new year 2003.

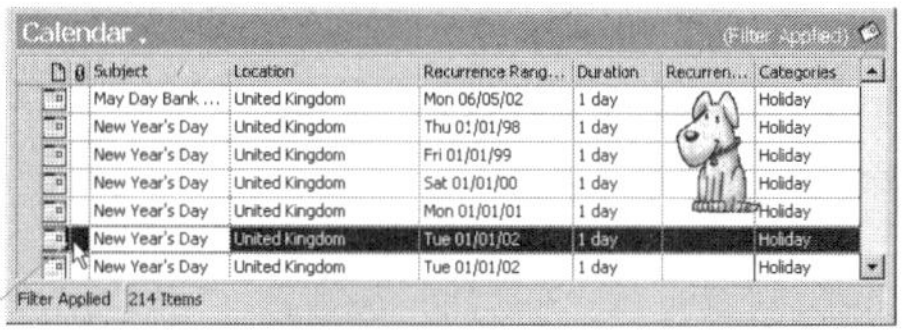

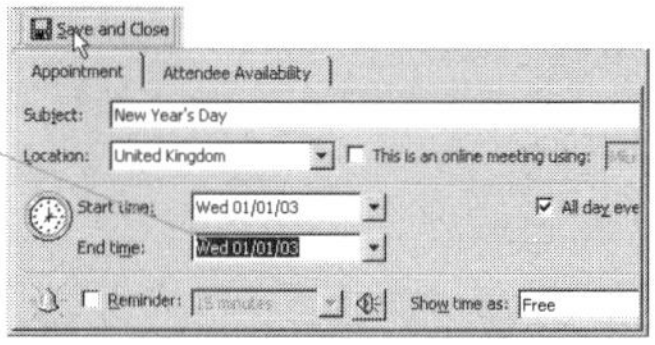

If you change the view settings – eg, expand column widths to see more detail – you can return to the original settings by:

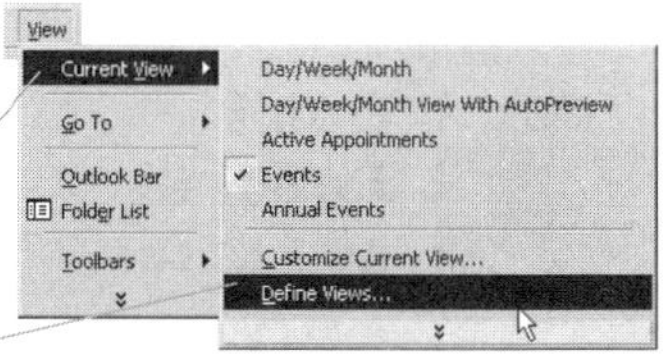

If the reset button is greyed, the view selected has not been modified, or it is a custom view (which has no original setting).

5. Choose View, Current View, Define Views.

6. Select the view you want to restore, click the Reset button and confirm that you do want to reset the view.

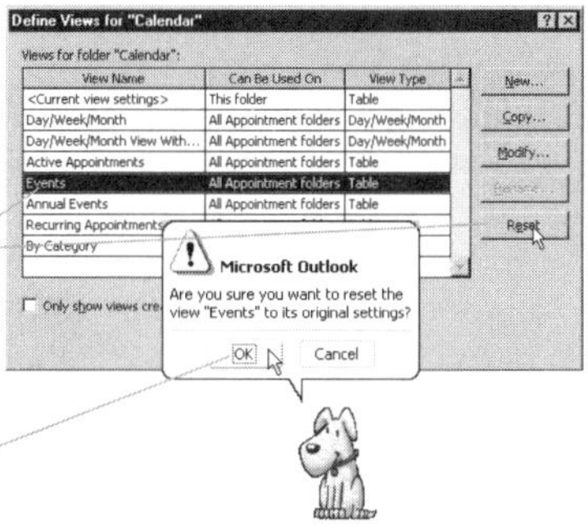

Modifying the list of holidays

To include the days you want, modify the Add Holidays list. This is a file with sets of event names and dates preceded by group names and counts. The size depends on the version of Outlook. You will also find a longer list of events for the USA than for the UK and other countries.

Change one of the groups, or make your own group of events, by editing Outlook.txt.

Put one example of regular fixed-date events such as Boxing Day, and convert them to recurring events later (see page 135).

1. Close Outlook.

2. Select Start, Find, and then Files and folder, and find Outlook.txt in the Office folder.

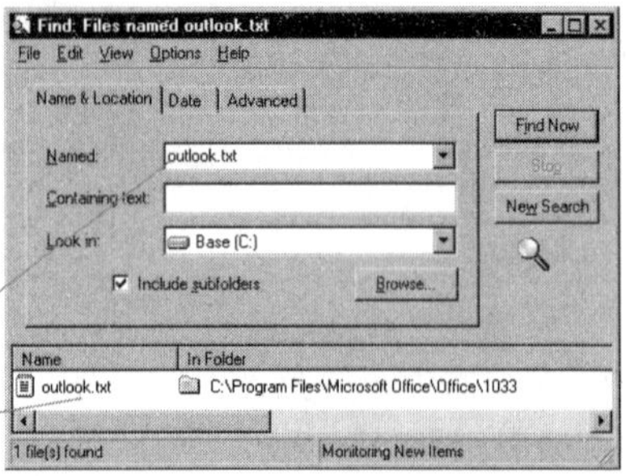

3. Select File, Open Containing Folder, and make a backup copy of the file.

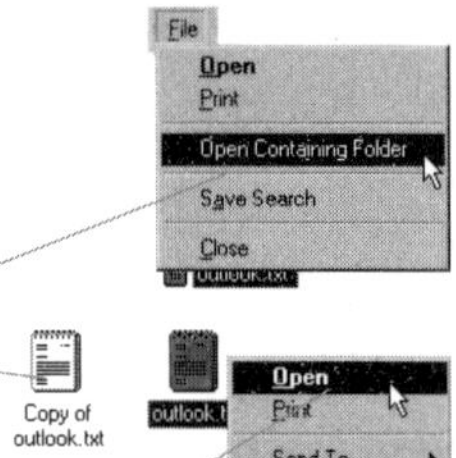

4. Right-click the file icon and select Open. Since it is a large file, you need Word Pad.

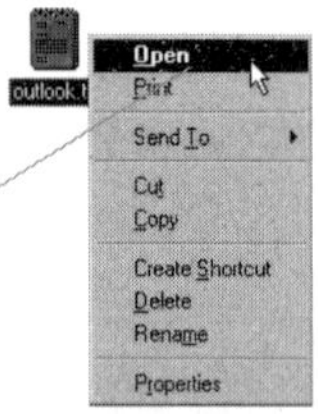

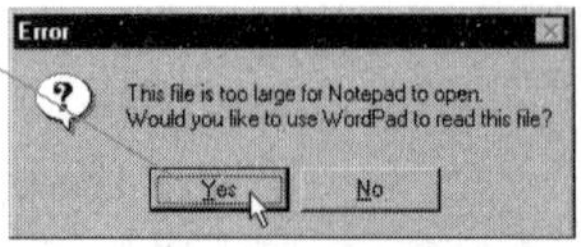

5. Modify entries, add new entries or add new groups to the file and save it.

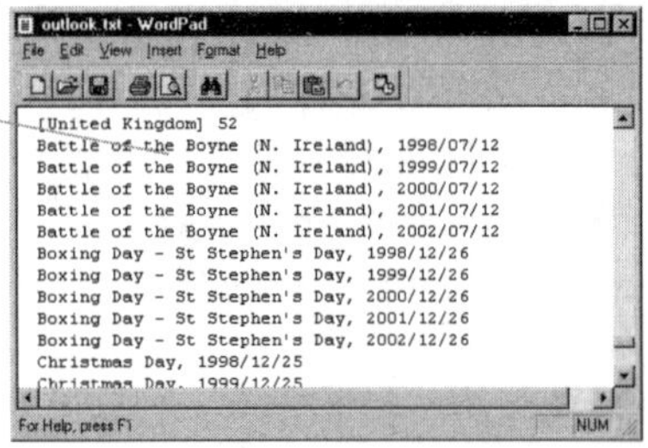

Don't forget to adjust the entry count or Outlook may ignore your additions.

The next time you run Outlook, you can use the revised holiday list to add holidays to your Calendar.

Creating annual events

When a holiday occurs on a fixed date every year, you can set it up as an annual event. This is entered once but appears as many times as needed. To specify Boxing Day as an annual event:

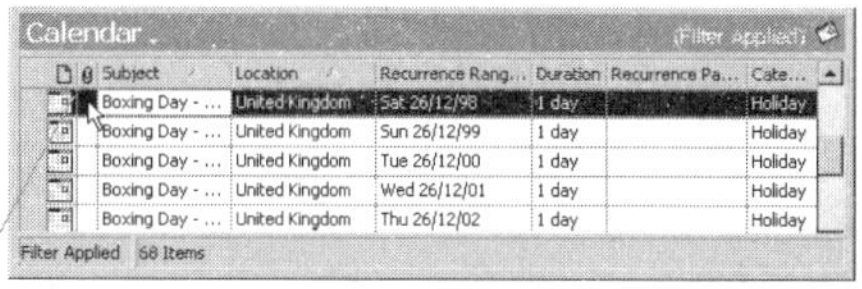

1 Open Calendar and select the Events view. Locate a Boxing Day event and double-click it.

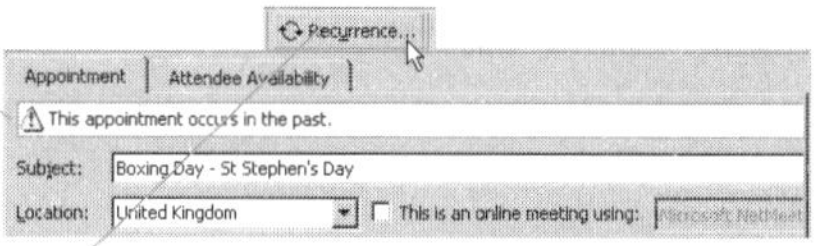

2 Press the Recurrence button. Click Yearly, and No end date, so that this event will be added every year. Click OK, Save and Close.

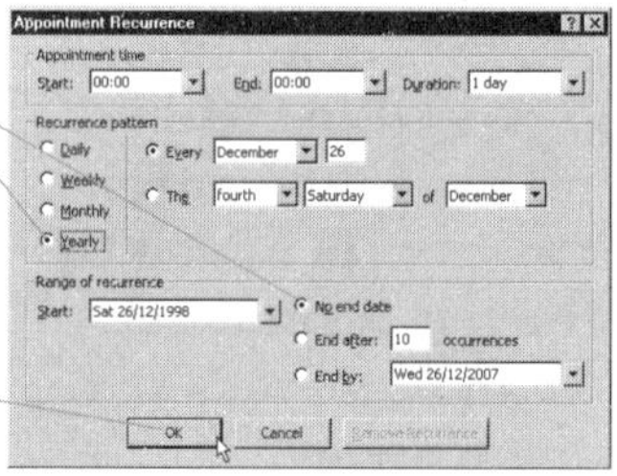

3 Delete other entries for that holiday or event.

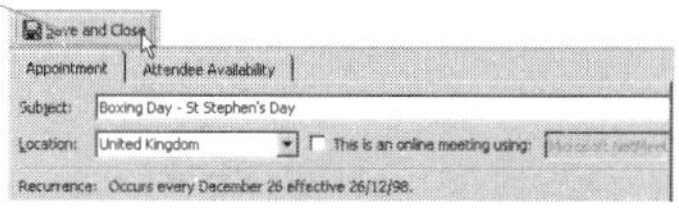

4 Repeat these steps for other fixed date holidays and events such as Christmas, Valentines day, etc.

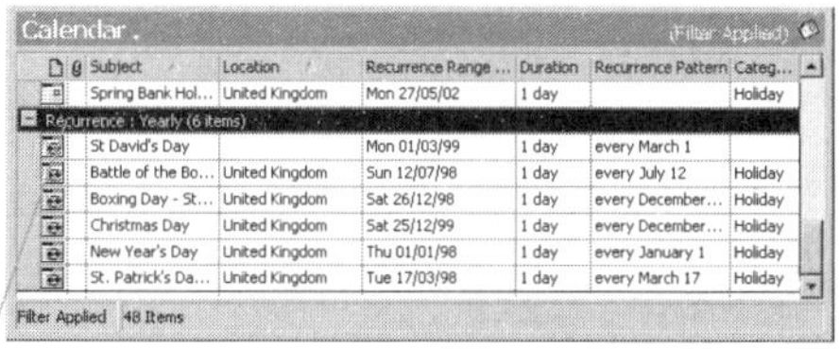

Recurring events do not have to be fixed dates. You can say "fourth Thursday of the month", for example.

When you return to the Events view, the recurring entries will be shown in its own section of the list, separate from the list of individual entries.

In the normal day/week views, the recurring entries appear with a circle symbol to indicate that they are repeated events.

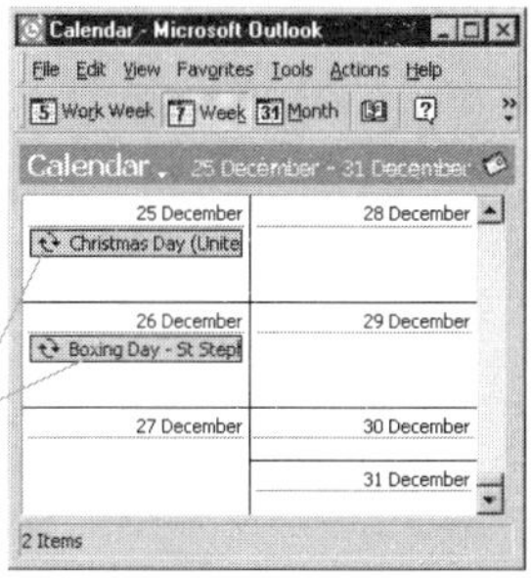

Scheduling appointments

You can schedule an appointment in your calendar to remind yourself that there is something you have to do or a place where you have to be. This can also signal to anyone with access to your calendar that you may be unavailable at the time concerned.

If the Calendar is displayed, just click the New Items button, and a new appointment is started..

1. Click the down-arrow on the New Items button, and select to create a new Appointment.

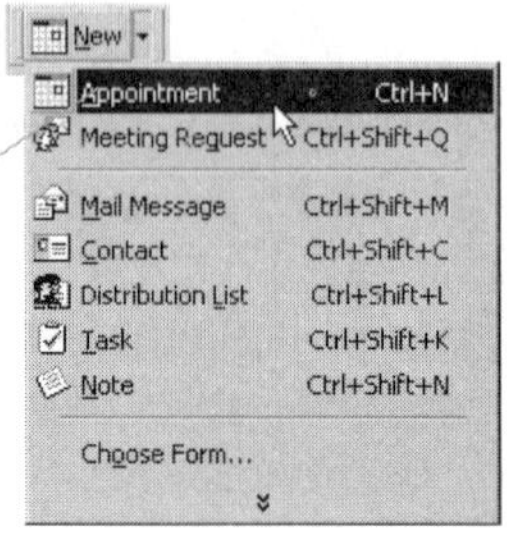

2. Enter the Subject and select the Location from the list, or type in a new location.

Each new location you enter is added to the list displayed when you press the down arrow.

3. Specify the start time and the duration. Say if you want to mark this period as Busy time or Out of Office.

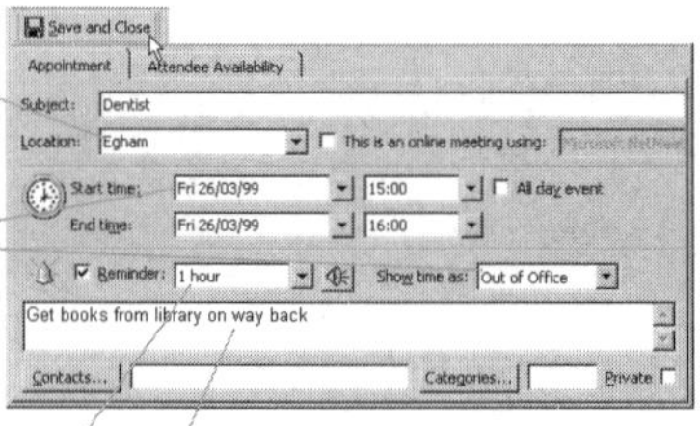

Flag your private appoint-ments so that they won't appear on your calendar lists viewed by other users.

4. Set the Reminder period if you want to be warned as the time approaches.

5. Enter a description (or specify a category) if appropriate.

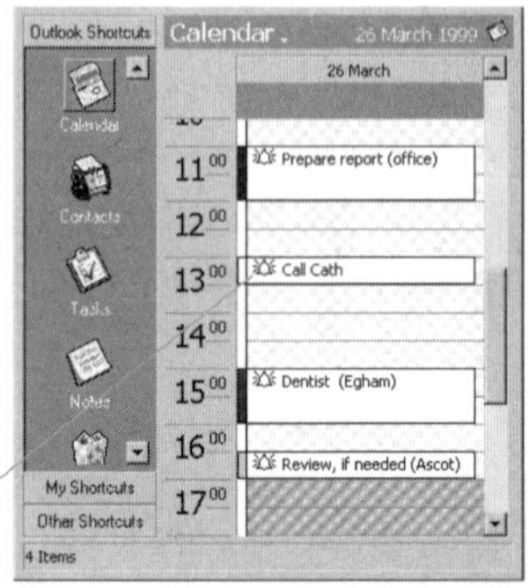

6. Click Save and Close to complete the action, and the appointment appears in your diary. The bell symbol shows that a reminder has been set.

If your plans change, move or copy appointments to a new time or date.

1 Point to the left of the item that you want to move.

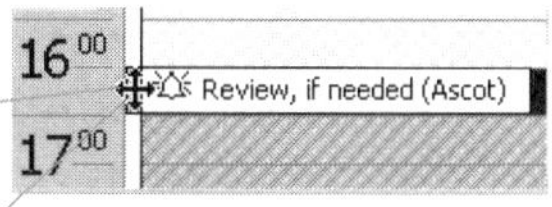

2 When the pointer becomes a 4-way arrow, click the item.

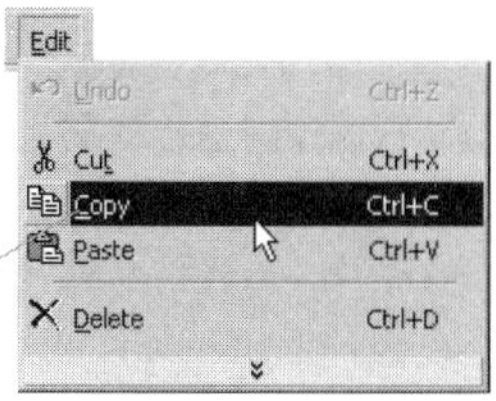

3 Click Edit on the Menu bar, and then select Cut (or Copy).

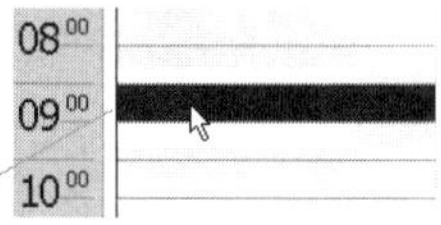

If an item recurs, only the selected instance is moved.

4 Select the new start time or the new start date, click Edit and then select Paste.

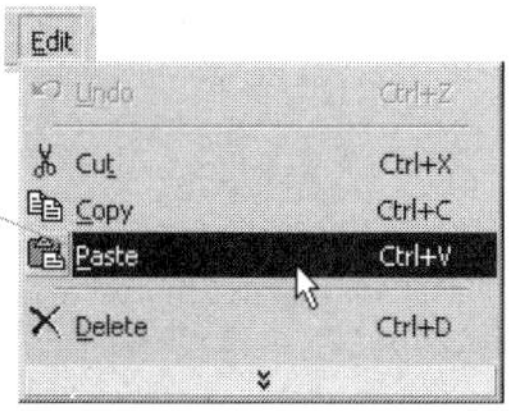

5 The appointment is moved (or copied) to the new time and date. The duration and other details remain unchanged.

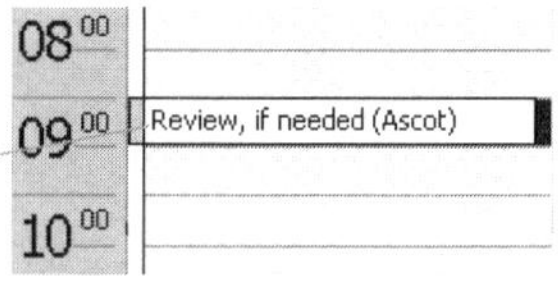

A quick way to rearrange appointments is to use the mouse to select and drag the item to the new date or time.

If you just select and drag the item with no Ctrl key, it will be Moved.

6 If you want to Copy the item, hold down the Ctrl key.

7 Click on the item and hold down the mouse button.

8 Drag the item to the new date on the calendar or the date navigator, and release it. The appointment is Copied (or Moved).

Meetings

HOT TIP **Add some attendees to turn an appointment into a meeting. You may also have resources to assign and invitations to keep track of. Calendar will help you manage all of these.**

The definition of a meeting is quite simple: it is an appointment that involves at least one other calendar as well as your own. In practice, a meeting can become a quite complex affair. You have to consider not only the availability of other people, but also the allocation of meeting rooms and of equipment such as projectors or video recorders, and you have to keep everyone informed when the details change.

This can all be done manually, with phone calls or e-mail messages to the attendees or the persons responsible for booking the room and equipment. Outlook however includes the facilities for fully managing meetings. Meeting requests and replies keep attendees informed. Resources are treated as Contacts, with entries in the Contacts list and special e-mail addresses to which meeting requests will be sent. These can automatically respond to requests, based on the current schedule in the calendars.

To allow you to plan a meeting without having to wait for responses, it would be nice to know about the free and busy times for all the attendees and for all the resources, before you make a request. Outlook allows you to share this data, and assists you to select meeting times that avoid or minimise conflicts. Meeting requests can then be sent to all the attendees and to the resource contact points, knowing that the request matches their calendars.

You wouldn't need to go to such lengths for ordinary meetings, but it is useful to be aware of the possibilities, so that as your needs develop you can take more advantage of Outlook. So the following pages step through the processes involved in planning a meeting, and identify the issues that can arise.

This will help you decide which of these facilities you need to use when you have to plan a meeting. It will also help you to understand what is involved, when you are the recipient of message requests for meetings that other people set up.

Converting appointments

Recipe for a meeting: take an appointment and add people.

Reserve time in your diary for an appointment, and then turn it into a meeting when you have all the details.

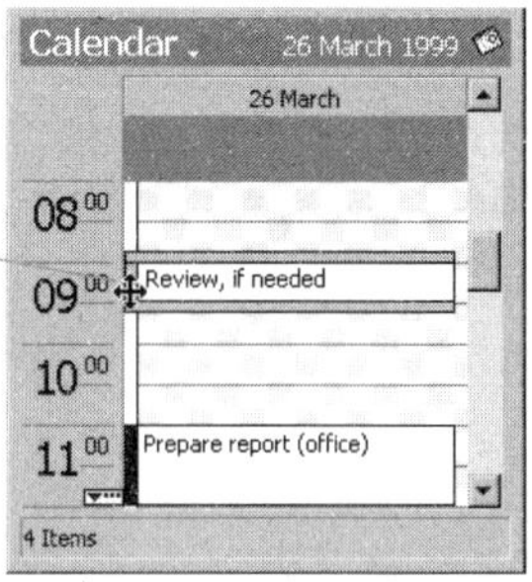

1 Select Calendar and double-click the appointment to view it.

2 Click the Attendee Availability tab and the status button.

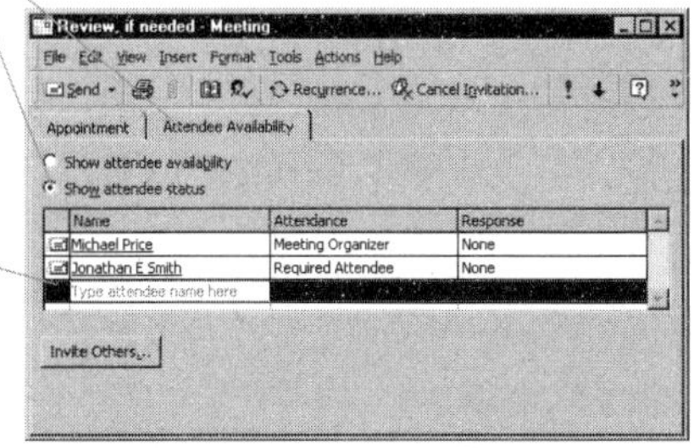

3 Enter the e-mail addresses or names of the attendees.

You can press Invite Others and select people and resources from the Contacts list.

4 Choose Appointment tab and make any required changes to the location, start time and duration.

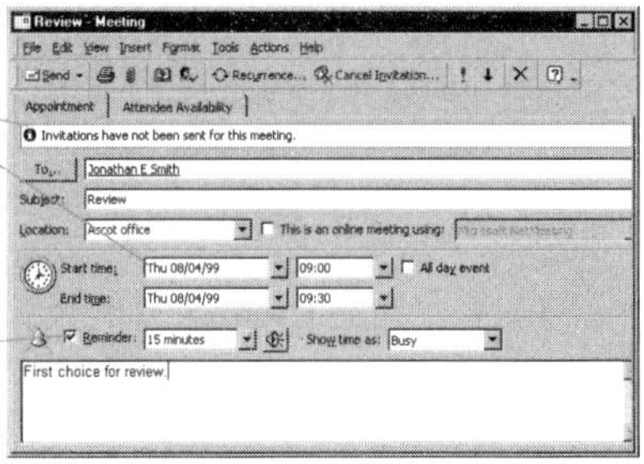

5 Choose a reminder and specify the notice period.

6 Press Send to notify the attendees who have e-mail ids.

When you Send a meeting request it is placed in the OutBox ready for your next Send & Receive.

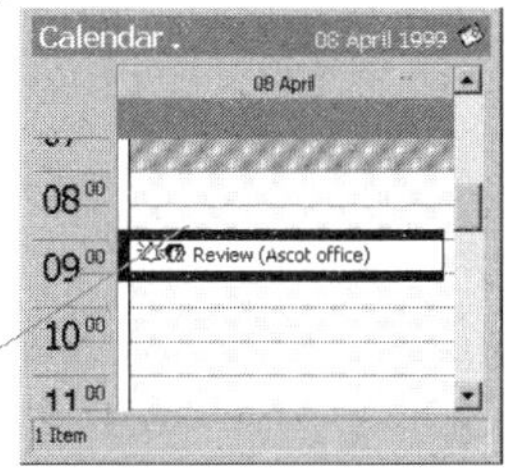

7 Press Save and Close to end message modifications.

8 The meeting appears in your calendar, complete with the people icon and reminder bell.

Planning meetings

Outlook helps you to book the room and the equipment, and invite the attendees.

1 Open the Calendar, select Actions from the Menu bar and click Plan a Meeting.

2 Press Invite Others, to open the Contacts list, and find the entry for each attendee. Press the Required, Optional or Resources button.

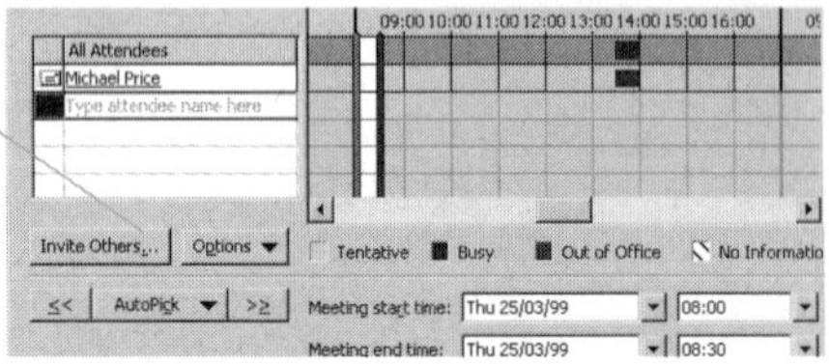

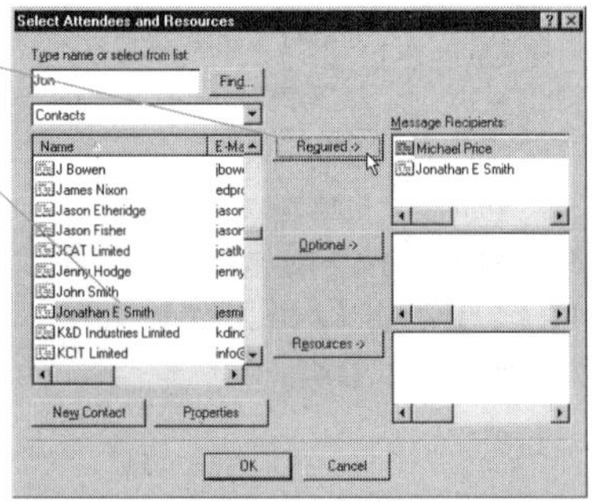

Required and Optional attendees appear in the To box, and Resources appear in the Location box.

3 Press AutoPick to establish a start time that fits with your schedule, and the resources you control. Select the end time or duration for the meeting.

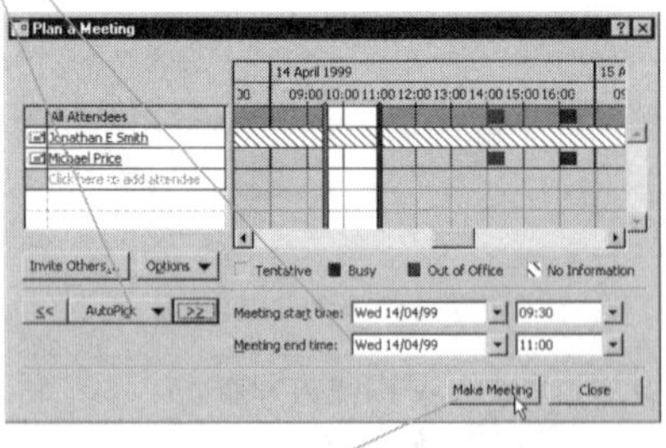

See page 143 for methods of reporting free/busy time over the Internet.

If you are part of a network, and you can access the calendars and the free/busy data for attendees, AutoPick will take their availability into account also when selecting a meeting time.

4 Select Make Meeting, and enter the Subject and the Location for the meeting.

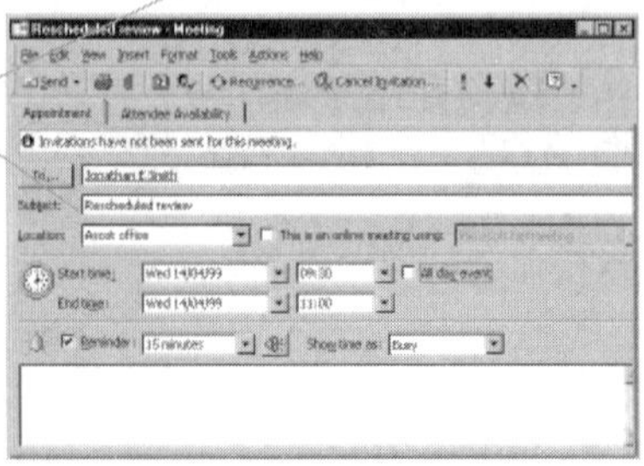

5 Press Send to create e-mail messages as invitations or meeting requests.

This is how attendees respond to meeting requests, or how you respond to the requests that you receive.

1 You can respond to a meeting request by right-clicking the title in the Inbox.

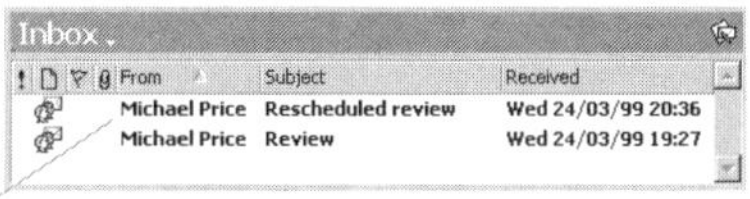

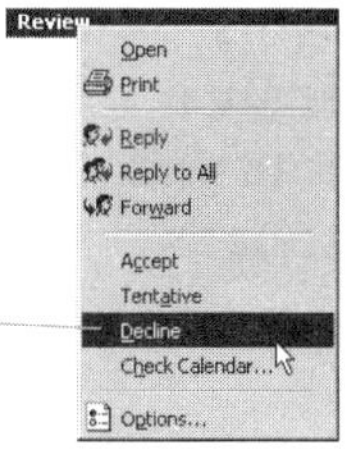

2 Click an action, and Send the response.

You can choose to open the message and add a comment to your response.

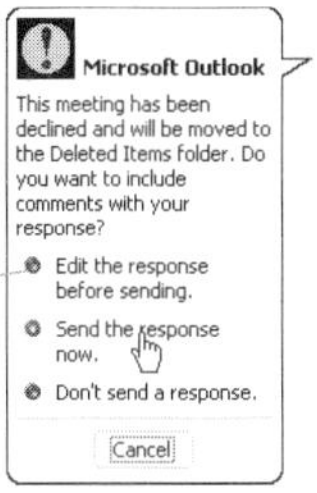

3 Your responses are added to the Outbox for sending later.

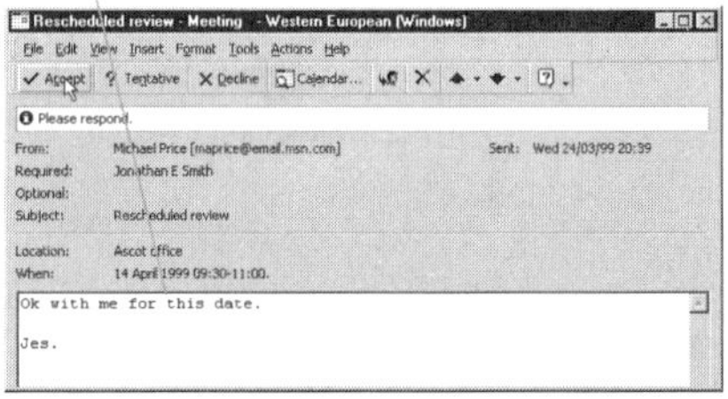

Outlook makes it clear when there are calendar conflicts but it does not prohibit double booking.

4 The request is removed from your Inbox. If you have accepted, the meeting appears in the calendar.

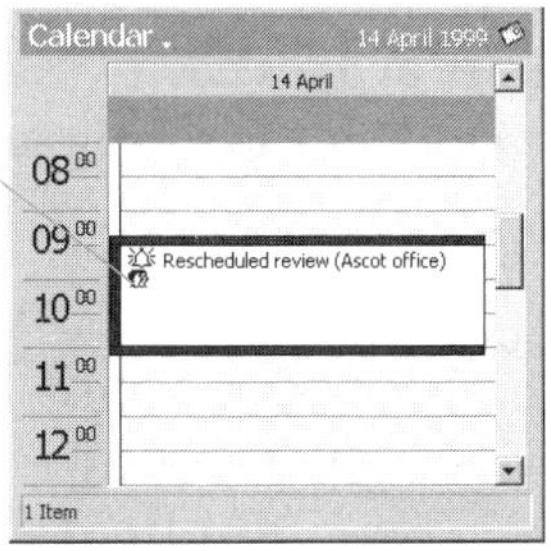

5 The responses are received as regular e-mail, and will show the summary of responses from the attendees and resource managers.

See page 116 for details of the Find and Advanced Find functions.

The replies are kept in the Inbox, and the original requests in the Sent folder, unless you have set Rules to redirect the messages to a different folder. Use the Advanced Find to group together a list of all the communications concerning the meeting.

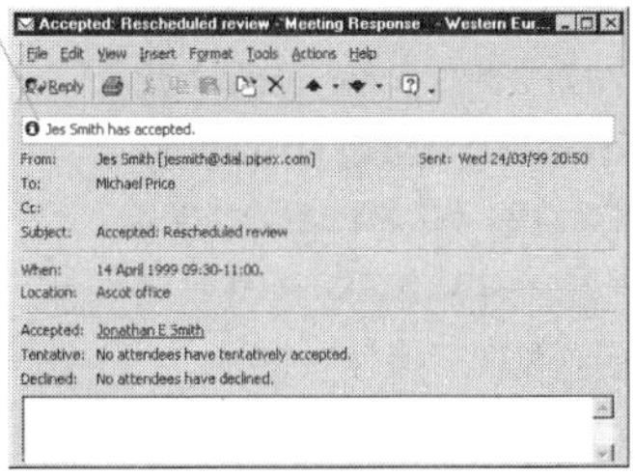

Changing meetings

You may need to change the details when you receive the invitations and receive responses.

1. Find the meeting in your calendar and double-click the meeting to open it.

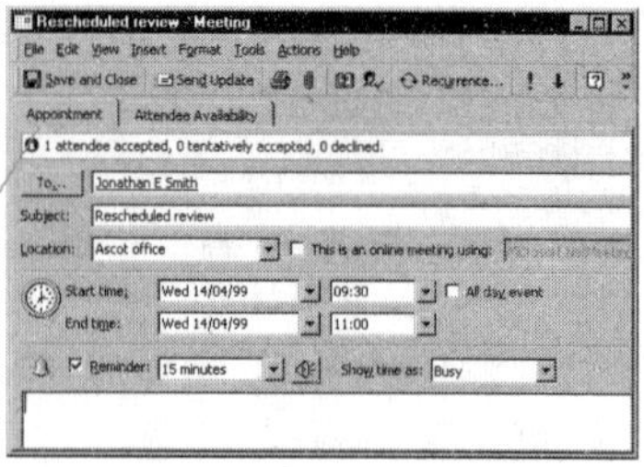

2. The Appointment tab shows a summary of the meeting details and the responses.

3. Click the Attendee Availability tab to see the current status. You can delete attendees or add new attendees.

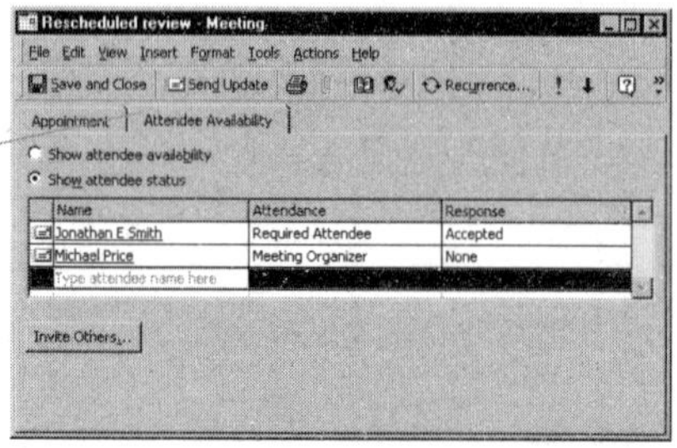

This will show only your own free/busy time, unless you have access to a server to share other people's data.

4. Click Show attendee availability to switch to the detailed view of the free/busy times for the attendees.

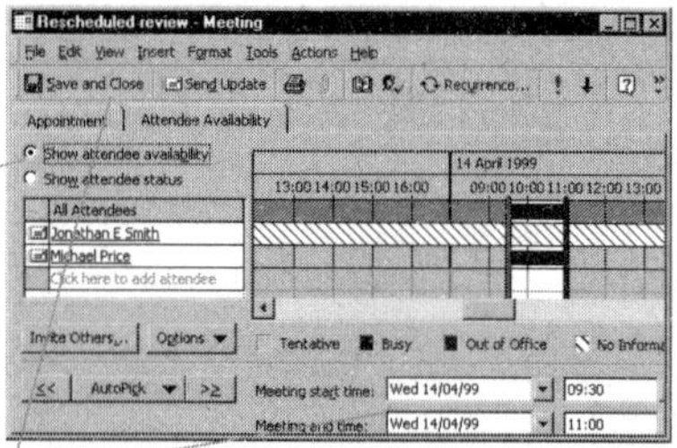

5. Make other required changes to the meeting details, and press Save and Close.

To avoid sending duplicate meeting requests to people previously invited, forward meeting requests to new attendees.

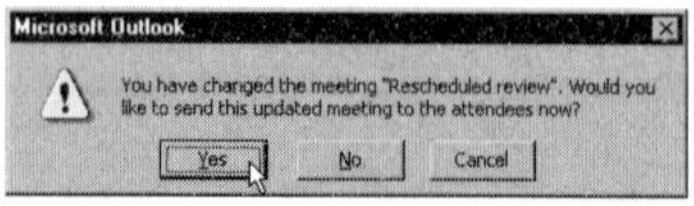

Outlook detects that you have made changes and gives you the opportunity to send a revised meeting notification to all the attendees.

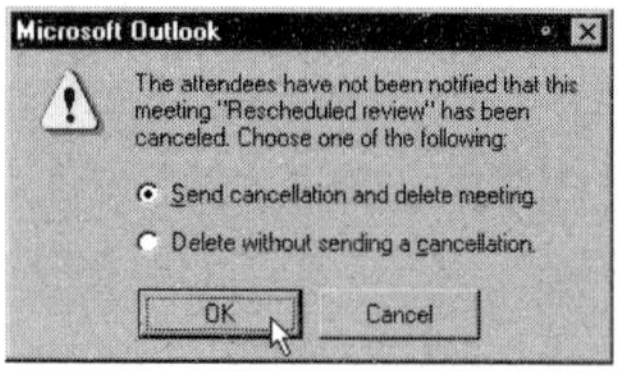

You'll get a warning whenever you make changes, even if you don't open the meeting notice – eg, if you select the meeting and press Delete to cancel it.

Reporting free/busy time

If you and your associates share access to a server on a local area network or to the pages on a Web server on the Internet, each of you can publish the details of your availability. One person can be designated to set up meetings using the combined availability data, and the AutoPick function, to schedule meetings that avoid calendar conflicts.

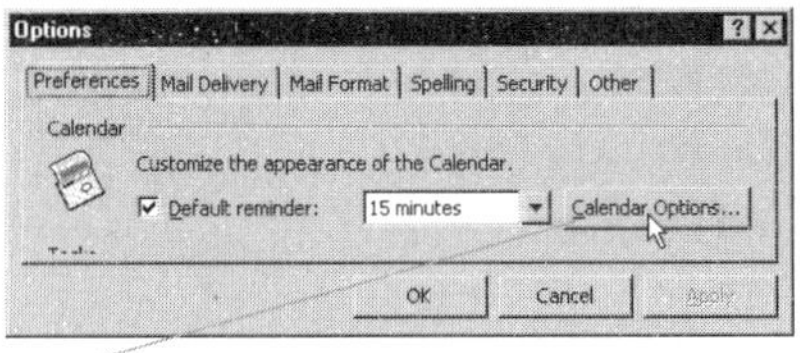

1 Select Tools from the Menu bar, then Options. Click the Preferences tab, and then Calendar Options.

HOT TIP **With an Internet connection, you may decide to enable this feature only when you want to update the data.**

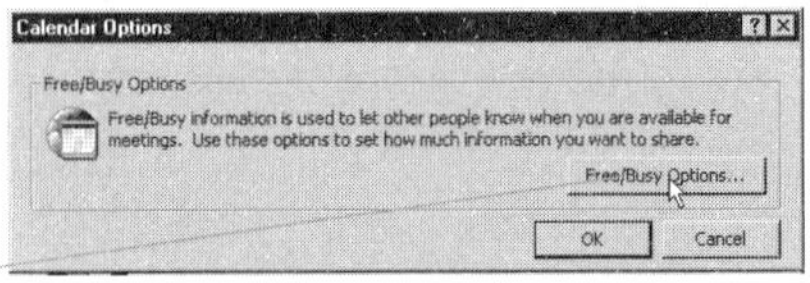

2 Select Free/Busy Options and say the number of months of your free/busy time to send to the server and how often to refresh.

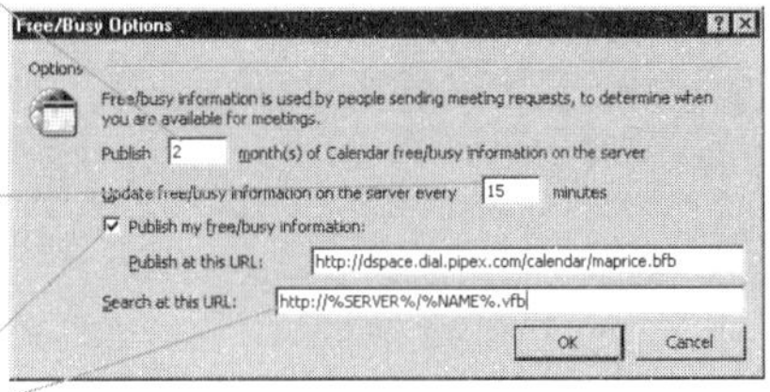

3 Select the option to Publish free/busy information, and enter the URL web page for Internet storage, or the server name for local area network connections.

HOT TIP **To request an update manually, select Tools, Send and Receive, Free/Busy Information.**

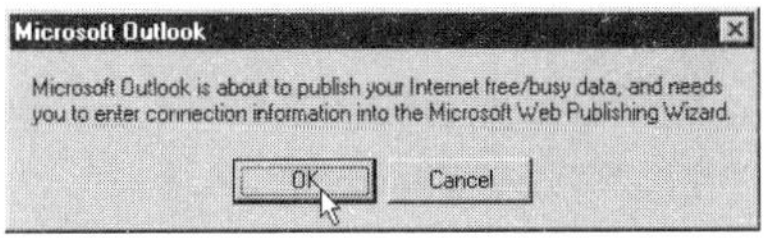

4 The Internet connection wizard records any additional details.

5 At the specified intervals, your free/busy information is transferred to the server or web page, for others to use in scheduling their meetings that may include you.

Meeting on the Internet

You can exchange video and audio also, with the right hardware and software.

E-mail messages are a poor substitute for real conversation because messages are not instantly transferred, and the recipient may not even be logged on when you send the mail. For active participation, to chat with others and share applications and documents, you need an online, real-time meeting. These functions are provided by NetMeeting, a component of Internet Explorer.

With Outlook you can add net meeting information to the details for your contact, and schedule meetings as online sessions.

1. Select Actions from the Menu bar, click New Meeting Request and mark it as an Online meeting.

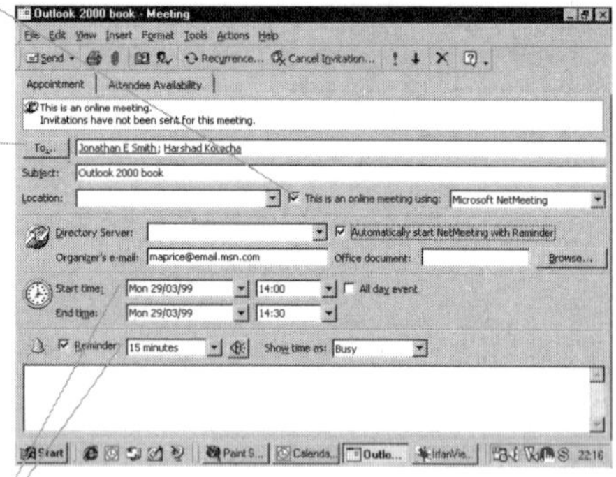

2. Choose the participants from the Contacts list. These entries must include NetMeeting details.

3. Enter the appointment details including the start time, the duration and the reminder notice.

If you set a reminder, connection happens that amount ahead of the official start time.

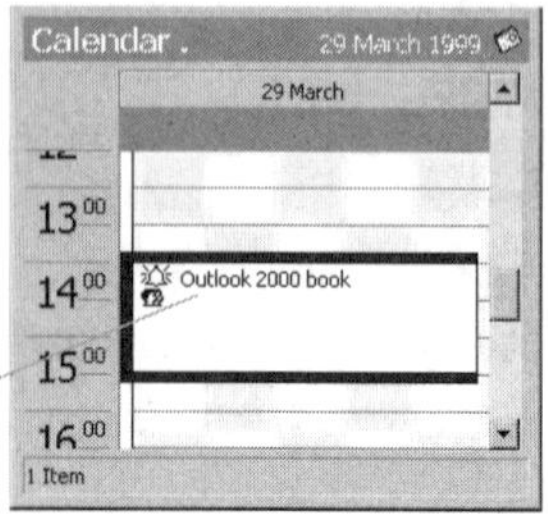

4. You can start the meeting immediately, or save the meeting on your calendar, and it will start at the specified time.

Task Manager

This chapter explores the Outlook Task Manager, showing how tasks are created, updated and assigned to others. It shows you how to keep everyone informed, and looks at the role of the TaskPad and the Today Tasks.

Covers

Chapter Nine

Setting up a task list

The Task folder in Outlook operates as a task list manager. In it you can enter a list of everything that you must do to complete the job or project that you have in hand. The list could include prompts for phone calls to make, meetings to prepare, letters or reports to write, travel arrangements to set up – in fact, anything that you need to do!

For each task you can specify details such as the subject, date required, priority and current status. You can also set reminders, as you do for meetings and appointments, so that you are warned when the critical time approaches. To open the task folder and enter a task:

1 Click Task on the Outlook bar or click the title in the Outlook Today window.

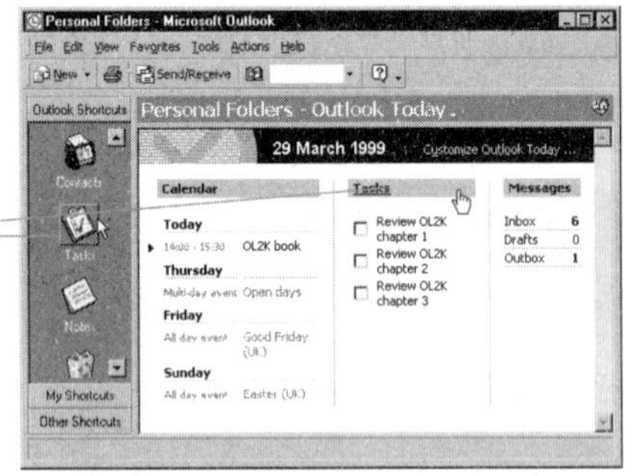

2 To create an entry in the list, click on the new task line, type the item title in the subject box, and press Enter.

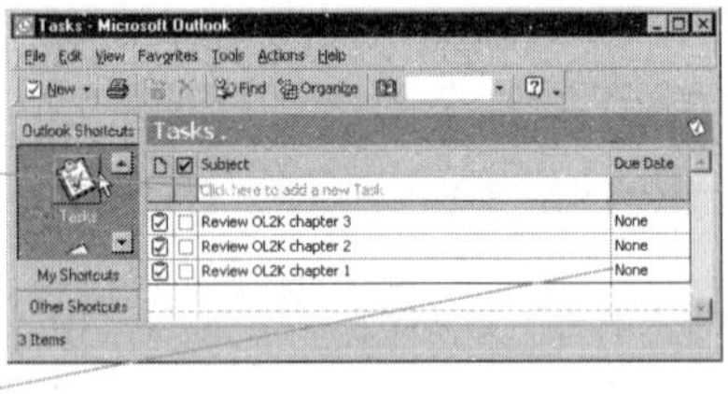

If you just enter the task titles you will create a useful to-do list for your project.

3 Outlook puts "None" as the due date, and adds default values for Status and % Complete.

4 The new entries get entered at the top of the list, but you can click the header to sort by task subject title.

5 Type the remaining tasks in your project to make your to-do list complete.

Task details

Describe the task more fully, when you create it, or when more information becomes available.

1 Press the New Task button on the toolbar, or double-click the New task line.

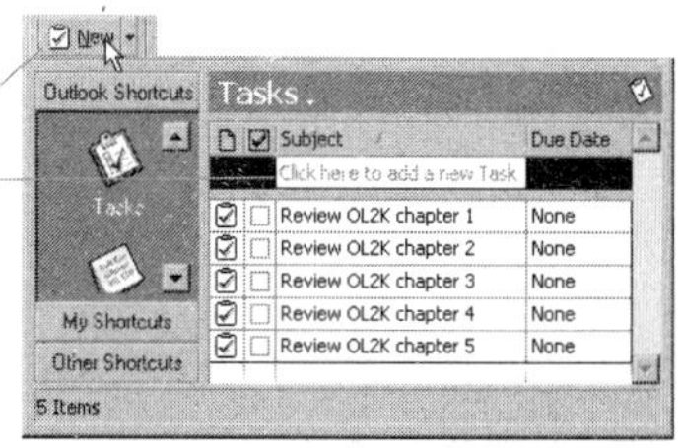

2 Select the Task tab and type in Subject, Notes, Contacts and Category.

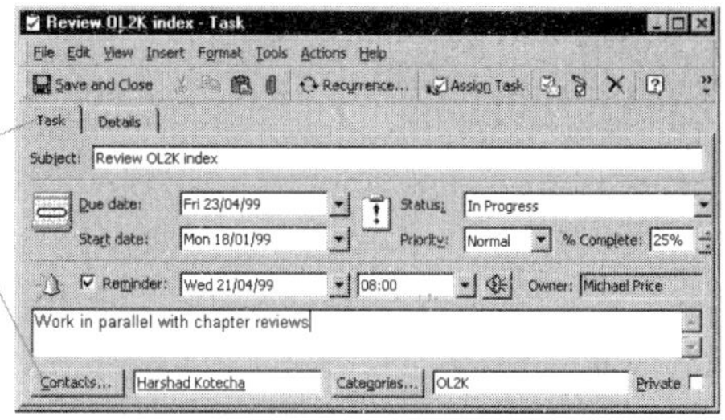

You can distinguish private tasks from business tasks by clicking the box.

3 Enter the completion date, and the start date. Click the down-arrow for a calendar to help find dates.

4 Choose the current status from the list offered. This entry should be updated regularly, as the tasks progress.

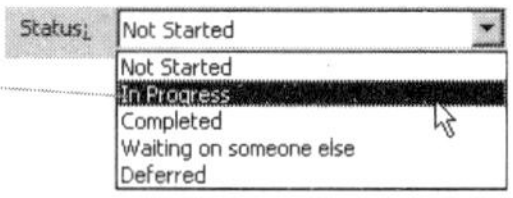

Put None, if the date is not yet known, and complete the details later.

5 Priority defaults to Normal, or you can select Low or High for the task.

6 Type in the % Complete to show the current position, or click the arrows for 25% increments. Update this value periodically.

Use the priority to sort tasks, and get the critical items to the head of the list.

7 The reminder date and time can be used as a prompt for starting or for finishing a task. You can also select a suitable .wav sound file to accompany the warning message.

8 Press save and close to record the task information.

Viewing the task list

In the Task folder, as in all Outlook folders, you can choose how you view the items.

1. Select View from the Menu bar, click Current View, and select one to try.

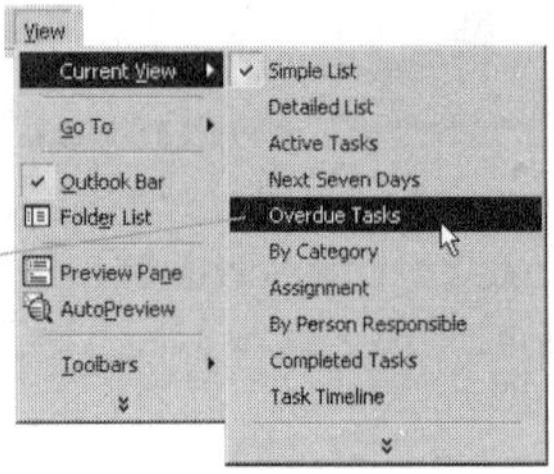

The Simple view shows the task subjects and completion dates, acts as a quick overview of the status of the project. You can double-click any task to open it.

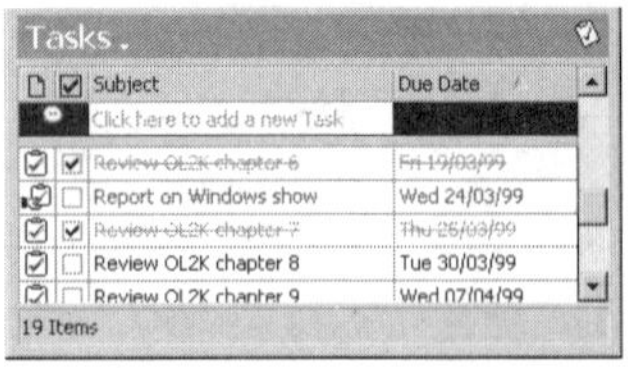

The Detailed view adds more information, so you can sort the tasks by status or category etc., by just clicking the relevant heading. It is a good place to update the status and completion data. You don't have to open each task separately.

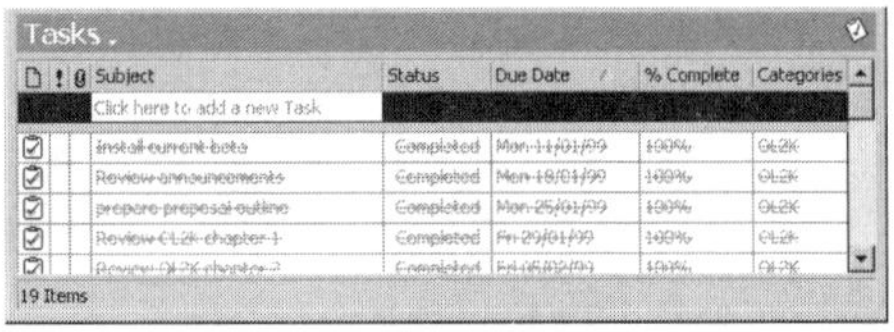

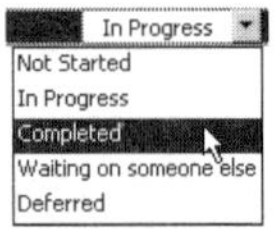

You can view selective lists – eg, the Active tasks which are those not yet completed. Other filtered views show tasks for Next week, Overdue tasks or Completed tasks. If you use categories to identify your projects, you can view by Category to group the tasks for the project. You can also view assigned tasks. All these are list views, but you can also see the tasks on a time line, to give you a better idea of the relative timings of the tasks, or to identify potential conflicts.

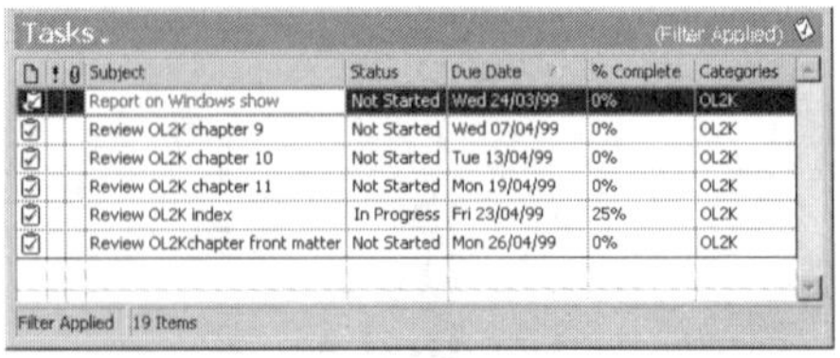

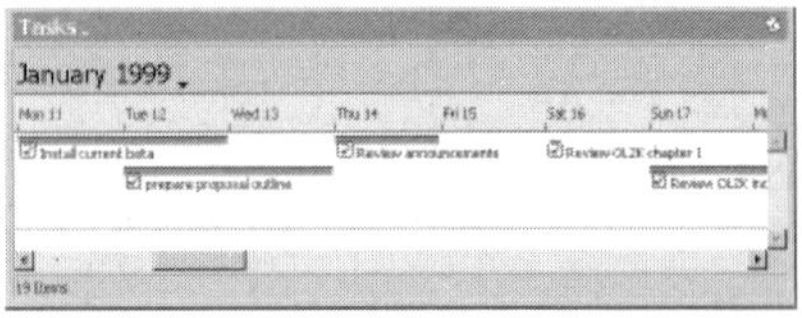

Tasks are tracked by whole days, so a task that starts and ends on the same day does not have any duration on the time line.

Working with tasks

As your project continues, reference the task list to remind yourself what needs to be done next, and update the entries to reflect progress. You may simply tick off activities when they are completed, or you can track intermediate status and update the amount completed.

Reminders only make sense if you sign on to Outlook at least once a day.

As the completion date for a task approaches, you get a reminder (if specified). You are also warned if the date passed without the task being marked complete. There are several possible actions to take:

1. Dismiss (cancel) the reminder. It will not be shown again, but the task will still be outstanding.

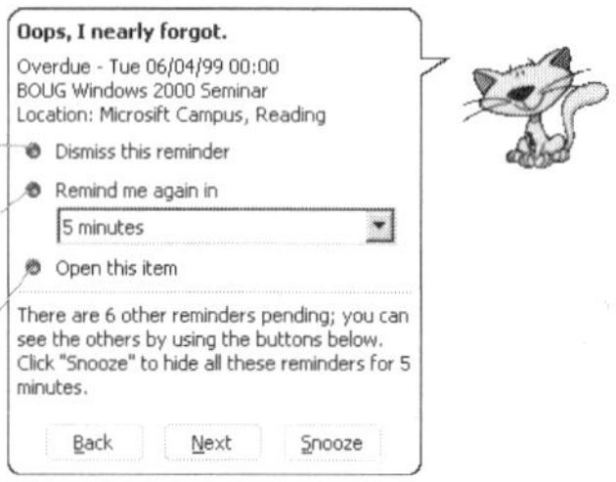

When two or more reminders are active you can scroll back and forward among them.

2. Postpone the reminder, for five minutes or for up to a week.
3. Open the task and update the status. Mark it complete, adjust the completion date, or change other details as appropriate.
4. Right-click the task without opening, for a quick menu of options for dealing with outstanding tasks.

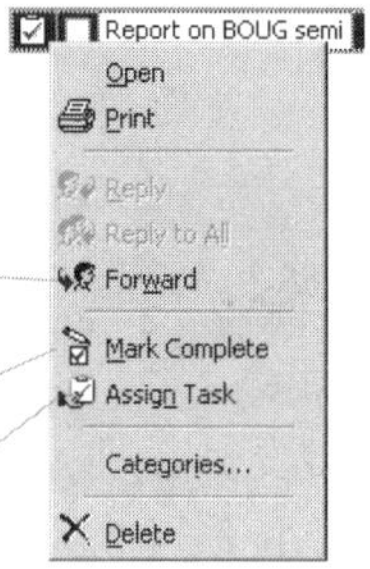

See page 150 for assigning tasks, and page 152–153 for status reports.

5. Forward a status report to anyone who is involved with completing the task.
6. Mark the task as already completed.
7. Assign the task for someone else to work on or complete.

Assigning tasks

You don't necessarily complete all the tasks in your folder yourself. You can define tasks as part of a project and then transfer them to someone else to complete. That person becomes the new owner, if the task assignment is accepted, and will send you updates on the status and notice of completion.

You can right-click the task in the list and choose Assign task.

1. Open the task and press the Assign Task button.

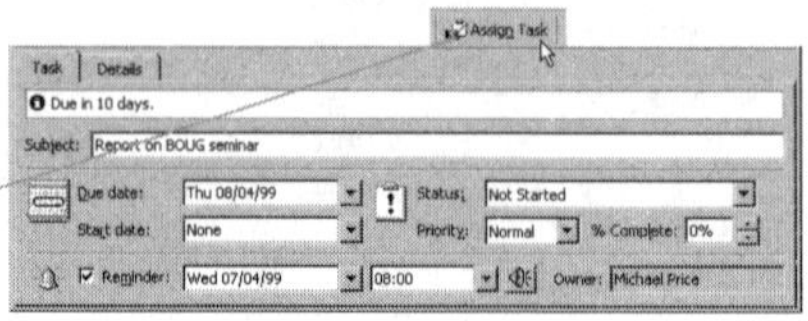

2. Enter the name of the new owner of the task, and add a note if desired.

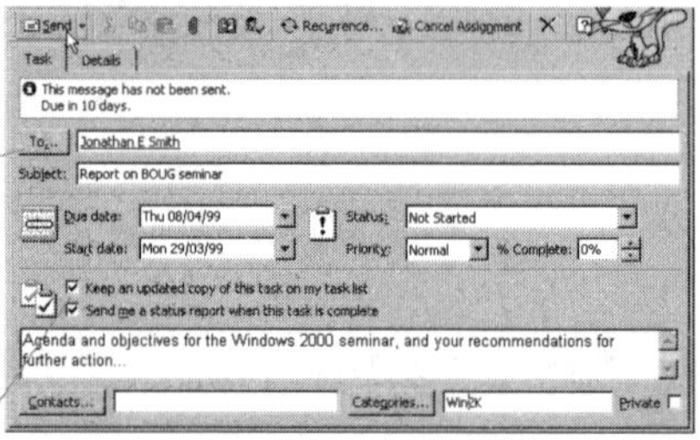

Outlook will switch off any reminders that were set:

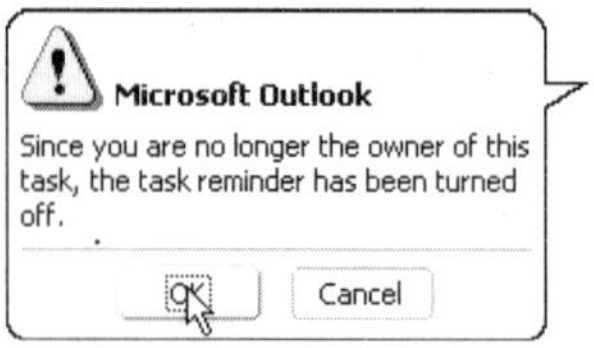

3. Leave a copy of the task in your folder if you want to keep track of the status.

4. Press Send to e-mail the task to the prospective new owner.

5. The icon for the task in the list shows that it has been handed on to someone else.

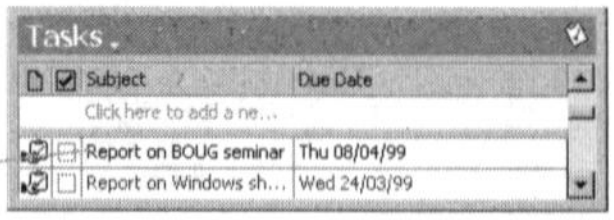

If you do change your mind before the message leaves the Outbox, you can cancel the assignment.

6. You can still open the task, and you will receive status reports and updates, but you won't be able to change any of the details yourself.

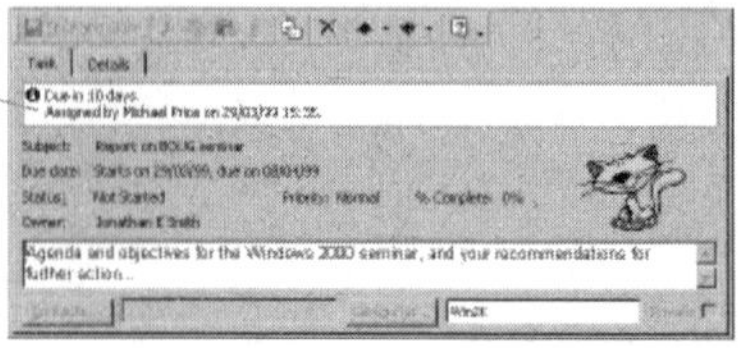

Task assignments arrive as normal mail in the Inbox. When opened, the prospective owner must decide what action to take:

1 Accept the task, and become the new owner.

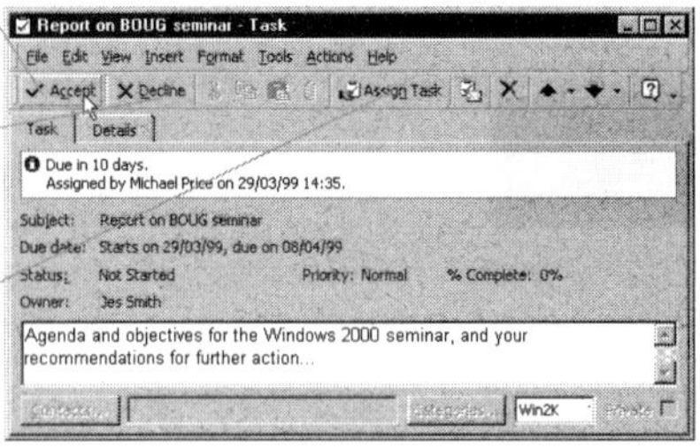

2 Decline the task, and return it to the sender.

3 Assign the task to someone else.

If the proposed owner does not reply, the task will be left in limbo. See page 155 for one way of claiming the task back.

4 The task will be added to the relevant folder, Task, Deleted, or Outbox.

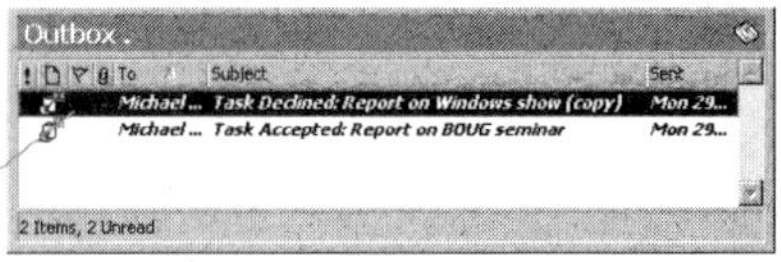

5 Messages are added to the Outbox to tell the sender the actions taken.

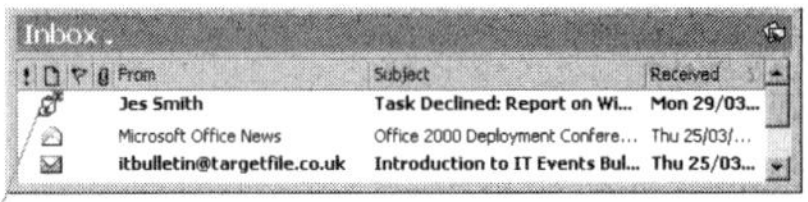

6 When the replies are received, any declined tasks are reassigned to the original owner.

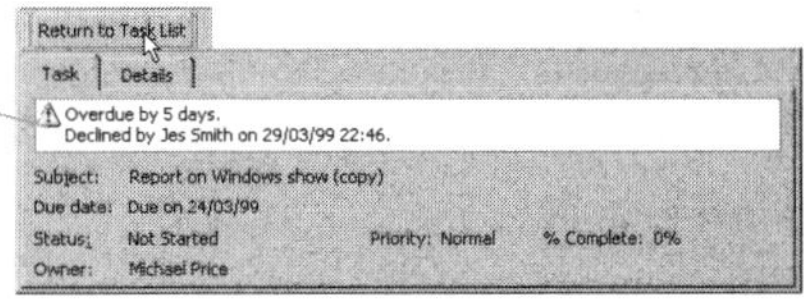

7 The task list shows the final status of the tasks after the assignment.

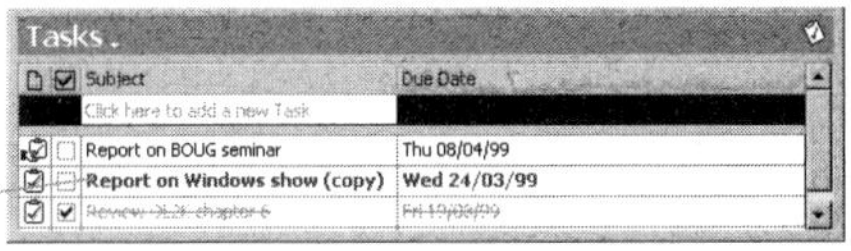

Updating an assigned task

When the new owner makes changes to the status of the assigned task – eg, a change to the % Complete – the change is automatically sent as a notice of update to the original owner, as long as an updated copy of the task was left in the task list. The new owner can also choose to send a status report to the original owner. To update the status of an assigned task:

1 Open the task and update status and % complete fields etc..

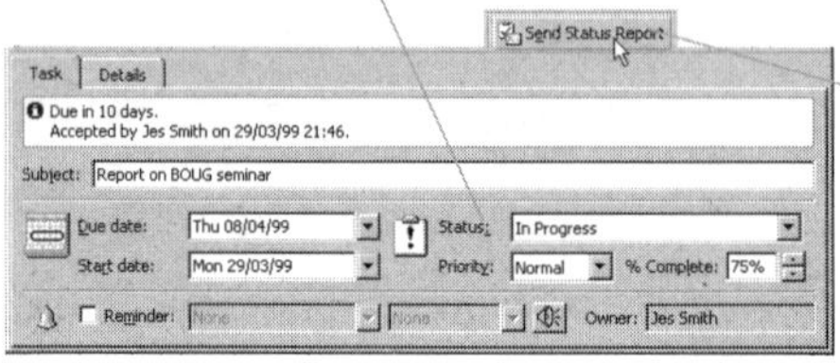

2 Press Send Status Report button to create a report.

3 Outlook generates a report with the latest values for the fields in the task record. You can add comments to this report.

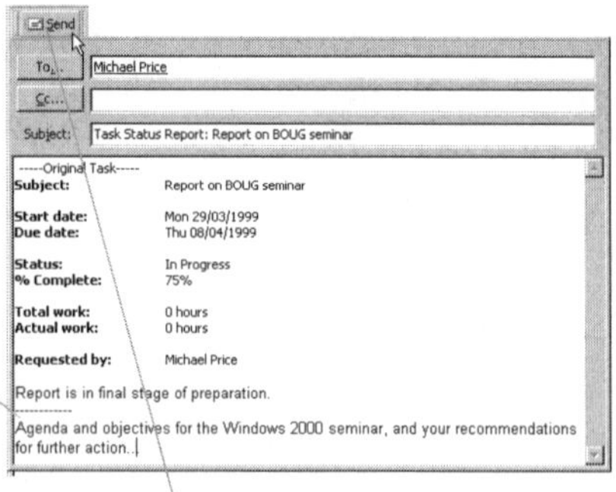

4 Press Send to add the status report to the Outbox for later transmission.

Outlook checks the Inbox for any task update message, adjusts the details in your task list and deletes the message from the Inbox for you.

5 The original owner receives a copy of the status report as normal e-mail, and can reply or forward the report. The entry in the Task list is updated with the latest progress, automatically.

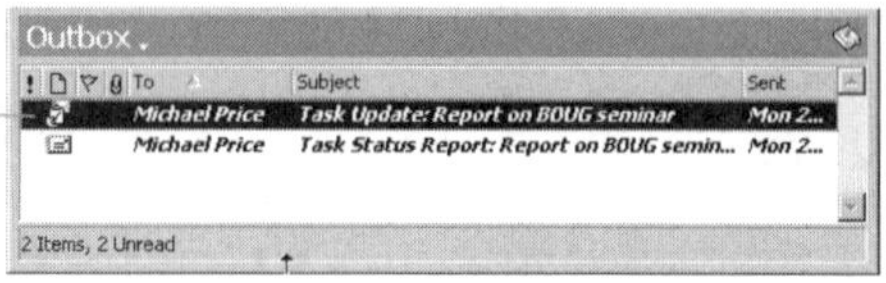

It isn't necessary to own a task to request and receive an update on what's happening.

You can send anyone interested in the project the latest information about its status and progress:

1. When you create a status report, you can add anyone from your mailing list to the To, Cc or Bcc boxes.

2. To send an existing report, open the task, and select Actions, Forward. Enter the names of the recipients. The task becomes an attachment.

Drag any additional tasks from the task list to the text box of the message you are forwarding.

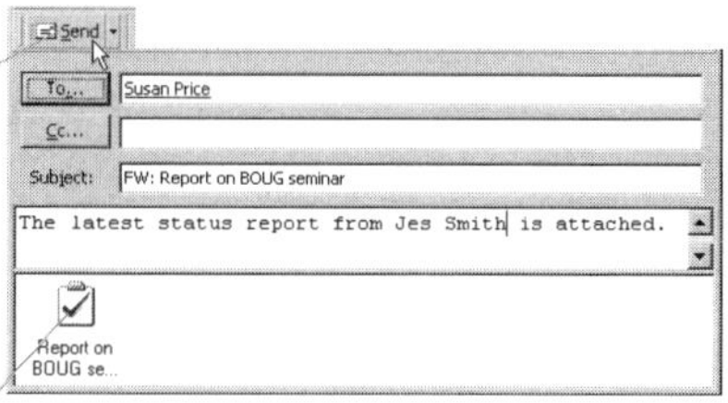

3. Press Send to copy the message to the Outbox ready for transmission.

4. The recipient should double-click the attachment to open the task, and then save it in the Task folder.

If the task has been assigned, the status report or comments can be addressed automatically. They will be sent to anyone who retained an updated copy of the task, or who elected to receive a status report on completion.

5. Open the task, and select Actions, Reply to All to distribute the report.

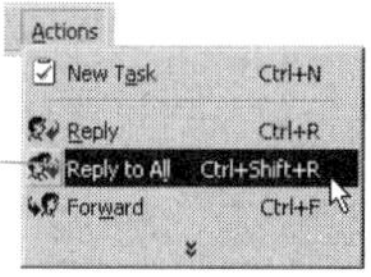

6. If you select the Reply option, your comments are sent to the new owner if you are the original owner, or vice versa if you are the assigned owner.

Keeping more information

For most tasks, all the data fields you need can be found on the Task tab of the input sheet. For simple tasks, just the title and the completion date will suffice.

If the tasks are large or complex, record more detailed statistics, and keep track of the time spent on the task, the people you deal with and the expenses involved. This data is very useful when you assign tasks to people and account for their time. To enter the data, open the task and select the Details tab. You can enter the following fields:

Those neat graphic symbols on the Task input sheet have no function – they are just decorations.

1 Total work: the estimated work effort to complete the task, in hours, days or weeks.

2 Date completed: the final completion date for the task, which may be different from Due date.

3 Actual work: the measured work effort to date, or in total for completed tasks, in hours, days or weeks.

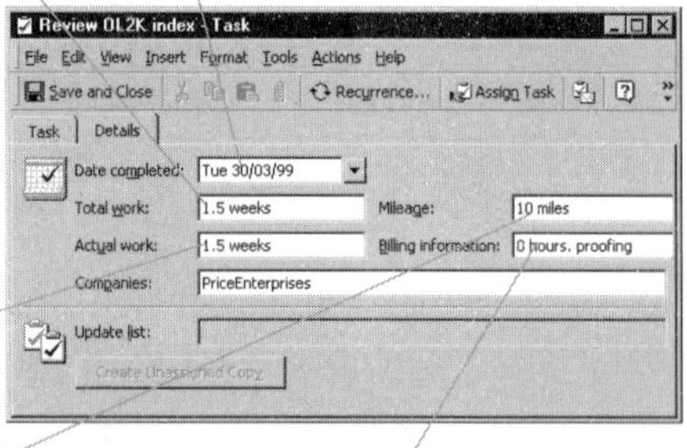

See page opposite for time conversion factors used by Outlook.

4 Mileage: space for mileage or other travel costs and factors, entered as free form text.

5 Billing information: Time or account details for chargeable work related to the task, entered as free form text.

This field is entered as plain text, and does not make use of the Contacts list.

6 Companies: Names of companies and people associated with the task.

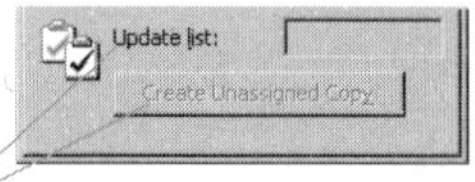

The remaining field, and the Create Unassigned Copy, and are used only with tasks that have been assigned or reassigned.

These two fields are used for assigned tasks only.

To assign a task to several people at once, make copies with similar names rather than reassigning the same task,

7 Update list: The people who keep an updated copy in their task lists. This entry is generated and maintained by Outlook.

8 Create Unassigned Copy: This button is used by the original owner to copy a task and reassign it to another person.

Hours, days and Weeks

When you enter a duration in the total work or actual work fields, Outlook assumes hours, unless you specify the unit as Minutes, days or weeks. No other units are allowed. Outlook converts the values to days or weeks, using factors of 8 hours per day and 40 hours per week. To change these factor values:

1 Select Tools from the Menu bar, click Options, Other tab, and then Advanced Options.

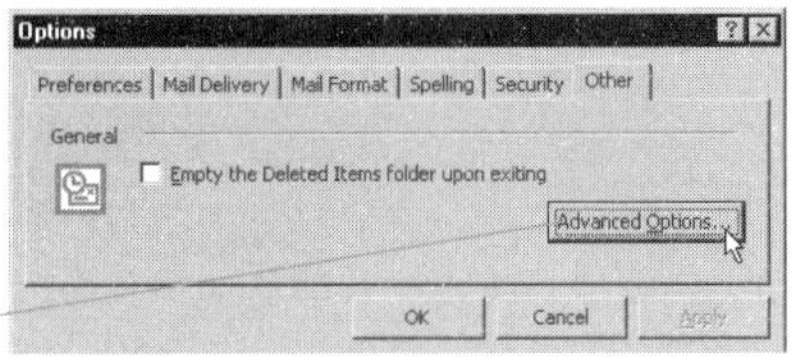

2 Adjust the number of hours in a working day, and the number of hours in a working week to suit your working practices, or to suit a part-time project.

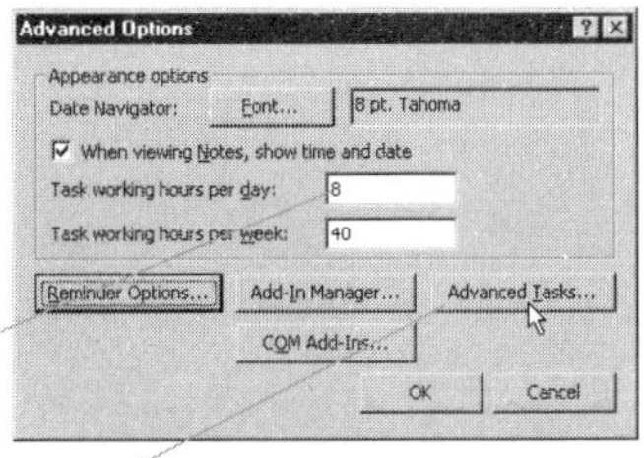

3 Select Advanced tasks, and set the default actions for reminders, assignments and status reports.

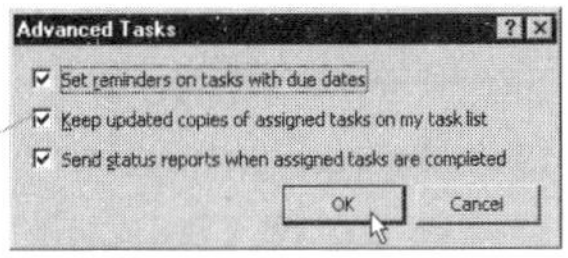

4 To end and save the settings, press OK (for three levels).

Calendar taskpad

The TaskPad in Calendar acts as a mini Task List.

You also find your task list in the TaskPad portion of the Calendar. This is displayed in the Day/Week/Month view. The TaskPad views are a subset of the views you use in Tasks itself. To display and adjust the TaskPad:

1. Click Calendar on the Outlook bar, or in the Today window.

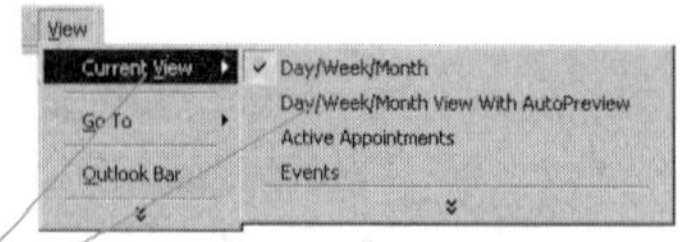

2. Make sure that the Current View for Calendar is Day/ Week/Month and then select TaskPad View.

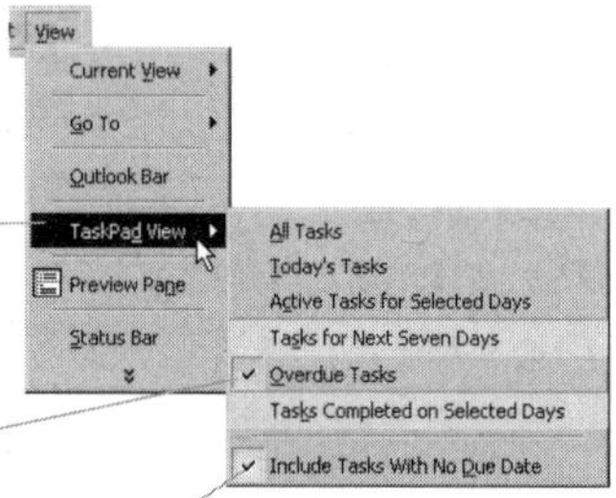

3. Select the view you want to see in the TaskPad.

4. Decide if you want to display tasks with no due date set.

You can display all the tasks in the list, or just today's tasks, and distinguish between active, completed and overdue Tasks. You can make changes to your task list straight from TaskPad:

Changes or additions that you make in the TaskPad will show up in the full Tasks list also.

5. Create new tasks by entering the subject here.

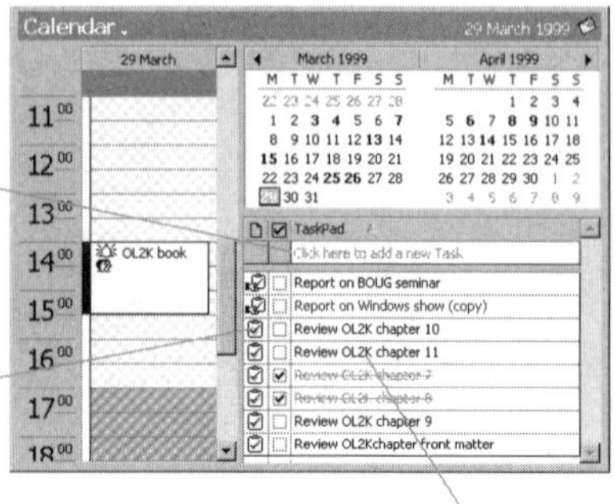

6. Amend the subject title or status of existing tasks.

7. Double-click the task title to open it and make changes.

Outlook Today tasks

Visit the Today page at the end of the day to rapidly mark off all the tasks that have been completed that day.

You don't have to open the Tasks list or the TaskPad to update the status of your tasks. The Outlook Today window carries an abbreviated task list. There are just a couple of options for this list. To choose the one you want:

1. On the Outlook Today window, select Customize Outlook Today.

2. 'All tasks' shows a list of all incomplete tasks. 'Today's tasks' shows a list of the tasks due today, together with any overdue tasks, and (optionally) those with no due date specified.

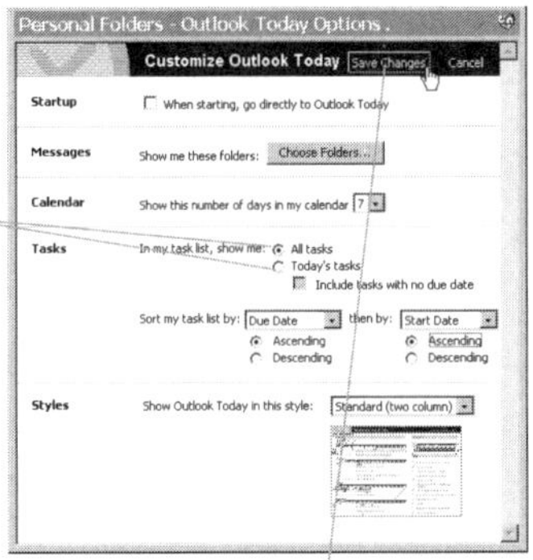

Sort the task list by up to two fields, in ascending order or descending.

3. Select the type of list you want and click Save Changes to record the changes and put them into effect.

4. Overdue tasks, past the due date without being marked complete, show in red. Click the box to update the task status. A tick marks it as completed (the title is struck through to emphasise this). Blank means that the task is incomplete.

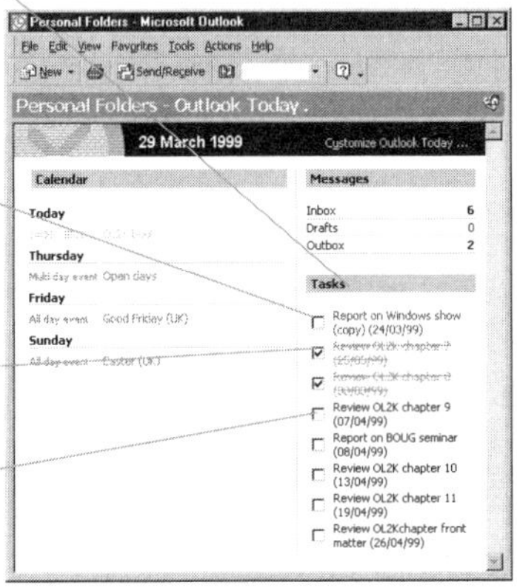

You can select different views for Outlook Today, with one, two or three columns, or using the Summer or Winter layouts.

To make any other changes to a particular task, double-click the task title and open the detailed input sheet. Click Task or the Task button to open the full task list if you have several tasks to update.

Scheduling task time

Let the Task list help you set up your Calendar to set up meetings and allocate work time.

When you have defined a task, you can use the entry in the TaskPad to help you to set aside time in your Calendar to complete the task.

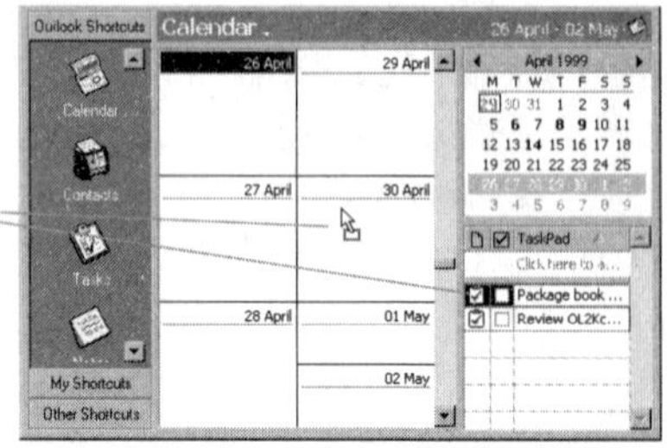

1. Select the task and drag it onto the Calendar page.
2. Release the task and the Appointment panel opens automatically.

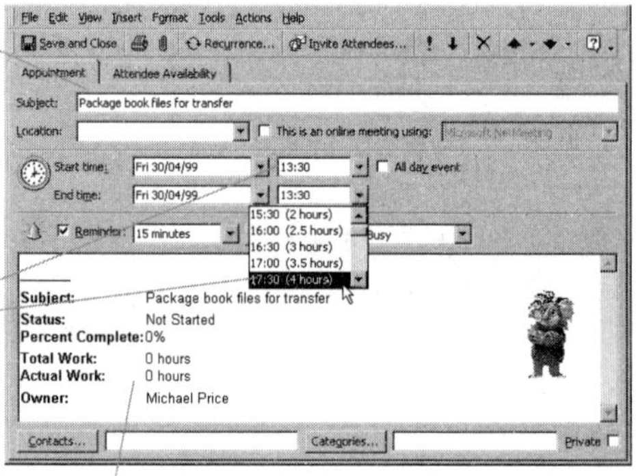

3. Select the start time and the duration, and make any other changes to the appointment definition.
4. The status information for the task is added to the appointment, as the comment field.

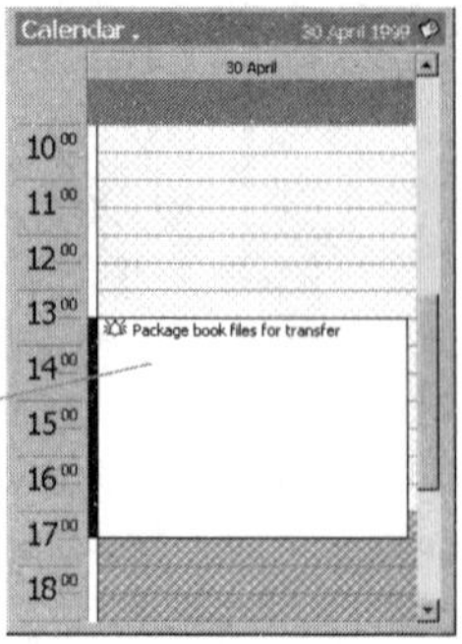

5. Press Save and Close to enter the appointment into the Calendar, and so reserve the time for the activity.

Alternatively, you can drag tasks from the full Tasks display and drop them onto the Calendar icon on the Outlook bar. This again opens the appointments panel, and you can specify the start date and time and the other information needed to describe the scheduled work item.

Journal activities

Outlook keeps track of your communications, whatever form they take, using the Journal. It also tracks activities by contacts. If these records don't tell you all about your projects, you can use Notes to complete the details.

Covers

Chapter Ten

Configuring the Journal

The Journal is a folder within Outlook which records the times of meetings, phone calls, message responses and other activities related to your project. It is really a kind of log book, since it deals with the start and stop times and other relevant (if minor) details of the item being recorded, rather than with the contents themselves.

You don't have to supply all these details yourself since it will automatically record Outlook items, including e-mail messages, meetings and tasks, for the contacts you specify. It can also record the work you do on Microsoft Office items, including database, spreadsheet, reports, presentations and documents.

Journal starts out inactive. It becomes inactive also when you deselect all items.

For items and contacts that are not being automatically logged, you can add details manually. This means that you can include other types of activities or work items, not just the ones Outlook knows about.

To specify the criteria and start recording:

1. Select Journal from the Outlook bar.

2. If Journal is inactive at this time, Outlook offers to turn the Journal on. Press No to view existing Journal entries, or press Yes to display Journal Options.

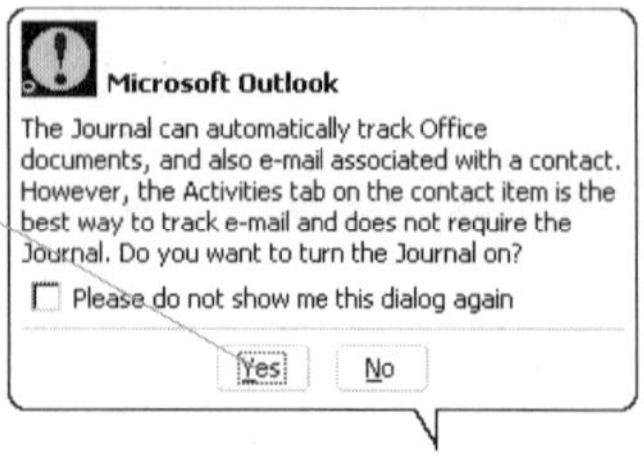

3. If Journal is already active, but you want to change the criteria, select Tools from the Menu bar, then Options, click the Preferences tab and then the Journal Options button.

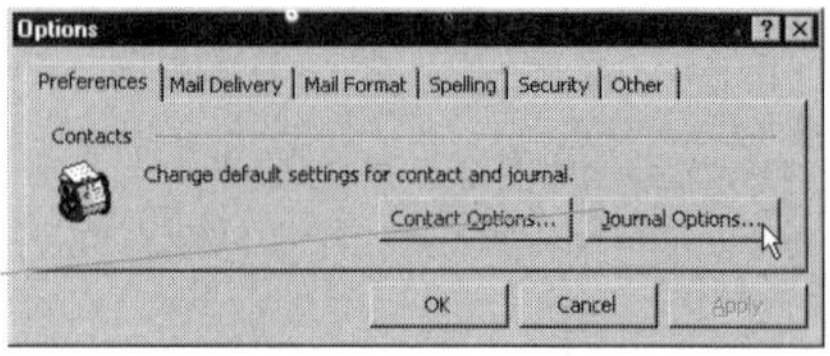

Set up or change the items and contacts that are recorded in the Journal.

4 Select the types of items and the Contacts for whom you want these items recorded.

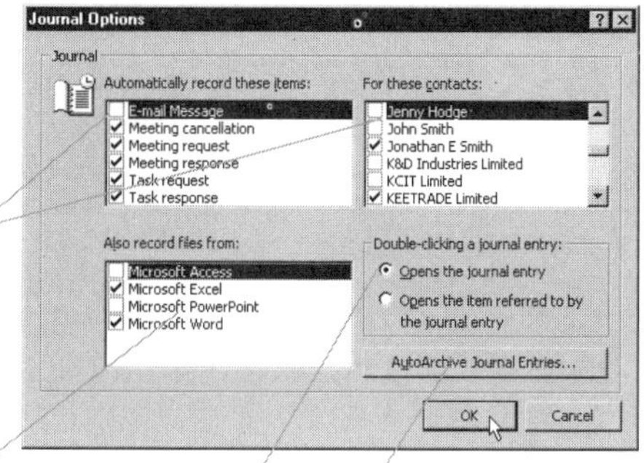

5 Choose the types of Office documents you want to record in the Journal.

The first time you select Auto Archive, you may need to insert the Office 2000 CD, to complete the installation.

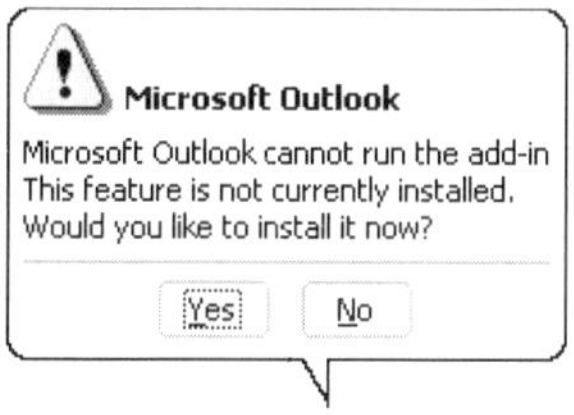

6 Choose the action to take when you double-click an entry in the Journal.

7 Press the AutoArchive button to specify what happens to older Journal entries, and when you archive or delete them.

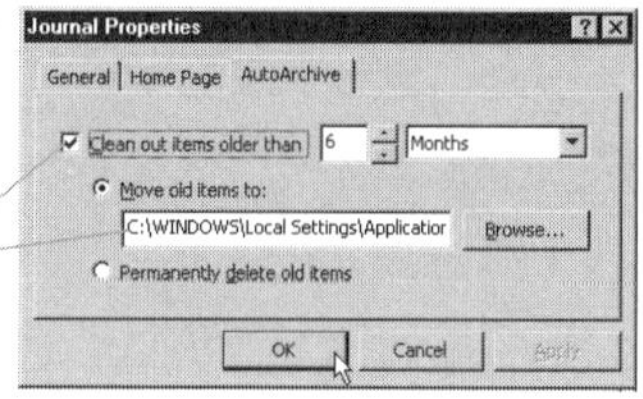

You can track activities by contact name without using the Journal. To see the details recorded for a particular contact:

Outlook reminds you when you start the Journal that you can track e-mail and activities by contacts without the Journal. See page 166 for more details.

8 Locate the entry in the Contacts folder, and double-click to open it. Select the Activities tab.

9 Choose the type of Outlook item to display, or select All Items. The list of relevant activities is shown.

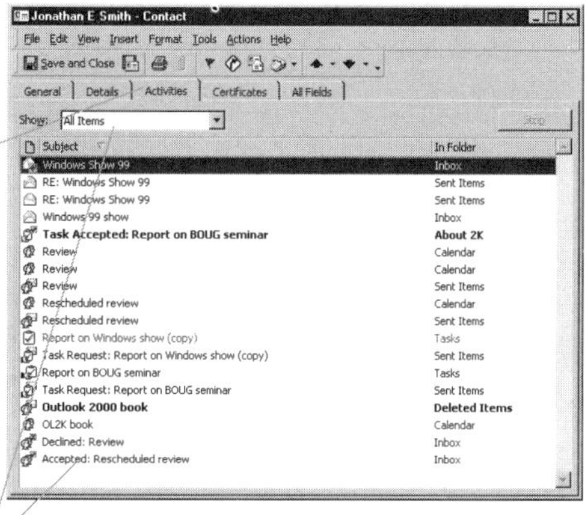

Viewing Journal entries

As with all the Outlook functions, you can change the manner in which items are displayed.

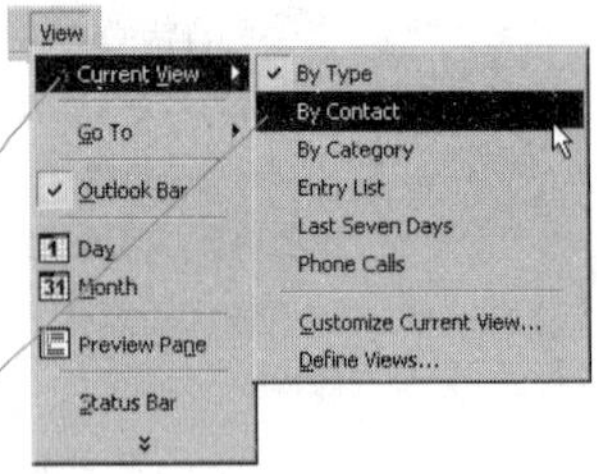

1 Select View from the Menu bar, and then click Current View.

2 Select another view, for example By Contact.

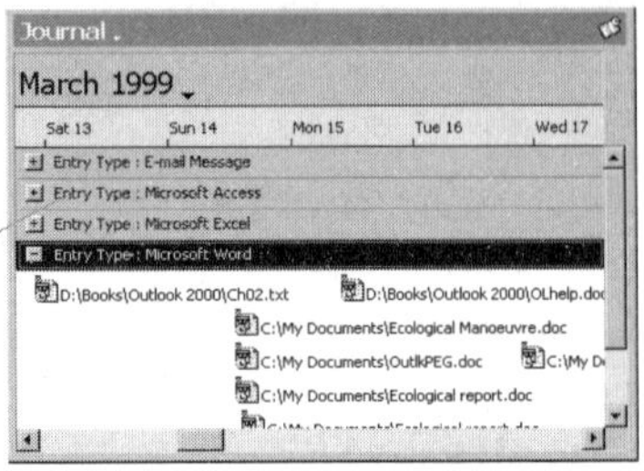

This groups the entries in a time line view, as do the By Type and By Category views. You can specify a range of a day, a week or a month at a time.

The items can also be displayed in a list or table format, with columns for the entry type, subject, start, duration, contact and category of item. You can view the full list, or just the entries for the last seven days.

3 Select View, Current View, Entry List.

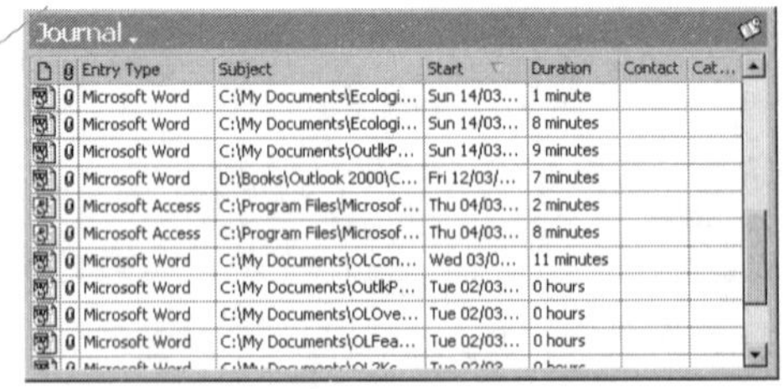

You can Filter the list to restrict the entries, and make it easier to spot the records you are interested in. To apply a filter to the journal, choose the view, then:

4 Select View, Current View. Customise Current View, and click the Filter button.

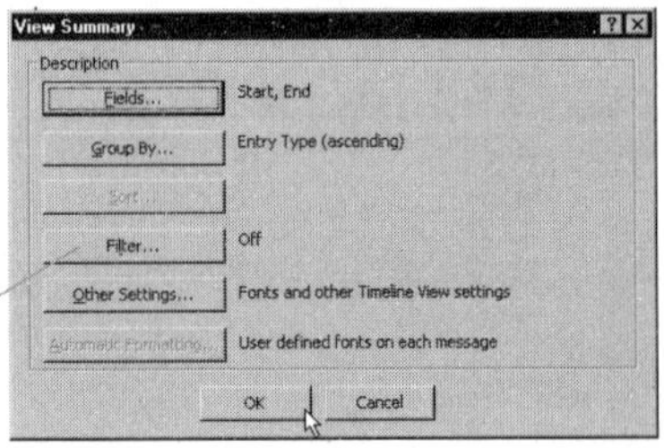

Journal symbols and meanings

Journal uses Outlook symbols to identify the types of items shown in the time line views and in the item lists.

Symbols like these are used for item lists in the Calendar, Contacts, Inbox and Tasks views.

Appointment in your calendar

Appointment or meeting request or response

Conversation record or informal meeting

Document record (manual or nonspecific type)

E-mail message sent or received

Fax message sent or received

Letter sent or received

Microsoft Access database activity record

Microsoft Excel workbook activity

Microsoft Office Binder report activity

Microsoft PowerPoint presentation work

Microsoft Word document preparation

Outlook Note record of activity

Phone call record, including timed calls

Task record

Task request or task response record

Indicates Journal item with an attachment

Manual recording

To record a journal entry for any item:

1 Open the folder that contains the entry you wish to record.

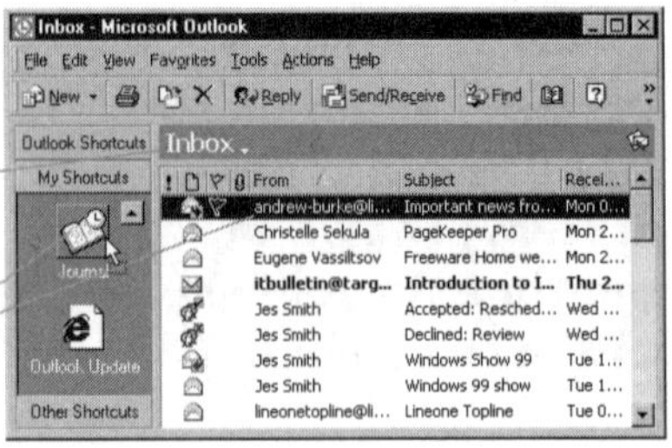

2 Select the item and drag it to Journal on the Outlook bar.

A shortcut to the item is added to the Journal entry. This may become invalid if the item gets moved or deleted later.

The Subject, Entry type, Contact, and Company boxes and other data are extracted from the item. You can supplement or amend any of this information. For example, add a category to group the records.

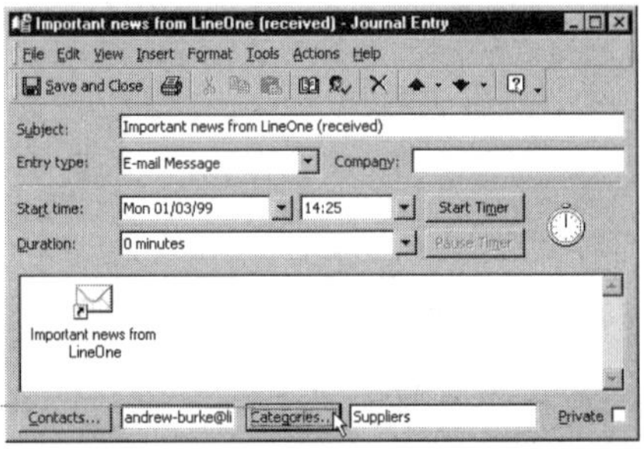

3 Click Save and close to record the entry in the Journal.

If you want to create a new journal entry, but you don't have an initial item to start from, you can create a new record from scratch:

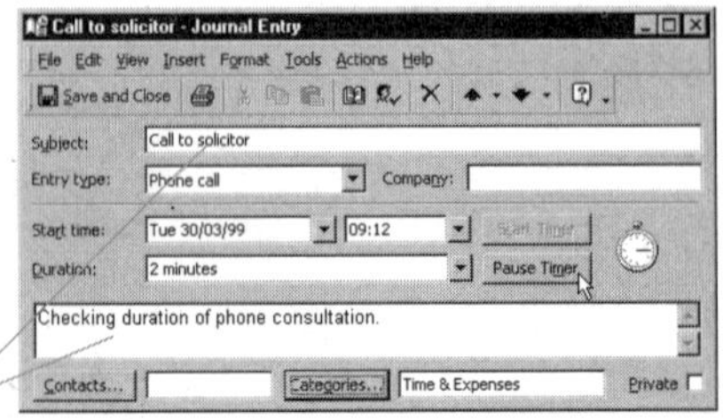

4 Open Journal and press the New Journal entry button.

5 Enter the subject, entry type, contact, time, or any other details you have available.

When you make a phone call or hold a meeting with clients, create a journal entry to record the event. Use the Start Timer and Pause Timer buttons to record the duration.

6 When you've entered all the details, press Save and Close to end and record the entry.

Using the Journal

The way you use the Journal depends on the type of projects you undertake, and the extent to which other people or other organisations are involved.

Journal entries may supplement the normal methods of tracking progress through the Outlook folders, by collecting information on specific types of activity or by concentrating on a certain contact. Such records will be useful for billable work, as an audit trail to support your charges, or to provide evidence when you need to challenge an invoice.

Use selective Journal entries to supplement the Outlook folders.

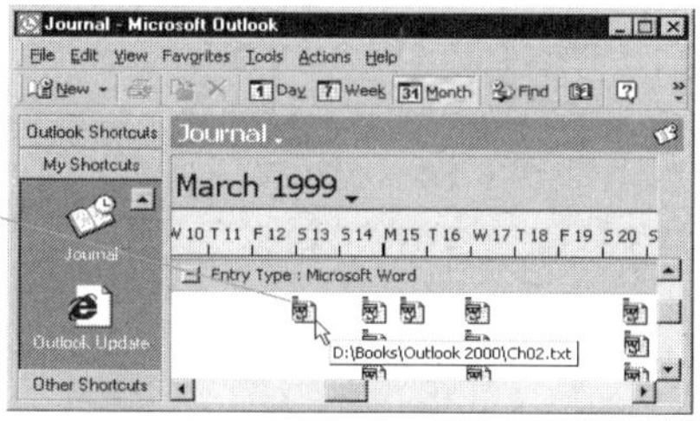

Another approach to the Journal is to allow it to capture all activities. You would not expect to review the data on a regular basis, but you could use them to analyse the overall activity, or to investigate issues such as how much time or attention you have devoted to a particular topic. For example, to see how much effort a particular document has required:

If you record everything, don't forget to archive or discard older records.

1. Select View, Current View and Customise Current View.

2. Choose Filter, and enter enough of the name to identify all related documents. Press OK (twice) to build the view.

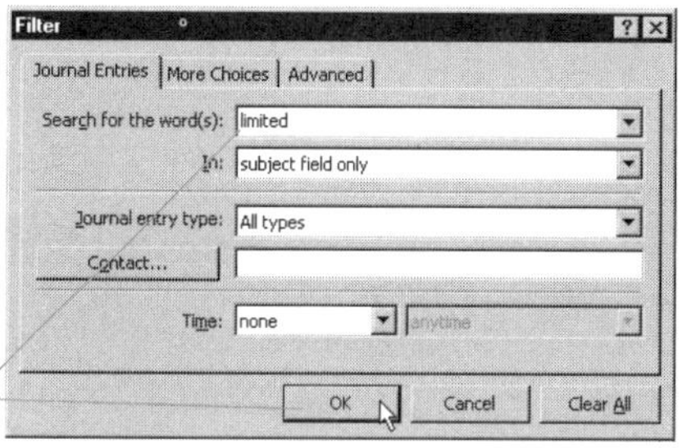

The list will show you how often you've referenced the document, and just how long you've spent reviewing or editing the text.

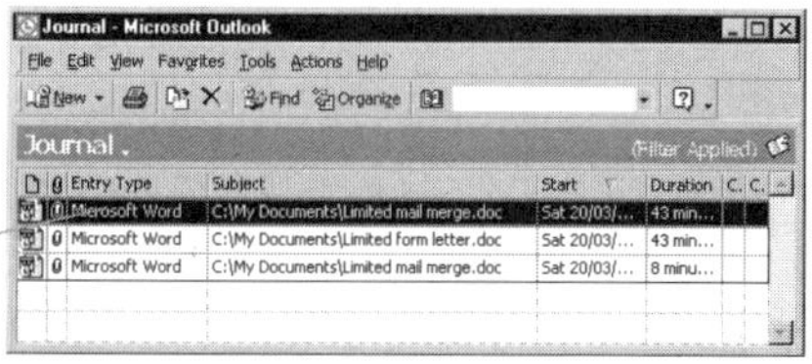

Contact activities

In Outlook 2000 it is no longer necessary to use the Journal to track tasks, appointments, e-mail, notes, or documents related to a contact. You can link any Outlook item or document to the contact, when you create the item. You can also link existing items or documents to the contact.

Hold down Shift or Ctrl as you select the contacts to select multiple contacts.

To link a new item to a contact:

1. Create an Outlook item such as an e-mail message.

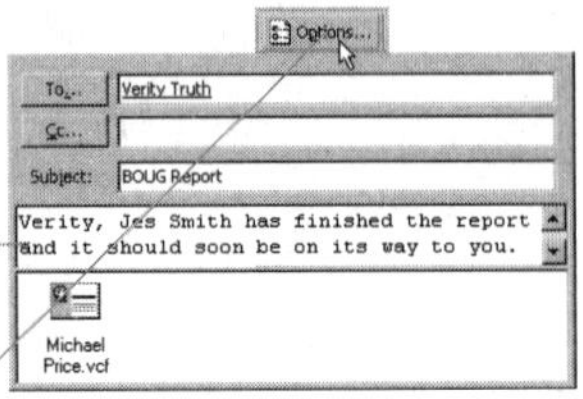

2. In the message, click Options, and then click the Contacts button.

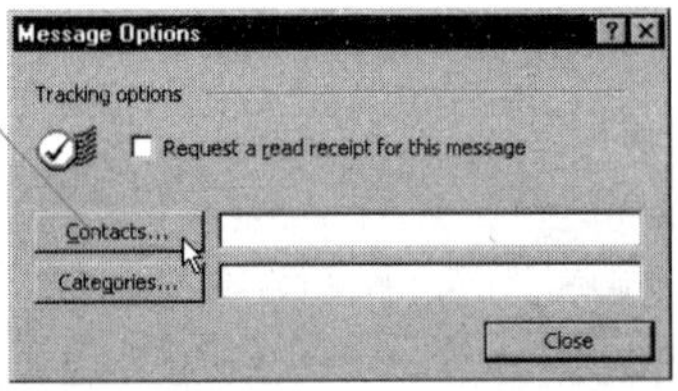

3. Other Outlook items have the Contacts field already displayed, so you'd click Contacts immediately.

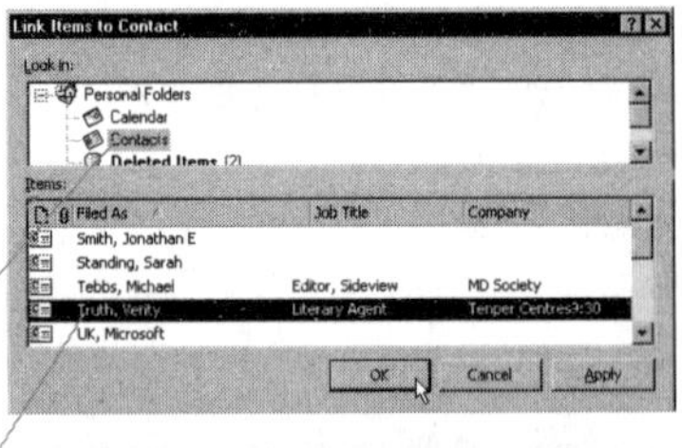

4. From the 'Look in' list, click the Contacts folder, or other folder that contains the relevant contact.

5. In the Items list, click the contact or contacts you want to link to.

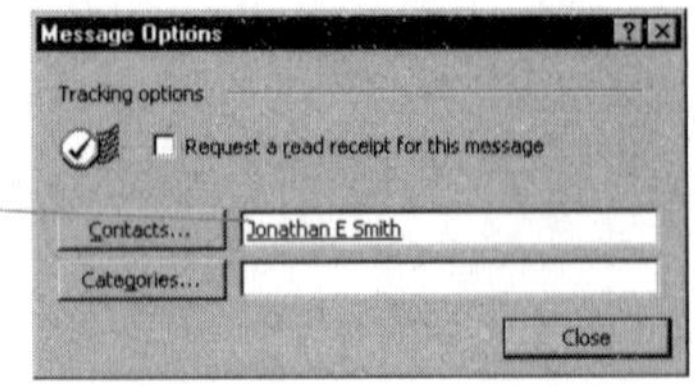

Suppose that there is an existing item, such as an appointment. This may already have a contact linked to it, or the Contact field may be blank.

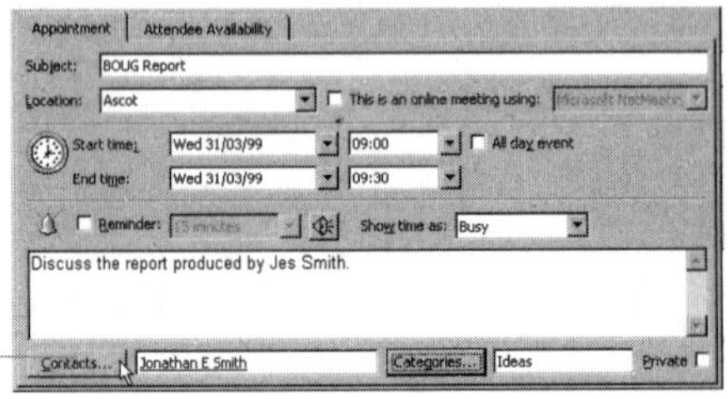

In either case, to link the item to a new contact:

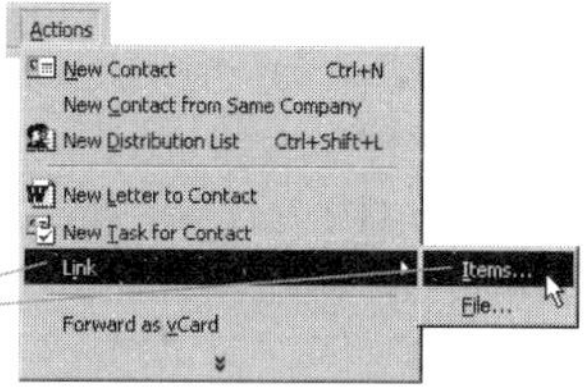

1. Open the contact you want to link items to.
2. Select Actions from the menu bar, click Link, and then Items.

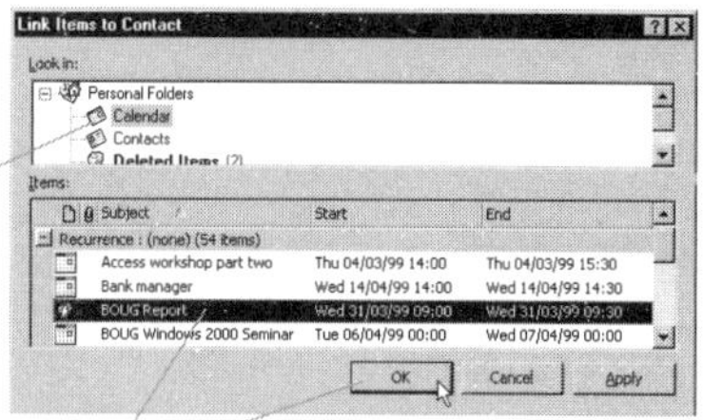

3. From the Look in box, select the folder that contains the item.
4. From the Items list, select the item or items you want to link to the contact and click OK.

You can open a contact from any item that's linked to it by double-clicking the contact name in the Contacts box in the item details.

To link a document to a new contact:

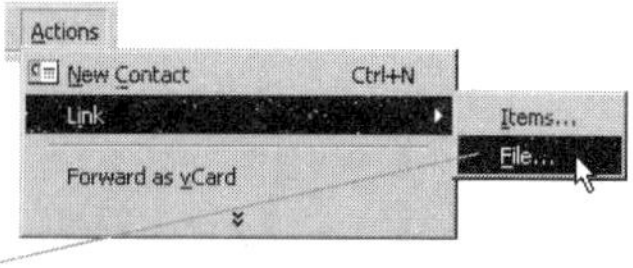

1. Select Actions as before but this time click the File entry.

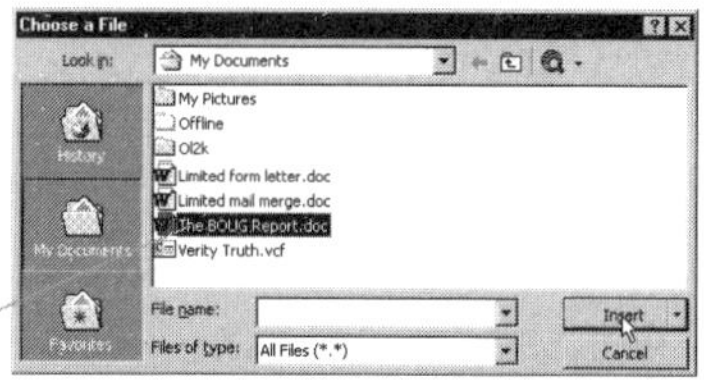

2. From the Choose file box, locate and double-click the file you want to link to the contact.

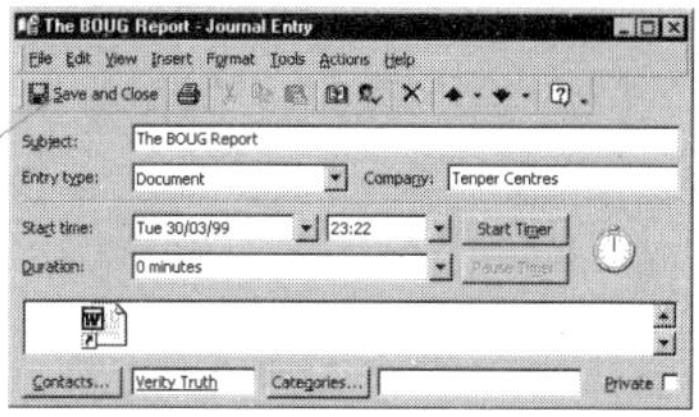

3. Click Save and Close to record the Journal item that this generates.

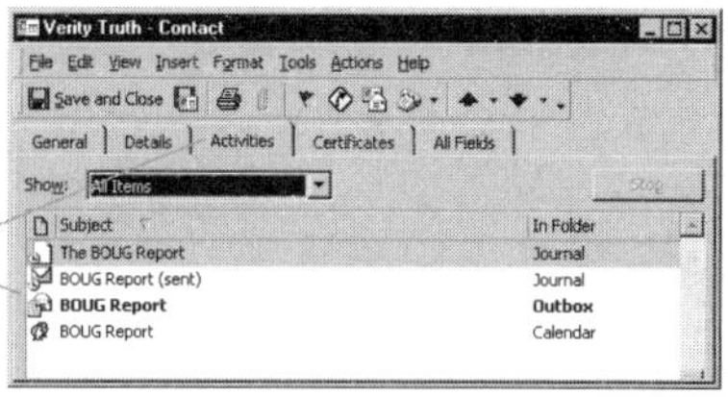

Open the contact and click the Activities tab to see the links that have been set up.

Outlook Notes

Notes are often brief reminders but you can make them as long as you like.

If messages, reminders and Journal entries are not enough, you can always write yourself a Note. Outlook Notes are the PC equivalent of the ubiquitous sticky notes, and even come in a variety of colours, yellow included. Notes can contain memory joggers, phone numbers, names or anything that you want to make a point of remembering. Notes are saved in an Outlook folder or you can leave notes open on the screen.

To create a note:

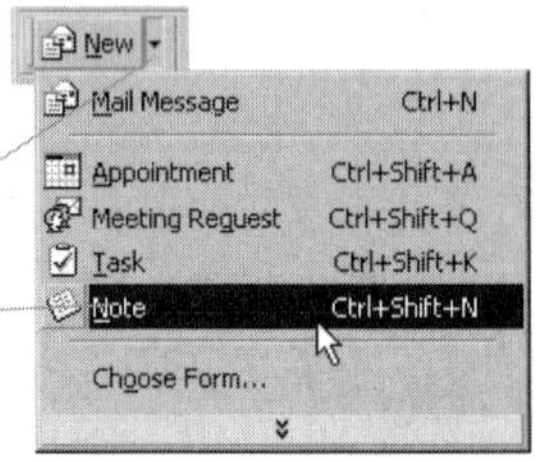

1 Click the down-arrow next to the New Items button, and select Note.

2 Type the text of the note.

3 Click on the taskbar to redisplay an open note.

4 Click the Close button to close the note window.

Notes are created in a standard window which you can move, resize or overlay with other windows. Each open note has a taskbar entry.

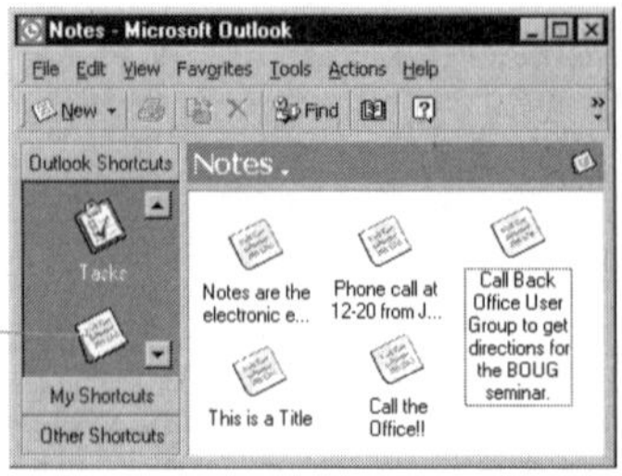

5 Select Notes from the Outlook bar.

Your notes appear as icons in the folder. The contents form the icon name. You can generate an explicit title by pressing Enter while creating the note. In that case, only the text before the first Enter is used. As usual, Windows abbreviates long names (except for the selected icon).

Working with Notes

Drag a note to the Windows Desktop and drop it there, so it will be seen when you start up the system.

Unlike reminders attached to tasks and meetings, the Notes do not display automatically, so you need to visit the folder to check them. To open one or more notes:

1 Press Notes from the Outlook bar.

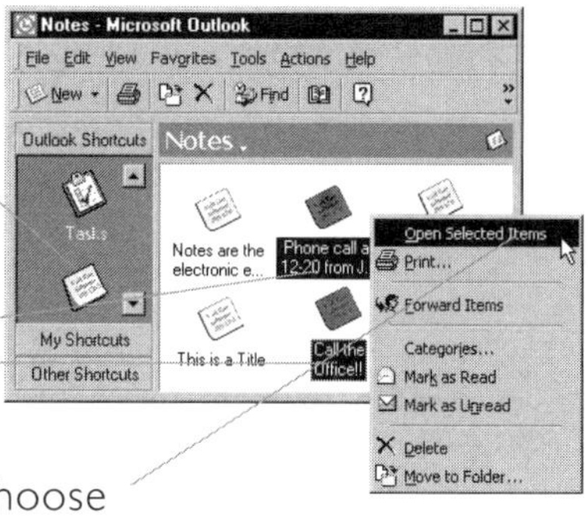

2 Select a note, or use Shift or Ctrl keys for a set of notes.

3 Right-click the selection and choose Open Selected Items.

Edit the text in the open note, to add to or change the contents. All the changes are written to the note in the folder. There is no need to save the contents. You can change the size of the note by dragging an edge or a corner. Move the note around the screen by dragging the title heading.

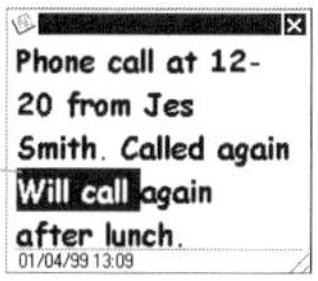

To see a list of other actions that you can perform on the open note:

4 Left-click the Control menu button on the note window to display the list of commands that are available.

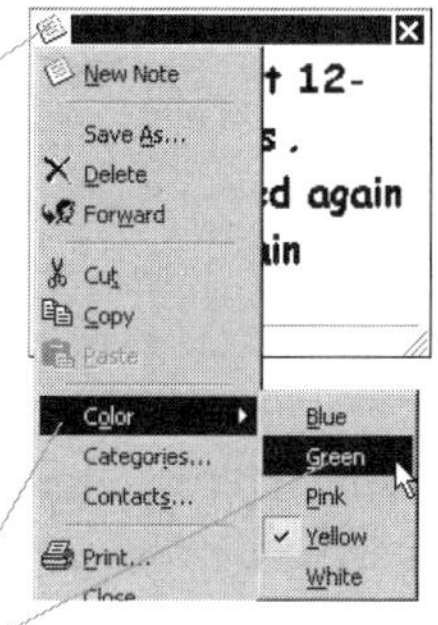

5 Select one of the actions. For example, you can choose a different background colour for the note. Copy and paste functions are also supported, though for unformatted text only.

Note settings

As well as changing the style of individual notes, you can specify the colour, size, and fonts to use for new notes. To view or change the settings:

1. Select Tools from the Menu bar, click Options, click the Preferences tab and choose the Note Options.

2. Pick the background colour for new notes (blue, green, pink, yellow or white). Existing notes won't be affected.

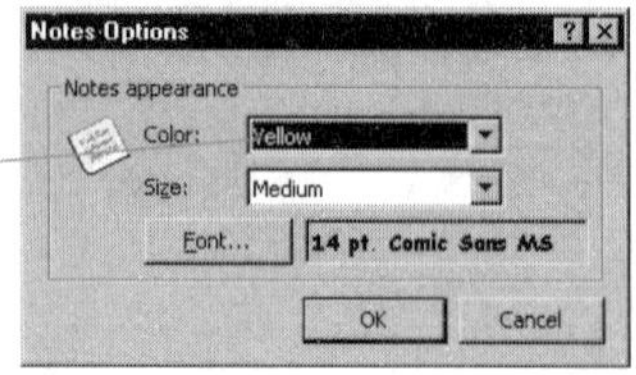

3. Choose the initial size for new notes (Small, Medium or Large).

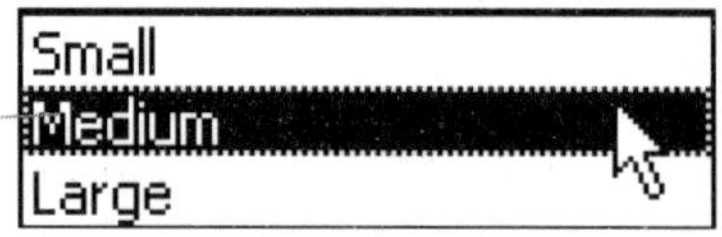

HOT TIP **Create a new note, and copy/paste from the old note, if you want to display it in a different font.**

4. Check the font settings. You can use any Windows font, and specify the style, size, colour and effects. The font settings are used for the whole of the contents, and they cannot be changed once the note is created.

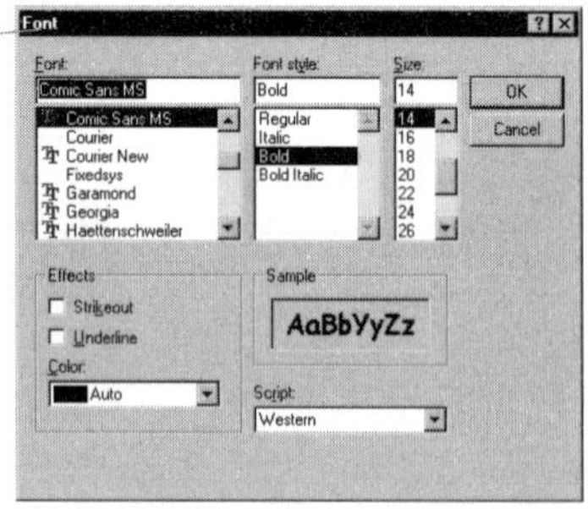

HOT TIP **Show or hide the time and date on notes. This applies immediately on all notes, including any open notes.**

5. Click Tools on the Menu bar, then Options, select the Other tab and press the Advanced Options button.

6. Clear or check the box in Appearance options to hide or show the date and time.

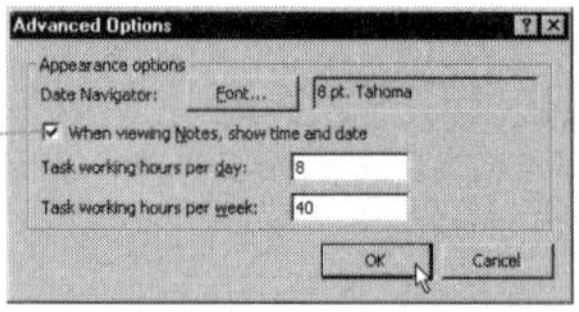

Viewing Notes

You can organise the way the Notes folder is arranged, using the View menu:

1 Select View from the Menu bar, then Current View, and choose the Icons view or one of the table views.

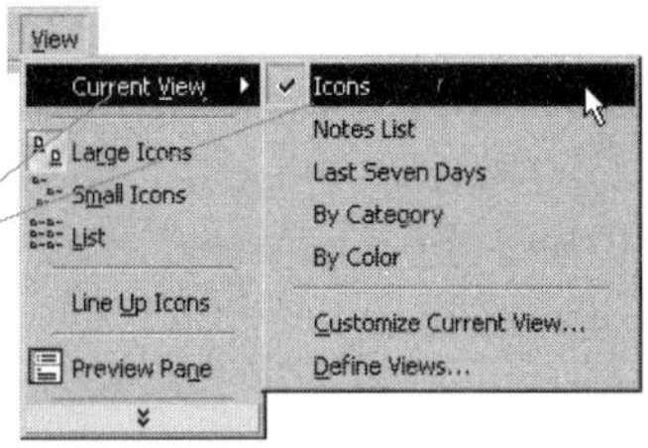

2 Show the notes as icons with the contents as title.

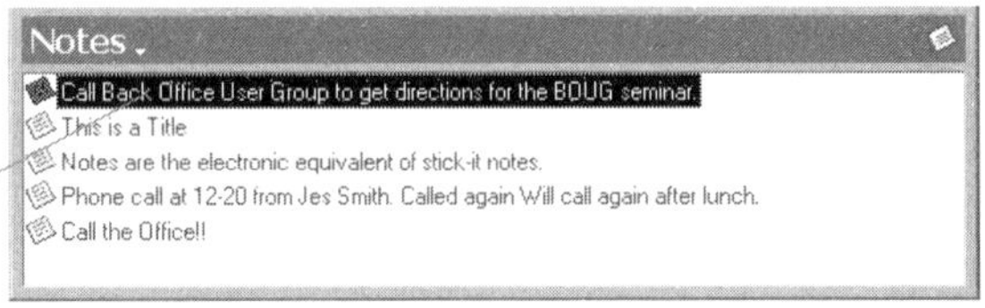

Choose large or small icons, or icons in a list.

3 The Note table lists the title, creation date and category for each note, and also offers an autopreview which shows the first three lines of each note.

4 You can restrict the list to show only those notes that were created within the last seven days.

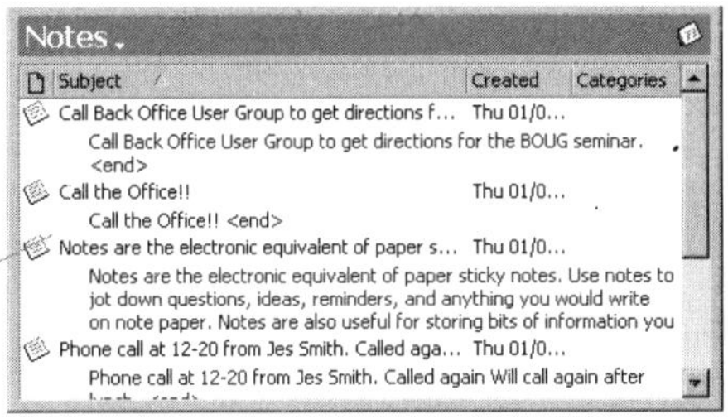

5 You can also display the lists grouped by category or by colour. This of course presumes that you have used categories or colours to classify your notes.

Select View, Current View, and Customise the current view to apply sorts and filters, or to change the fields displayed in the lists in the table views.

HOT TIP **Colour coding is a simple but effective way to separate business and personal notes.**

Starting up with Notes

Check your notes every time you start Outlook, so you can check for action items.

1 Click Tools, Options, select the Other tab and press the Advanced Options button.

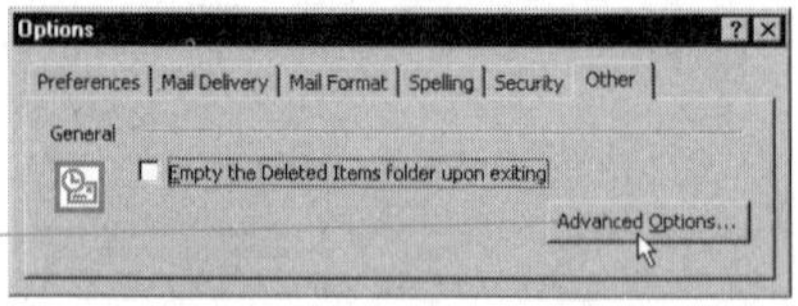

2 You can choose to start up in any of the main Outlook folders: Today; Inbox; Calendar etc..

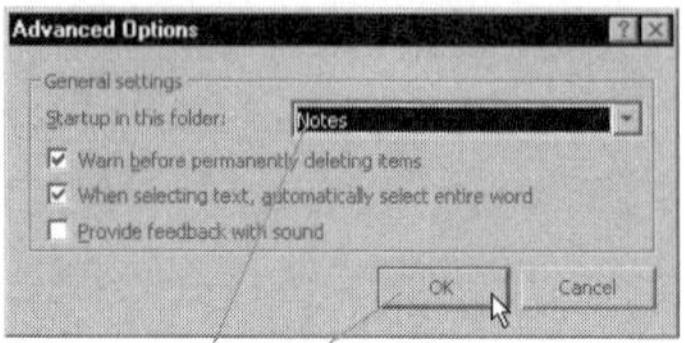

3 Choose to start up in the Notes folder, and click OK to save and end.

Leave a note for yourself without having to run the full Outlook.

Add a note for yourself or the next Outlook user, on screen and in the Notes folder. This uses a shortcut to Outlook with the appropriate startup parameter.

1 Find Outlook.exe and create a shortcut on the Windows Desktop.

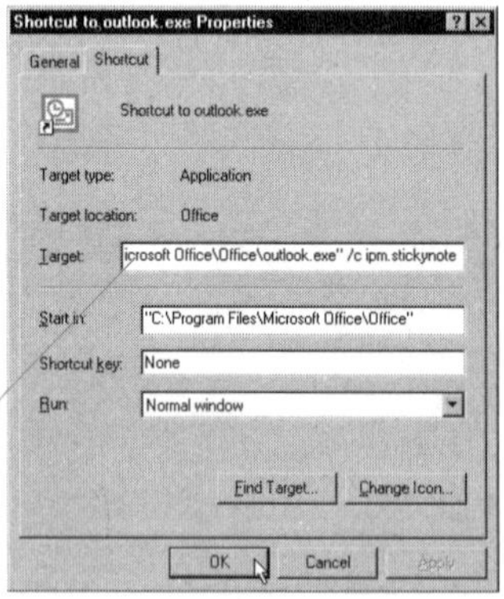

2 Right-click the shortcut and select the Properties command.

3 Add the following parameter to the Target program execution line:
/c ipm.stickynote

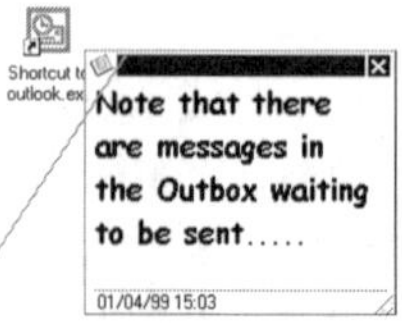

4 Double-click the modified shortcut, and start up with a blank note sheet. Enter your message and leave it on the screen or in the Note folder.

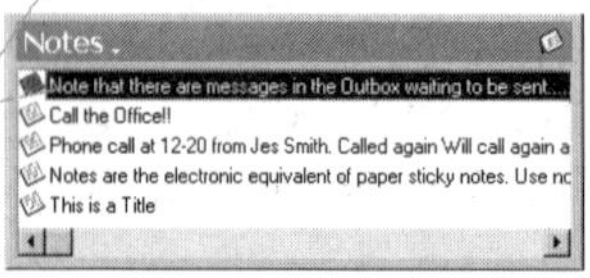

Add-in extras

Add-ins and extra applications extend existing functions and add new capabilities to Outlook. They include Forms Design, Net Folders and WinFax, supplied with Outlook, but there are many others available from Microsoft and other Internet sites, as free or shareware products.

Covers

Chapter Eleven

Add-in components

Parts of Outlook will be reserved until the first time you have a need for them, and then they are installed.

Outlook uses the Microsoft Fax from windows with the CW e-mail service.

Some features of Outlook are omitted from minimum or standard Setup, and some are not even included for the full Setup. However, in many cases, the links to the extra features are already in place, and they can be installed on first use, or added later using the maintenance wizard to transfer the new components.

This applies to components such as:

- Animated office assistants.
- Development Tools for form design and Outlook Visual Basic.
- Expression Service support for creating formulas in custom fields.
- Net Folders for sharing information without a network server.
- Stationery for e-mail and fax.
- Symantec WinFax Starter Edition fax program.

When you select one of these components for the first time:

1. Outlook recognises that the feature is not yet installed. Insert the Office 2000 or Outlook 2000 CD and click Yes.

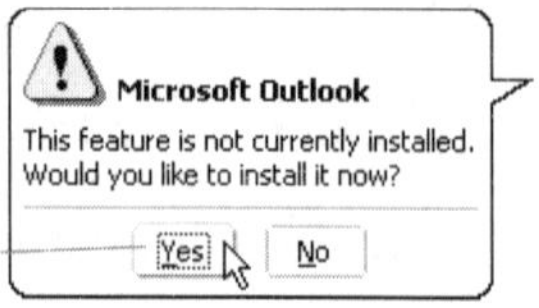

2. The required files are copied, and the feature is installed.

3. Follow the instructions to complete the installation. You may be requested to restart Outlook or restart Windows to activate the feature.

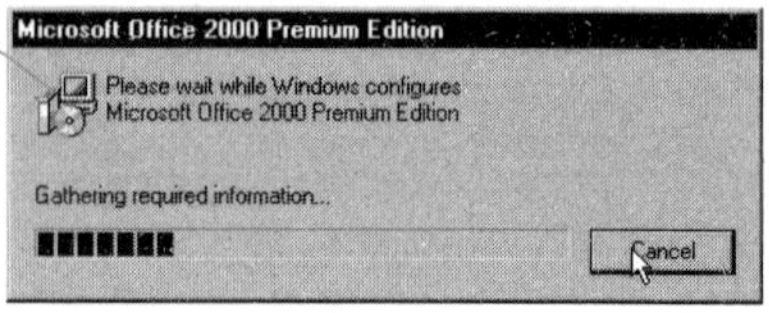

Sometimes you need to take explicit action to install or activate a new application or function in Outlook.

When you install new components, you may need to activate them in the Add-in manager, by clicking the relevant box.

Some of these are mutually exclusive, for example, they may be used for Internet Only mail or for Corporate and Workgroup mail.

4 Select Tools from the menu bar, then Options and then the Other tab, and click the Advanced Options button.

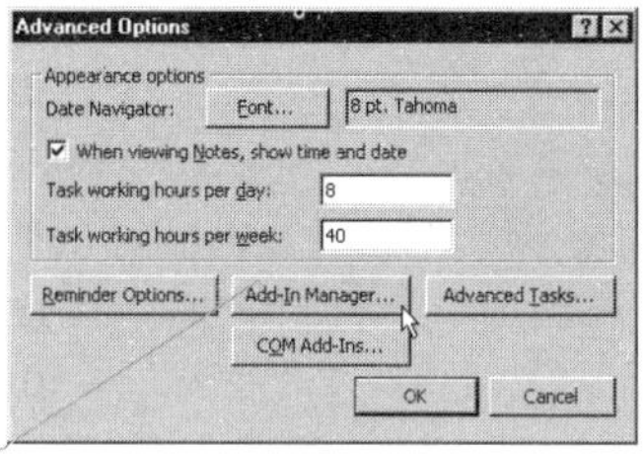

5 Click the Add-In Manager button to see a list of installed applications.

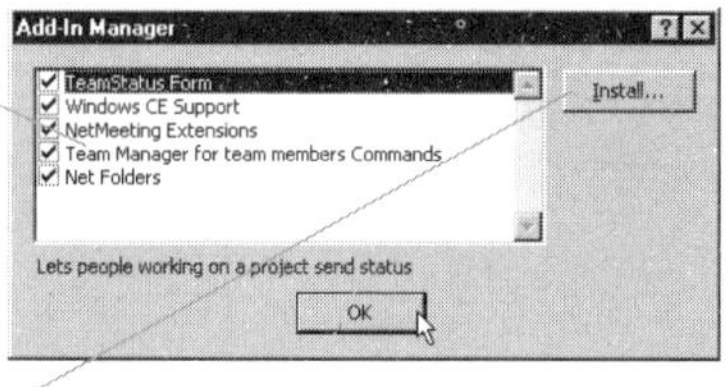

6 Click the Install button to see the list of available applications.

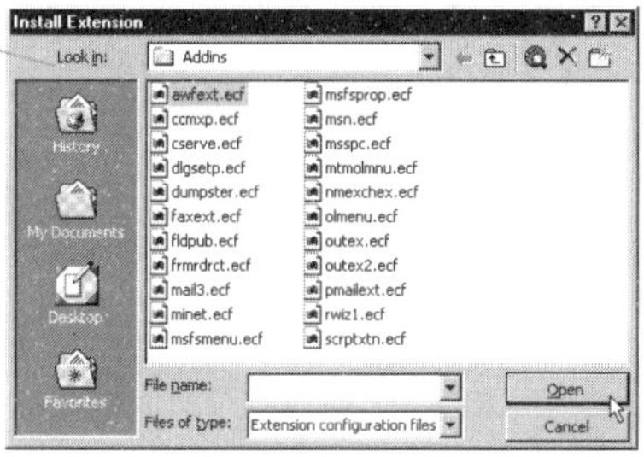

These add-ins are usually installed "on demand" when you first use them.

Some add-ins however can only be installed manually, using the maintenance wizard.

7 Run Add/Remove Programs from Control Panel. Select Office 2000 and then Outlook 2000.

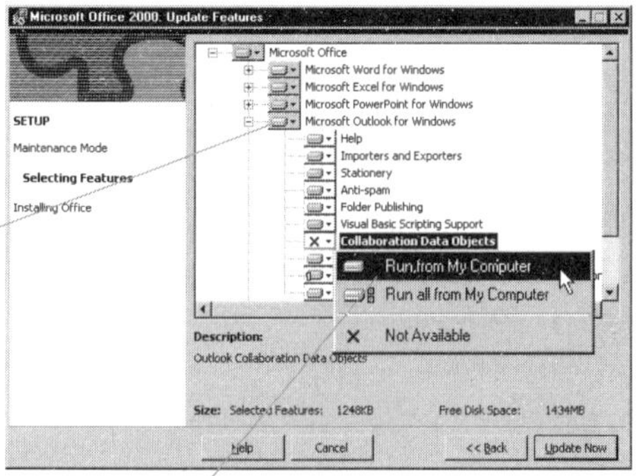

8 Right-click an item marked Unavailable and select Run from My Computer.

Forms design

Outlook uses built-in forms for messages, contacts and other items. You use the New Message form when you create a message, and the New Contact form when you enter details for a contact. Every action and item in Outlook is based on a form. You are not restricted to the built-in forms, since you can create your own forms to standardise the way information is stored or distributed. If you have a network, or use shared folders, you can create forms that anyone can access, for example to order supplies or to take telephone messages in a standard format.

To design a new form:

1. Select Tools from the menu bar, click Forms and then Design a Form.

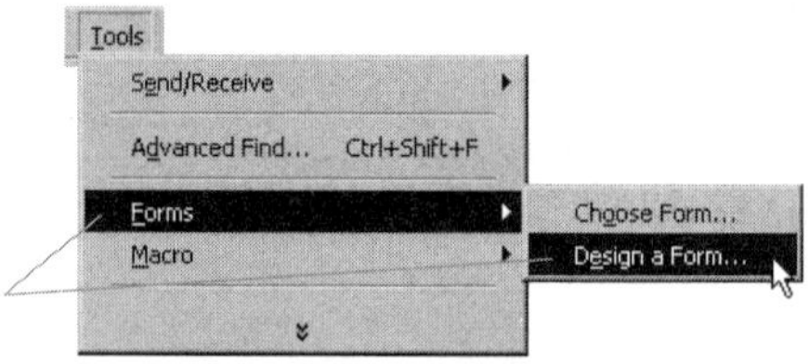

2. Choose an existing form as a starting point, or select one of the standard form templates.

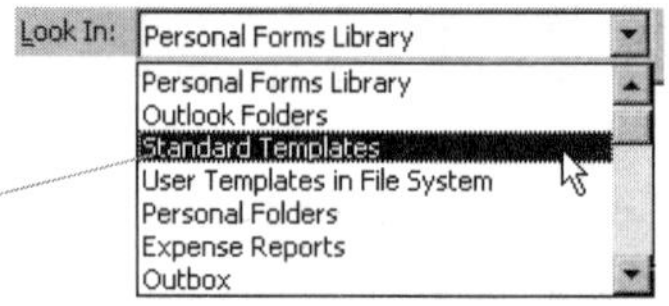

3. Use the Field Chooser to add fields to the form, add labels and define tabs.

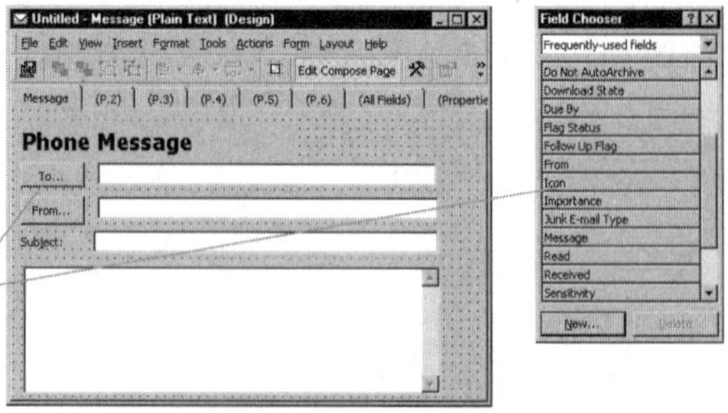

4. Select Publish Form, specify the display name and file name, and save it in the Personal Forms Library.

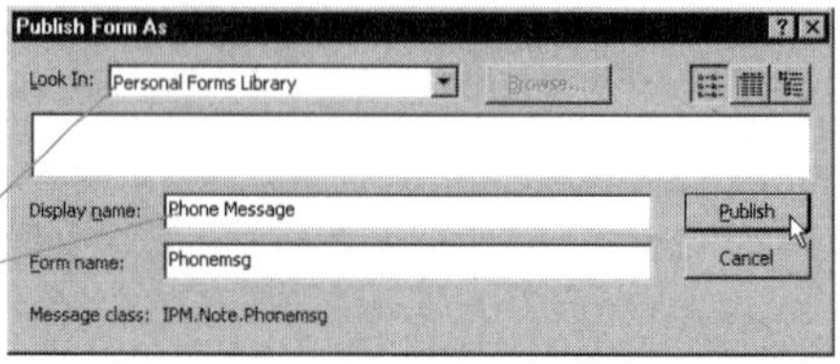

Save the form in a public folder or a shared folder if you want it to be available to other users.

To use a custom form that you have designed:

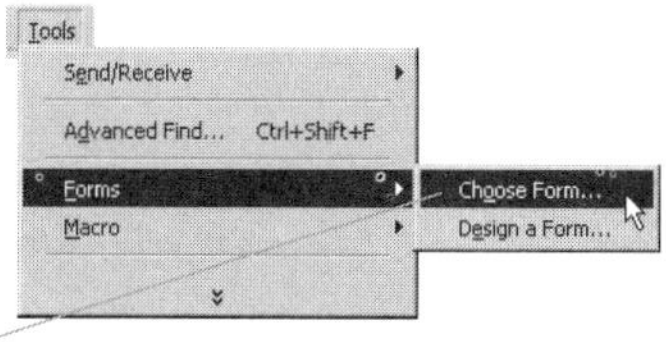

5 Select Tools from the menu bar, click Forms and then Choose Form.

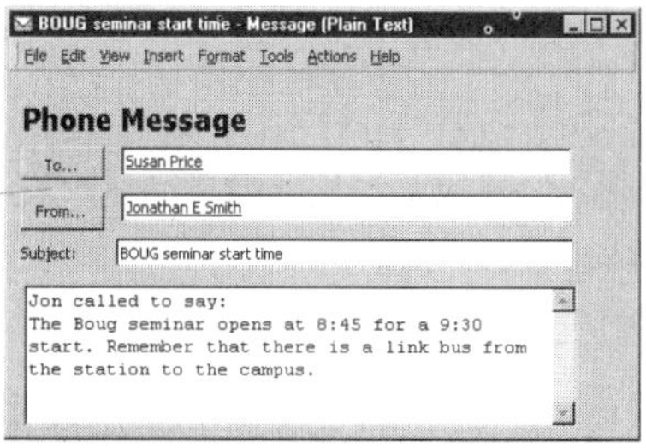

6 Select your custom form and fill in the details, then Send it or Save it.

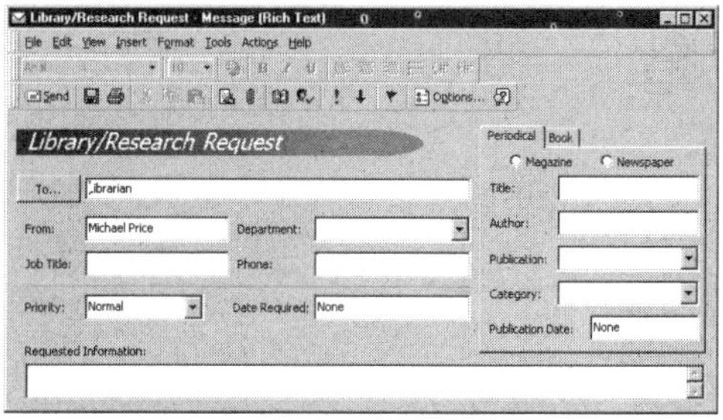

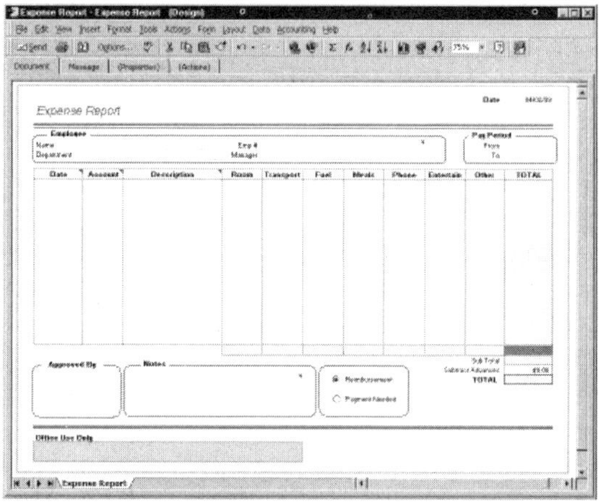

Designing forms can be a complex operation. However, you can find forms already created for you, to suit a variety of applications. For example, there is a form for Library requests in the Outlook sample groupware applications, which are provided free by Microsoft. The same applications include an expense report, which uses an Excel spreadsheet to help you fill in your expenses and calculate your balances.

The Internet has many predesigned forms or procedures for you to take advantage of.

Sharing folders

The Net Folders add-in allows you to share Outlook folders on a local network or even across the Internet.

If you work in an office with a local area network, it is easy to share documents and data files with your fellow workers. You will all have access to a network server, so you could have a folder space set aside for shared information. Selected files and folders on your own hard drive, or on your own network drive space, can also be shared with others. This needs specific permission, so the security and privacy of your data are not compromised. Shared folders and network drives can be added to the Other Shortcuts bar, so that you can access the contents from Outlook.

It is more difficult to share the contents of your Outlook folders, because these are not directly accessible from Windows. The e-mail facility and the support for exchanging requests and responses for meetings and tasks provide ways of exchanging information. However you cannot view the contents of another user's folder and browse through its entries.

Net Folders provide a different way to share Outlook Folders, by shipping the contents and changes as e-mail. The facility is designed for the small office using Outlook on a local area network, but you can share folders with anyone on your mailing list. With Net Folders you can maintain a shared appointments calendar, host a news or discussion service, or keep track of project activities.

To share an Outlook folder, one person in the group creates and maintains a master copy, and sends subscriptions to the others in the group, giving them access to the folder. The master folder is copied to their computers, and changes are exchanged automatically, using hidden e-mail messages.

To set up sharing:

1. Open the Folder List and select the folder you want to share.

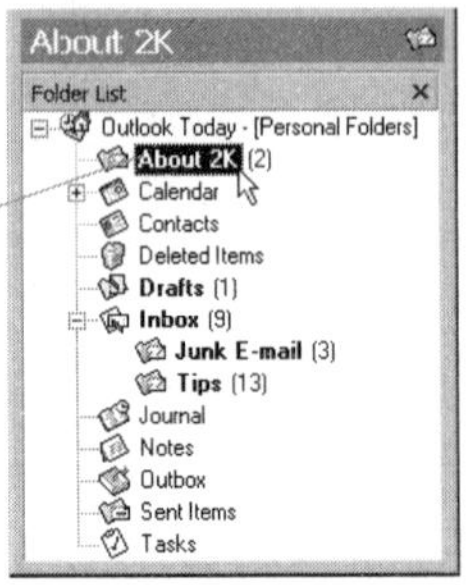

Share any Outlook folder, except for the Inbox, since that's where changes are sent.

2 Select File from the Menu bar and click Share.

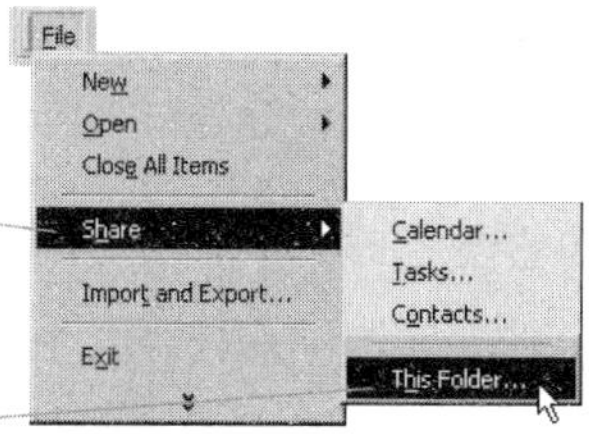

3 Select This Folder and the Net Folder Wizard starts up.

4 Press Next, and then click Add to choose names from your Contacts list.

5 Select a group of subscribers with the same access needs and press Permissions.

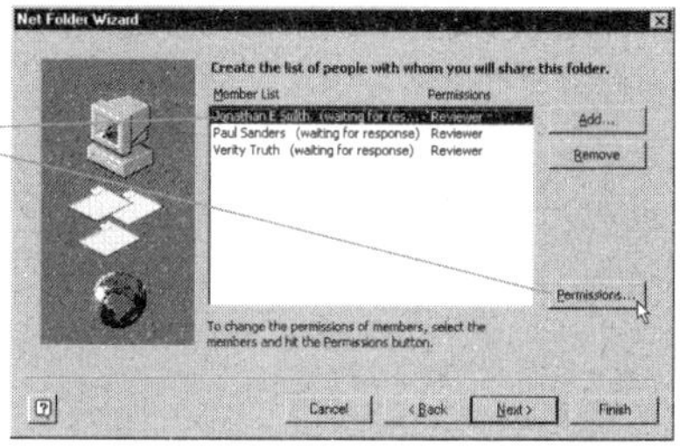

6 Choose the appropriate level: Reviewers can only read items, Contributors can add items, Authors can change their own items, and Editors can change items from anyone.

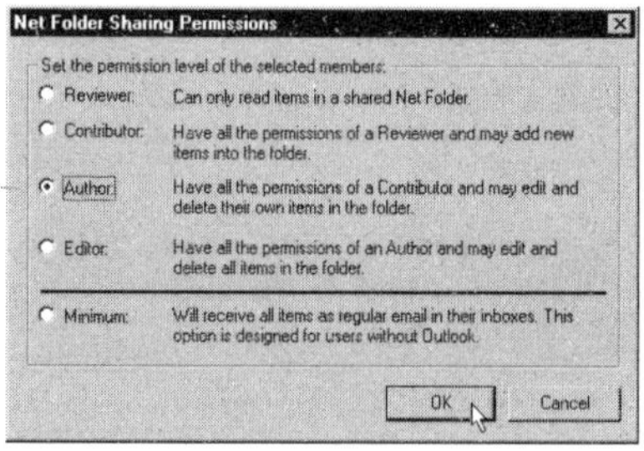

Select the Minimum level for subscribers who do not use Outlook for their e-mail service.

7 Repeat these steps for other groups, then press Finish.

8 When all the subscribers have been added, press Finish, and the wizard sends the e-mails to the Outbox, offering the subscriptions to the selected users.

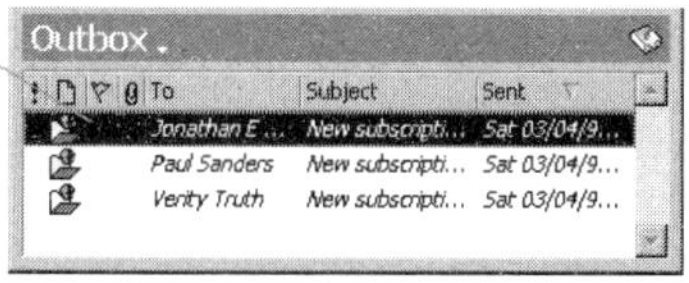

Receiving an invitation

The e-mail invitation arrives in the subscriber's Inbox as a normal message. When opened, the contents describe the access being offered, and the subscriber can accept or decline the invitation.

1. Open the invitation from the Inbox.

2. Check the details, and note the level of sharing allowed.

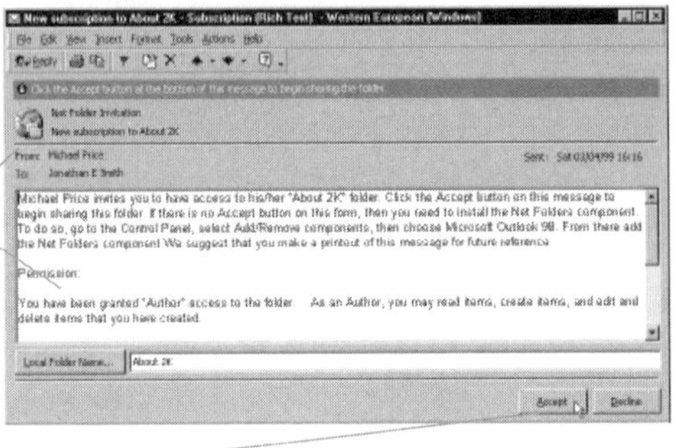

Supply your own local name for the Folder if you wish.

3. Press Accept in order to participate, or else press Decline.

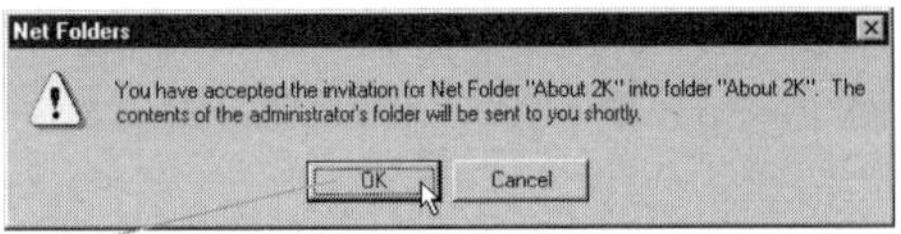

The subscriber's response is placed in the Outbox, ready to be sent.

When the administrator has received the reply, the whole contents of the folder are sent as an e-mail message, and any changes that are made will also be logged, ready to be sent on the next connection.

It may take some time for messages to be exchanged and updates sent, so the various copies of the folders will not always be in 'sync' with one another.

When the subscriber in turn receives these messages, the contents of the folder are inserted. Any views or forms associated with the folder are also replicated. Updates and changes, including updates from other subscribers with higher than reviewer status, will also be sent as appropriate.

WinFax starter edition

You can send and receive faxes, as well as e-mail, using Outlook.

Although WinFax starter edition is supplied with Outlook, it is not installed, so the first time you try to use it, the install is carried out.

1 Select New Fax from the New Items list, or from Actions on the menu bar.

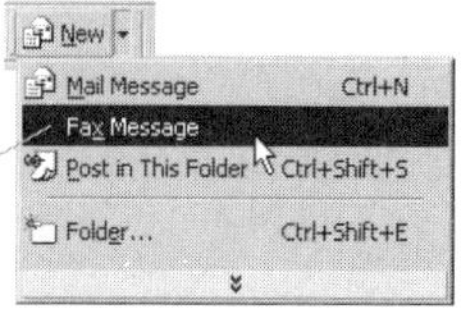

2 Insert the CD and the application files will be copied to your hard disk.

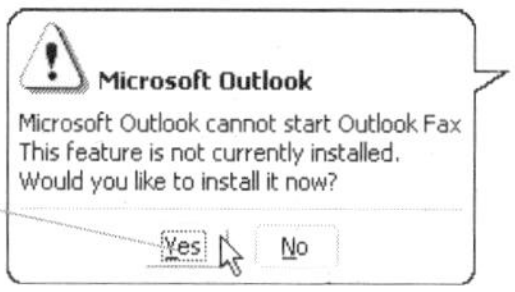

When WinFax has been installed, close Outlook and restart it to activate the feature. The WinFax wizard will help you configure your fax system:

3 Provide your name and phone numbers to show on your outgoing faxes.

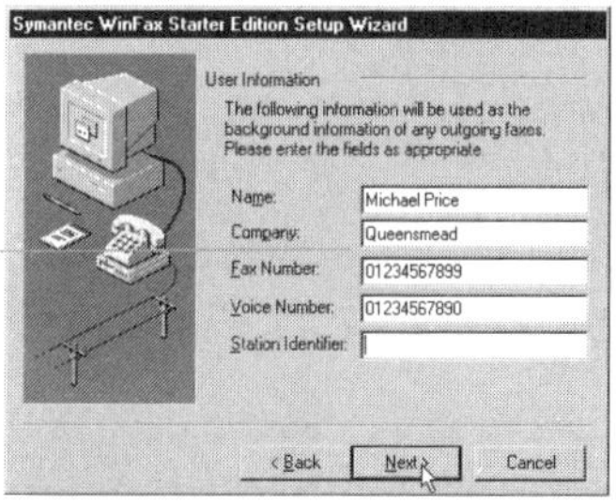

4 Click the box to receive faxes automatically, and specify the number of rings before WinFax should take the call.

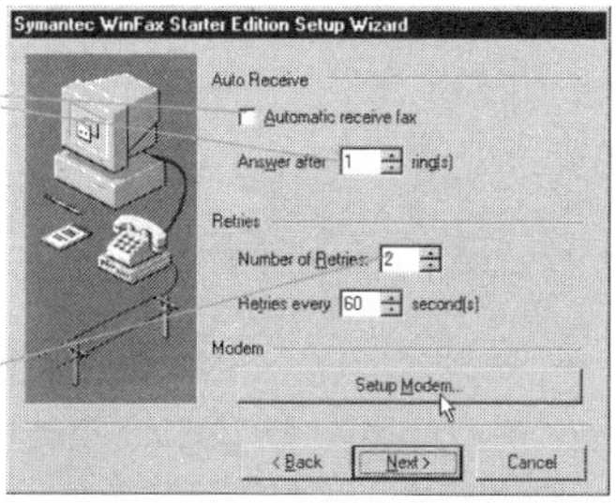

5 For sending faxes, specify the Number of Retries and the delay between retries.

6 Set up the modem and complete the configuration of WinFax.

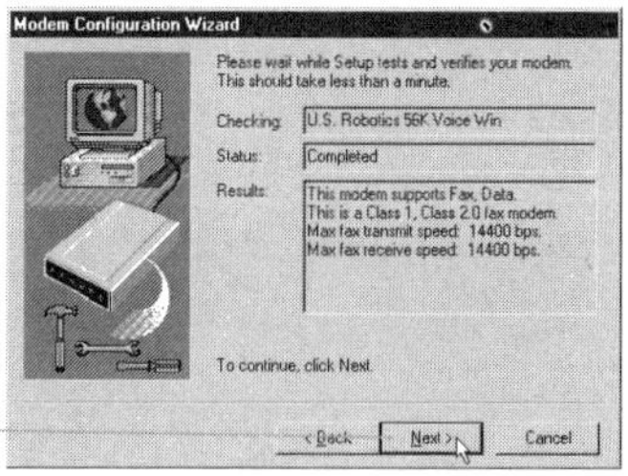

There are several WinFax cover page designs to select from, but you can't edit their contents.

Sending a fax

With WinFax installed, you can create and send a fax just as you create e-mail messages:

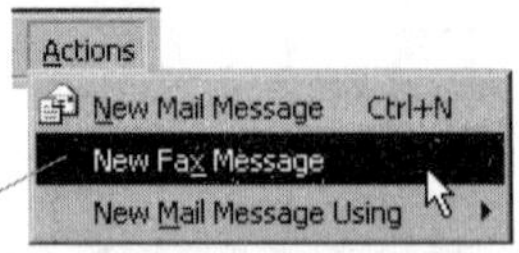

1. Select New Fax from the New Items list, or from Actions on the menu bar.

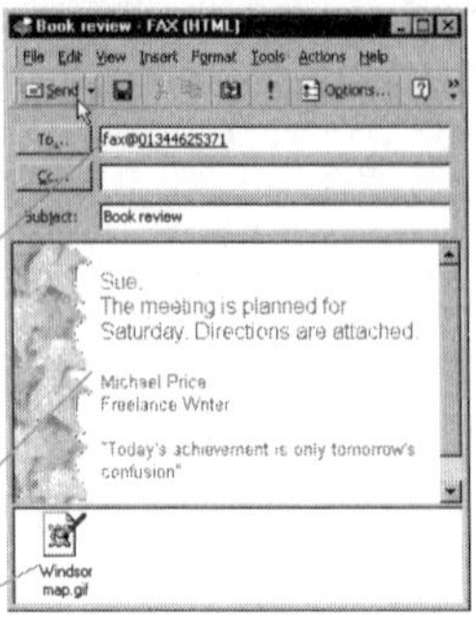

2. Enter the fax number, e-mail style, or select a Contact with fax numbers recorded in the address details.

Faxes use the HTML message format and default stationery.

3. Type the message and attach any documents or image files.

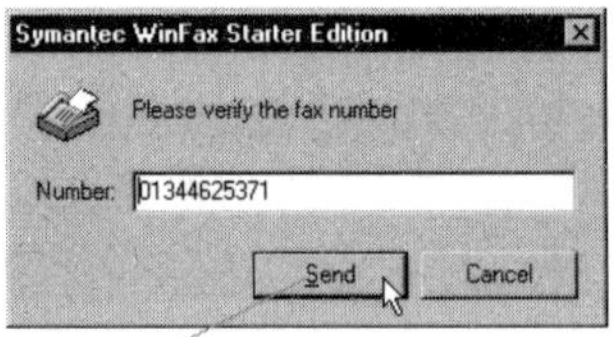

4. Select Send to start the process, and verify the fax telephone number, or select one if the Contacts entry has several.

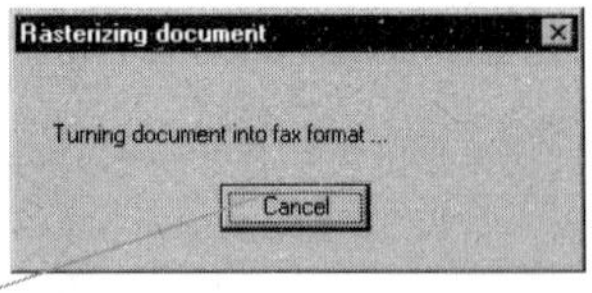

The pages are converted to fax format, and the fax message is prepared for transmission.

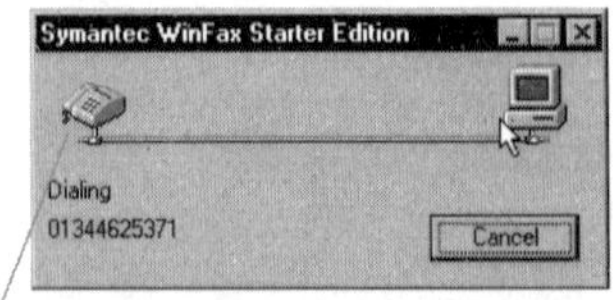

If your web browser is active, or if any other application is using your modem, WinFax will wait until the modem is free. Then it will attempt to connect.

WinFax displays a status panel while the fax is being sent, so you can tell it is active, but it gives no indication of the rate of progress, or of the amount of data that is being transferred.

Finding the fax in the sent folder is no guarantee that it has actually been transmitted.

The fax message will be moved on, from the Outbox to the Sent folder, without waiting for the transfer to be completed.

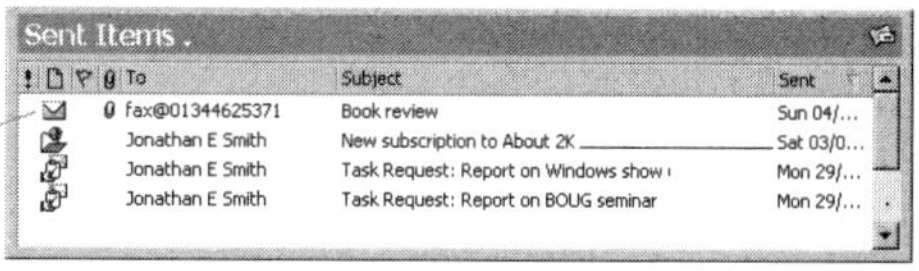

You receive a message in your Inbox, giving the reason for the failure (eg, the line could be busy, the transfer interrupted part way through, or the fax number invalid or unobtainable). To resend the fax, having corrected any error, open it from the Sent folder and choose Actions, Resend this Message.

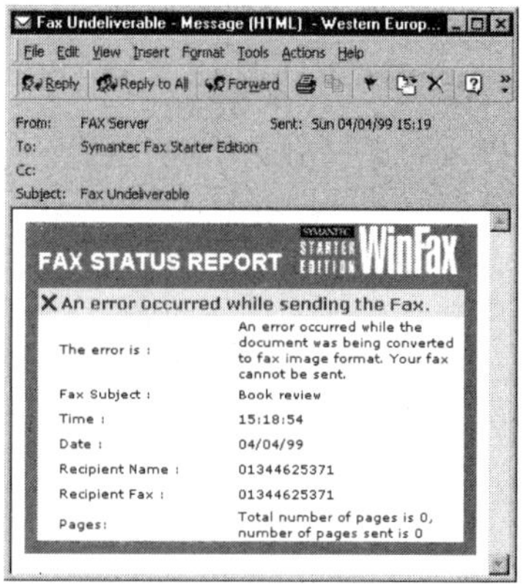

By default WinFax will make two extra tries at sending the fax before letting you know there's a problem.

You can change the settings to have WinFax retry the transmission more often:

1. Select Tools from the Menu bar, then Options, and click the Fax tab that will now be shown.

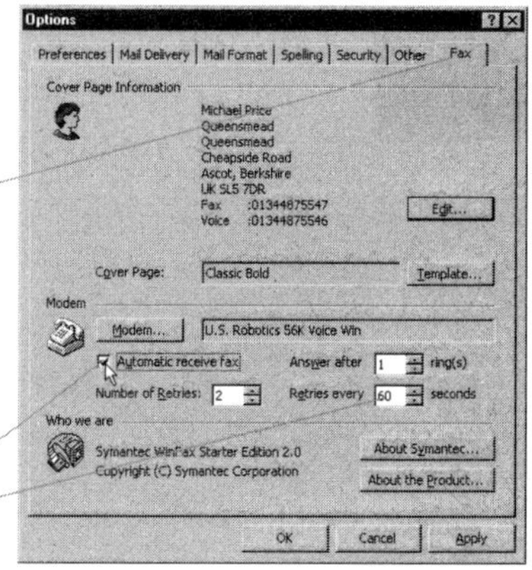

2. Change the settings as required. You can adjust the number of automatic retries, and the delay between retries.

3. This panel also allows you to specify Automatic Receive Fax, the only form of fax receipt that is offered.

Receiving a fax

You can only receive faxes with WinFax if Automatic Receive is enabled, and both the fax server and the modem controller are active. This means that Outlook must be running and your modem must be turned on, and not in use by any other application.

The modem will pick up all calls and try to process them as faxes, even if they are voice calls, so switch off Automatic Receive when you are not expecting a fax.

When a call comes in, the modem detects the ring signal and answers the call. The modem controller processes the incoming fax, displaying a status box, but giving no progress details.

When the transmission is complete, a standard Fax Received message is placed in your Inbox. The actual fax appears as an attachment to the message. To view the fax, double-click the attachment.

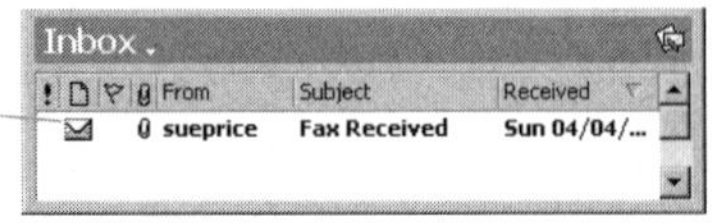

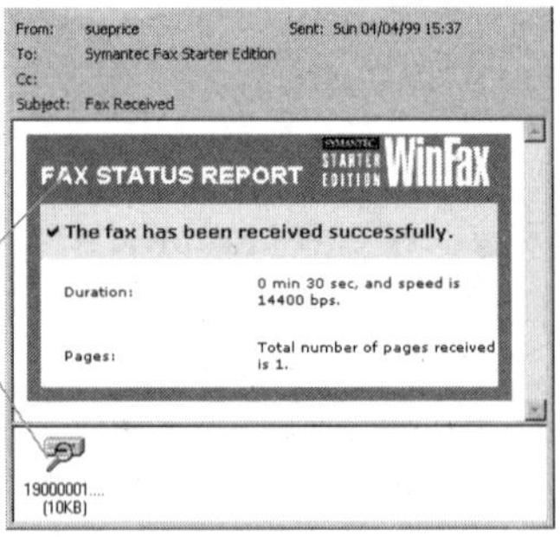

The QuickView accessory must be installed for you to view a fax.

The Quick Fax Viewer displays the fax, providing functions to zoom or rotate the image, and to switch between the parts of a multipage fax. There is no function to save it as a different file type, but you can print the fax. You may also view the fax using other file viewers such as Quickview Plus.

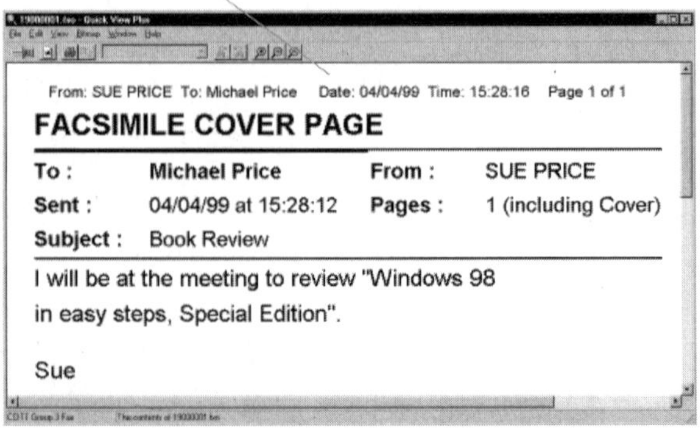

Cool add-ins

The URL addresses for web pages do change. If the page is not found, start at the higher level (e.g. at the .com), and look for any references to the data you want.

Many applications for Outlook can be found on the Internet. Microsoft maintains a list of third-party add-ons for Outlook and related products. The document can be viewed at the following URL:

Application cross-reference lists are maintained at the Slipstick web site, which specialises in Outlook and Exchange. The URL address for this site is:

Some add-ins are free, while others are shareware and must be registered for a fee, after a trial period. Most add-ins will run on any type of Outlook installation, but some are version or configuration dependent.

The list of add-ons can be found at the URL:

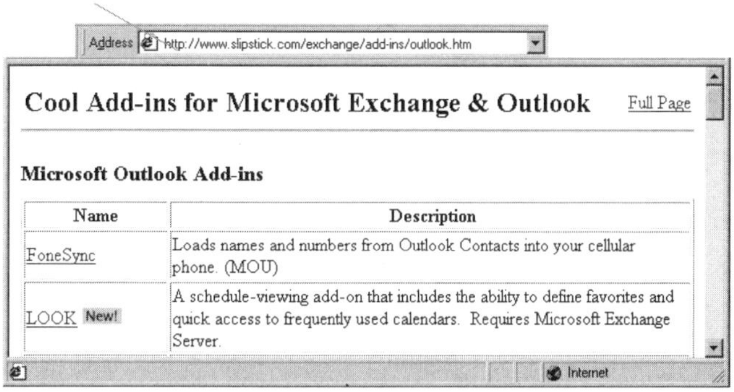

Integrated Outlook

You don't have to run Outlook 2000 to take advantage of its functions. You can send e-mail directly from Office 2000 applications. For example, to send the contents of a spreadsheet as an e-mail message:

Outlook 2000 is integrated with the other Office 2000 programs; they share each other's functions.

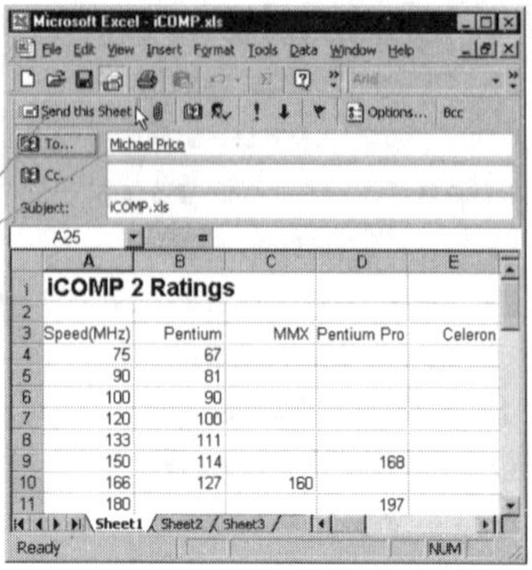

1. Click the Send button, enter the e-mail details and press Send this Sheet to send it in the body of the message.

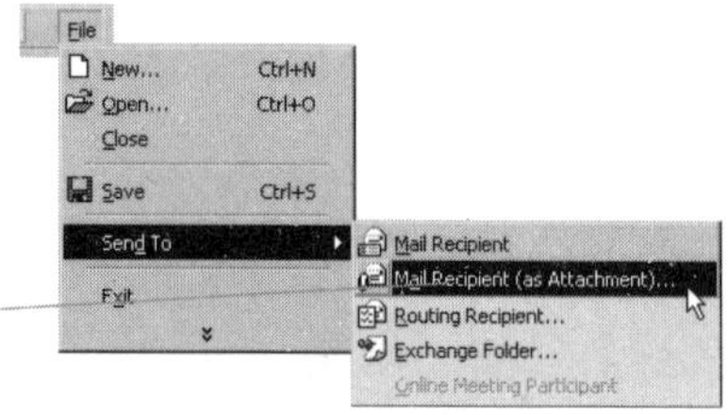

2. Alternatively, select File on the menu bar, click Send To and choose to attach it to a message, or to add a routing slip.

You can create and send an e-mail from within Word 2000:

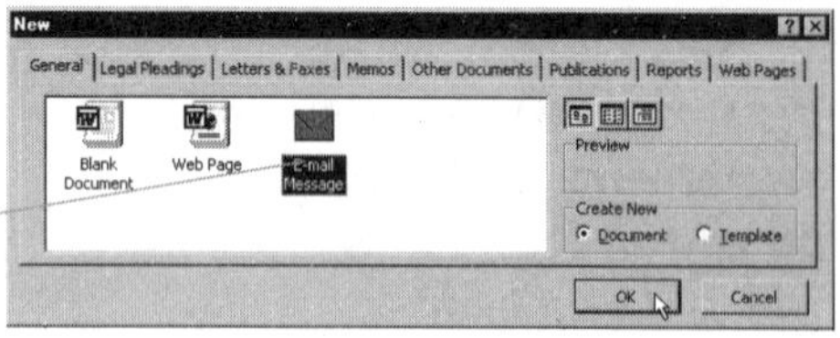

3. Click New document and select E-mail message as the template.

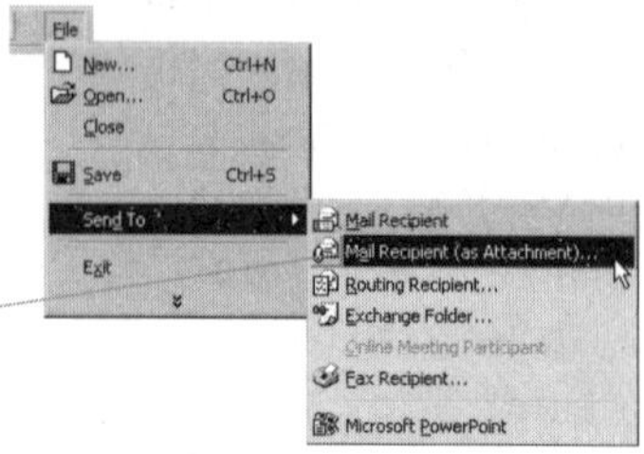

4. For an existing document, select File on the menu bar, click Send To and attach it, add a routing slip, or send it as a Fax.

Word 2000 can also be used as the e-mail editor within Outlook 2000, providing background spelling checks, and supporting Word, HTML or plain text formats.

Index

A

B

C

D

E

L

M

N

O

P

Q

R

S

T